The Murder Mystique

The Murder Mystique

Female Killers and Popular Culture

Laurie Nalepa and
Richard Pfefferman

 PRAEGER

AN IMPRINT OF ABC-CLIO, LLC
Santa Barbara, California • Denver, Colorado • Oxford, England

Library of Congress Cataloging-in-Publication Data

Nalepa, Laurie.
  The murder mystique : female killers and popular culture / Laurie
Nalepa and Richard Pfefferman.
      p. cm.
  Includes bibliographical references and index.
  ISBN 978-0-313-38010-5 (hbk. : alk. paper) — ISBN 978-0-313-38011-2 (ebook)
1. Women murderers—United States—Case studies.   2. Murder
in mass media.   I. Pfefferman, Richard.   II. Title.
  HV6517.N35   2013
  364.152'30820973—dc23   2012037964

ISBN: 978-0-313-38010-5
EISBN: 978-0-313-38011-2

17 16 15 14 13   1 2 3 4 5

This book is also available on the World Wide Web as an eBook.
Visit www.abc-clio.com for details.

Praeger
An Imprint of ABC-CLIO, LLC

ABC-CLIO, LLC
130 Cremona Drive, P.O. Box 1911
Santa Barbara, California 93116-1911

This book is printed on acid-free paper ∞

Manufactured in the United States of America

Contents

Acknowledgments

This book would not have been possible without the constant love of Carl Boggs and Terrence LeBleu. A special thank you to our families, friends, and colleagues who provided encouragement along the way. We are truly grateful to our editor Jane Messah for "putting a gun to our heads" to make sure we met our deadlines. More importantly, without her guidance and encouragement, this book would never have been completed.

Many sources need to be acknowledged for providing in-depth accounts of the cases studied in this book. Faith McNulty's 1980 work *The Burning Bed* (New York: Harcourt Brace Jovanovich) provided information on Francine Hughes for Chapter 1. Ann Rule's book *Heart Full of Lies* (New York: Pocket Books, 2004) and Gary Fletcher's articles for *The Observer* were instrumental for the discussion of Liysa Northon also found in this chapter.

The crime of Betty Broderick, addressed in Chapter 2, relied on the accounts provided by Bella Stumbo in her 1993 work *Until the Twelfth of Never* (New York: Simon and Schuster) as well as *Hell Hath No Fury* (New York: St. Martin's Press, 1992) by Bryna Taubman.

We are indebted to numerous works for information related to Chapter 3. Two books assisted in our understanding of Kristin Rossum. These include *Poisoned Love* (New York: Kensington Publishing Corp., 2005) by Caitlin Rother as well as the account by John Glatt, *Deadly American Beauty* (New York: St. Martin's Press, 2004). Significant contributions to the discussion of Susan Smith were from *Sins of the Mother* (New York: St. Martin's Press, 1995) by Maria Eftimiades, Andrea Peyser's 1995 book *Mother Love, Deadly Love* (New York: Harper Collins Publishers), David Smith's *Beyond All Reason* (New York: Kensington Publishing Corp., 1995), and Gary Henderson's chronicle of events *Nine Days in Union* (Spartanburg, SC: Honoribus Press, 1995).

Jeanne King's *Signed in Blood* (New York: St. Martin's Press, 2009) as well as articles by Paul Pringle and Hemmy So for the *Los Angeles Times* provided information on Olga Rutterschmidt and Helen Golay in Chapter 4. In addition, we are grateful to Susan Braudy's account of Ann Woodword, *This Crazy Thing Called Love* (New York: Alfred A. Knopf Inc., 1992), which was also discussed in Chapter 4.

A number of books contributed greatly to Chapter 5. Information on Aileen Wuornos came from Sue Russell's *Lethal Intent* (New York: Kensington Publishing Corp, 2002), the account provided by Michael Reynold's in *Dead Ends* (New York: St. Martin's Press, 1992), and *Monster* (London: John Blake Publishing Ltd, 2006) by Aileen Wuornos and Christopher Berry-Dee. We are indebted to numerous authors of books related to Andrea Yates. In particular, we want to acknowledge Suzanne O'Malley's account *Are You There Alone?* (New York: Simon and Schuster, 2004) as well as *Breaking Point* (New York: St. Martin's Press, 2002) by Suzy Spencer.

Introduction: The Killer Inside Each of Us

Admit it! There's something about a woman who commits murder that makes us look at the crime in a little more detail, makes us shudder a little deeper, and makes us a little more judgmental as we ask ourselves, "Why did she do it?" We are socialized to believe that most ordinary women would never dream of killing someone. There has to be something "deviant" about them, something so pathological that they've turned against the laws of nature and become evil incarnate. However, I know from personal experience that this viewpoint is overly simplistic.

I am a law-abiding person. The worst crime I've ever committed is probably running a red light when I was tired. But I have to confess that I too was once filled with a murderous rage that was so overpowering I thought about killing someone. I walked in on my boyfriend having sex with another woman. They were in our house, in our bedroom, in our bed. I literally could not believe my eyes. As my mind started to process the information, I was filled with the most overpowering physical anger I have ever felt in my life. I walked out of the bedroom, through the living room, and into the kitchen, where I stood shaking over the kitchen sink. My glance fell on a large knife that was lying on a cutting board. For one infinitesimal moment, one second in time, I considered picking up the knife and thrusting it into both of them. I didn't. But I realize that I could have. And who knows? I could have been one of those women you see on the reality show *Snapped,* or watch on Court TV, or read about in the *National Enquirer,* or even had a best seller written about me by Ann Rule.

If someone asked you "Would you welcome more drama in your life?" your answer would probably be no. Who among us consciously seeks confrontation, violence, or disruption? Right-thinking people don't want to invite situations that place them outside their comfort zones, demand that they make difficult moral judgments, or shatter their perceived notions about how the world works. No, we have television for that.

In entertainment, drama is precisely what we crave, and it's made all the more enticing when it crosses lines we would never consider traversing in real life. That's why murder, especially when committed by a woman, is such a staple of books, films, television, Internet blogs, video games, and pop music. Writers, producers, and program developers can always rely on this topic to get our attention, whether in a fantasy novel or an investigative crime show. In fact, it's almost axiomatic that those whose lives are void of dramatic impact are the best bets to consume depictions of extreme or violent acts in the media. It's no wonder then that as our daily activities continue to move steadily into the realm of cyberspace, where the most intimate tool of social interaction is an on-screen keyboard, our thirst for tangible dramatic impact in our universe of news and entertainment is becoming unquenchable. As technology grows, personal power shrinks. We want to be reminded that a person can perform a real, physical act that has an undeniably meaningful effect on another human being.

Murderers are not heroes. But killing—whether motivated by passion, greed, thrills, madness, ideals, or desperation—is an extraordinary act; not an honorable one, to be sure, but undeniably extraordinary. And extraordinary acts—even depraved ones—tend to have the effect of elevating the perpetrator to iconic cultural status. Society *bestows* this exalted place upon genuine heroes. Murderers *seize* their exalted place. That's what makes them sexier. This book explores how the taking of a life, and the subsequent spectacle surrounding those who commit murder, provides an antidote to the mundane activities that fill our world. Murderers take control.

But these days, even acts of murder are becoming commonplace: drive-by shootings, terrorist bombings, disgruntled workers "going postal," etc. Our regular servings of murder on the ten o'clock news, *CSI* reruns, and Halloween movie marathons are becoming ho-hum. Isn't it time for something different on the menu? How about something we really don't expect? Something that may even unearth some long-held beliefs or assumptions we take for granted? Please, Nancy Grace, won't you give us something that will intrigue, titillate, and horrify us, all at the same time?

Female murder cases fit this bill because the topic is located where three of our most common areas of interest intersect—crime, gender, and pop culture. When a woman kills, we're intrigued, hoping that some nugget of insight about any or all of these interests buried in the story will somehow be revealed to us: What was her motive? Was it in any way justifiable? How will she be portrayed in the media? How will society judge her? In what ways is this murder different from those committed by men? Does the explanation fit our common notions about women? If not, how should our beliefs about women change in light of this event? And if women *have* changed, how has our culture contributed to those changes?

Over the past several decades, media attention to female aggression and violence—and particularly to murder—has increased dramatically, both in real and fictionalized portrayals. We see Oprah interviewing female murderers in prison. We watch case after case of accused female killers depicted in detail on investigative news shows. We listen to popular songs about women taking violent revenge against men who have wronged them. You'd think that the number of killings perpetuated by females has steadily grown; but not, according to the U.S. Department of Justice. In 1976, females committed 3,295 homicides. By 2005, the number had dropped to 1,826.[1] More surprising is that in 1976, fully 16.2 percent of all murders in America were committed by women. In 2005, females accounted for only 9.5 percent. So in actual fact, not only did the number of female homicides decline during that time, but by the end of that nearly 30-year period, we see not a larger, but a *smaller* proportion of murders committed by females, compared to males. These statistics belie the common perception that female killings are on the rise. How can this be?

The only explanation for this discrepancy between our observations and the facts is that female killers are now more prominent *in our minds*. The notion that women are capable of killing is steadily pervading our collective consciousness through popular culture. The circumstances that lead up to the murder, the milieu in which the murder takes place, the mindset of the murderer, the publicity of the murder and trial, people's reactions to both the murder and the verdict, and any folklore that may later be associated with the murder all of these are directly influenced by cultural values. And cultural values are purveyed by media images. So in order to understand the phenomenon of female homicide, we need to examine not only the stories of the incidents and trials themselves, but also the thematic messages of the culture that provide the context. What images were fed to the public during that period that may have influenced or even shaped perceptions, opinions, and judgments?

In the chapters that follow, we explore 10 cases of killings by American women. These cases span a variety of motives—love, money, revenge, self-defense, and psychopathology. They cover an assortment of different circumstances—from crushed spirits trapped in genuine desperation to advantaged souls with myriad options and potentially sparkling futures ahead. Women of different ages and backgrounds—some glamorous and sexy, others plain and unattractive; some passionate and impulsive, others calculating and strategic; and some overly confident, others completely lacking in self-esteem. Their stories also encompass a broad range of victims—from husbands and children to professional colleagues to homeless men and virtual strangers. All of these factors contribute to society's ultimate judgments of the palatability of these women's crimes and the degree to which each deserves our sympathy. But there's another piece to this puzzle.

The earliest of the cases we explore occurred in 1955; the latest in 2010. American culture has undergone continuous and dramatic evolution during that 55-year period: The Women's Movement was born and has progressed and evolved through a number of iterations. The country rejected materialism and then embraced it again. The political environment has swung from right to left more than once. High-profile celebrities have come out and candidly confessed their fears, faults, and transgressions, and as a result, many Americans have become more open and forgiving of imperfections in themselves and others. For the most part, we've become more accepting of different lifestyles, and sometimes we are even willing to entertain the possibility that extreme acts may be justified. Since murders don't happen in a vacuum, each one is, in some way, a manifestation of the prevailing cultural norms at that time. In this book, we examine how, for example, a not-guilty verdict could be reached in the mid-1970s, while the defendant in a case with similar characteristics—30 years later—could receive a prison sentence.

Some of the changes in our cultural mindset can be attributed to the new ways technology has altered how we receive and process information. In 1955, television was just coming into its own. Newspapers, magazines, and radio were still the main sources of news and entertainment for the majority of Americans. The most cutting-edge TV format was *Person to Person,* a show in which respected news reporter Edward R. Murrow, sitting in a comfortable chair in the studio, interviewed celebrity guests at their homes, which viewers could see on a large projection screen. The signals were transmitted to the network through a microwave link. Interactive messaging was pretty much limited to telephone calls and the *Dear Abby* column in the daily newspaper. For information, there was the *Encyclopedia Britannica,* and for news, whatever events were perceived to be of mainstream interest were fed to the public, *en masse,* on the nightly news report.

The Internet utterly changed all that, affecting the way a potential killer might enable herself to commit a crime, as well as the eventual moral judgments the public might make about that crime. Information of every variety, in as much detail as you could imagine, has become available on demand. No matter how esoteric or arcane your interest—whether it be *8 Steps for Cooking Snakes,* lyrics to the theme song from *Petticoat Junction,* or *The Bottom 50 Sexual Fetishes*—you can find it, fast and easy. And now you can do it all on your phone or iPad. So if you happen to have a predilection toward something a little out of the ordinary—say, you're looking for chemicals that can be fatal without leaving much residue or you want to find stories of women who successfully took revenge against their abusers—you could conceivably spend all your time retrieving and digesting information on your preferred topic, and without having to wade through other material that might present a different perspective. Gosh, there's probably even a cable TV channel devoted exclusively to your particular pleasure. So it's now possible, more than ever before, for someone to fill her or his mind exclusively with carefully selected information that may be used to justify a crime.

Interactive media tools such as blogging and social networking sites have taken public discussion to an entirely new level. No longer are discreetly selected opinions delivered through the one-way channel of a newspaper's editorial page. Now anyone can post and retrieve thoughts to and from just about anywhere in the world, in real time. This change in the forum of public debate makes the tides of public opinion more volatile and subject to uncontrollable influences. It is an environment where a lone, subjective comment—posted in the right spot at the right time—can grow into a pervasive public sentiment or even a national political movement virtually overnight. Whether overt and conscious or concealed and subliminal, the influence of pop culture on our thoughts, opinions, and values is more powerful than ever before.

In exploring cases of women who have killed, this book highlights how each one in some way parallels the media images fed to the American public through pop culture during that era. When we consume media depictions and perceive real-life events at the same time, they intermingle in our palates. And they are bound to mix as we digest them. Consequently, it may be impossible to decipher exactly which ingredients are responsible for the aftertaste left in our mouths.

—Laurie Nalepa

Women Who Kill in Self-Defense

"Every Home a Safe Home" is the slogan promoted by the National Coalition Against Domestic Violence organization. But what happens when you are not in a safe home? What happens when you are the one out of every four women who is abused by a spouse or intimate partner and you decide you are not going to take it anymore? Are you justified if you kill your assailant, or are you just looking to get away with murder?

Media interest and depictions in popular culture have tended to always fall into two camps: either the woman is perceived as a cold-blooded killer or a sympathetic victim. However, this simplistic dichotomy does not take into consideration the intertwined complicated issues of gender, equity, and violence that can be found in the cases of Francine Hughes and Liysa Northon. Both women claimed they were abused wives. Both women killed their husbands while they were sleeping. Both women claimed they had no choice but to kill or they would be killed. One woman was freed, the other one wasn't. In either situation, the public is deeply curious to know why she did it. The cases of Francine Hughes and Liysa Northon reflect our fascination with this dynamic.

FRANCINE HUGHES

Once the match hit the gasoline, there was no turning back. Flames quickly danced around the room and made their way to the bed. A naked man slept soundly unaware of the looming danger. The person who lit the match, his abused ex-wife, hurriedly left the room. Panicked, she gathered up her children, grabbed her car keys, left the house, and drove away. Francine Hughes took matters literally into her own hands when she ended the life of Mickey Hughes. As a result, she was charged with premeditated murder in the first degree in a case that seemed clear cut. She had time to think about what she was doing as she looked for the can of gasoline she planned to use to start the fire. She voluntarily turned herself into the police, confessing, "I did it. I did it" while in custody.[1] The victim was not threatening to or causing her harm at the exact time of the crime. She herself, along with the general public, was horrified over his violent gruesome death.

However, as the details of Francine's story came to light, a more complicated picture emerged. Francine suffered 13 years of brutal physical and emotional harm from Mickey. Her family, in-laws, and neighbors all knew what was going on. Law enforcement and social agencies were aware of her situation. According to Francine, "They wouldn't do anything. I just felt like I was alone and no matter what I did it wasn't any help."[2] Domestic violence was a topic few people talked about and little could be done about. Ann Jones writes in the book *Women Who Kill,* "Throughout most of the twentieth century, wife beating was against the law, but the police, the courts and the public winked at it." In fact, in 1977, the year Francine killed Mickey, abusers were not even arrested unless the abuse occurred in the presence of the police.

As media attention swirled around Francine, the house of horrors she lived in became national news and the inability of authorities to do anything became a damning indictment. A best-selling book, *The Burning Bed,* turned her into a celebrity. The book led to a television movie starring Farrah Fawcett, which become a cultural touchstone focusing the spotlight on domestic violence. In the end, the story of an ordinary housewife changed our perception of battered women and impacted the judicial system. Where and how did it all begin?

Francine came from a small town in Ingram County, Michigan. And while small towns often evoke a quaint way of life with an emphasis on charm and folksiness, the reality is often much bleaker. People often married young and struggled to make ends meet. Girls of her background didn't often have career ambitions, and even if Francine did, there were limited opportunities. Instead, she had a romantic ideal of getting married to a man who adored her, having perfect children, and living in the suburbs. When she was 15, she met Mickey Hughes. Francine was used to attracting boys. However, Mickey's interest was different. He wanted to spend all their time together and demanded Francine's full attention. He told her he loved her and could not live without her. He proposed again and again. The repeated proposals made her anxious. While she liked Mickey, she wasn't even sure she loved him. All his talk of the suffering she caused him by rejecting his proposals and refusing to sleep with him made her feel pressured. She wanted to break up with him, but he wouldn't accept it.

Feeling restless and uninterested in school, she impulsively dropped out. At the same time, she decided to have sex with Mickey. She immediately regretted it. "It used to be that a girl was taught to save herself for somebody. We had intercourse before we were married. I felt like I should marry him because of that. He wanted to marry me so bad. I never felt I had anyone who loved me so much."[3] Pushing aside her concerns, Francine married Mickey in 1963 when she was 16. She lacked the self-confidence to explore other options.

The teenage couple lived with Mickey's parents and his siblings. Mickey was used to having his family turn a blind eye toward his angry outbursts. Francine got her first glimpse into this dynamic a few weeks after her wedding. In a jealous fit, Mickey became upset over an outfit Francine was wearing at home, literally tearing the clothes off her body. His mother and father were aware of the attack, but did nothing to stop it. Eventually, Mickey calmed down and apologized. Yet the apology did not take away the physical hurt of the attack or the emotional hurt she felt over his misplaced anger. Faith McNulty notes in the book *The Burning Bed* that it also did not take away the guilt that she had provoked his reaction.[4] Francine didn't know it yet, but this was the first step in a scenario that would take place over and over again for the rest of their life together.

A short time later, another incident in which Mickey started to beat Francine for a perceived slight. As his father tried to intervene, his mother called the police. When they arrived, Mickey took a swing at one of the officers. Because he committed a violent act in their presence, he was arrested. For the first and only time, Mickey's parents blamed him and not their daughter-in-law for causing the trouble. Despite their support, Francine had enough. She decided to go back to her mother's house to escape the turmoil.

Mickey was released the same day and came looking for Francine in a contrite mood. Turning on his charm to both Francine and her mother, he promised it would never happen again. Francine wanted to believe him, so she relented. They moved into their first apartment in an effort to make a fresh start. Unfortunately, Mickey took to hitting his wife on a regular basis—not just in private but also in public. When Francine disagreed with him in the presence of their friends, he punched her in the face. After the friends left in embarrassment, he gave Francine the worst beating yet. She fled back to her mother's for safety. Although she initially refused to see her husband, Francine eventually gave in to his pleadings to return. She learned she was pregnant shortly after. The teenager was barely 17 and married only 6 months. Right before the baby was born, Mickey walked out.

Despite everything, Francine loved Mickey and did want him back. She said, "My love for Mickey grew out of being with him, depending on him, being pregnant with his child. During the good times together we were very close. When he left me I realized I loved him more than I had known."[5] Giving in to parental pressure, Mickey rejoined Francine. The birth of their daughter seemed to stabilize the marriage. The couple was getting along, he took an interest in the baby, and the beatings stopped. But as the novelty of fatherhood wore off, Mickey's temper flared. Within months, he was hitting her again. Francine accepted the beatings as just part of the marriage. If she could just anticipate his needs, know what he was thinking, and always give him what he wanted, there would be no need for him to hit her. On those occasions when he did hit her, Mickey would usually cool down and make an effort to be loving and attentive. In fact, during the "kiss and makeup" intervals, like many women who are married to abusers, Francine would experience periods of happiness and contentment.

Francine's marriage followed the classic description of the battering cycle developed by Dr. Lenore Walker, one of the nation's most prominent experts on battered women. Walker describes a three-phased model: there is a tension-building phase where the abuser is restless and unpredictable no matter how solicitous the victim is trying to be, an acting out phase in which the abuser attacks the victim, and a honeymoon phase when the attack is over and the abuser is remorseful for their actions.[6] By the time Francine was pregnant with her second child, the periods between the cycles of abuse were getting shorter. To make matters even worse, Mickey started seeing other women. His infidelity, his continual bouts of unemployment, and the need to constantly move because of lack of money took its toll on her mental state, causing her to suffer from depression. All the while, the beatings continued.

Coping the best she could, Francine struggled to make a home for her husband and growing family. When the situation became too overwhelming, she applied for welfare and quietly filed for divorce. Her husband's anger was so great on the day she left that a friend had to call the police. Mickey tracked her down, begging her forgiveness. She reluctantly allowed him to move back in with the family. "I loved the kids so much I thought I could take any amount of hardship and abuse to keep the home intact. I kept hoping that if I stuck it out Mickey might change and our life [would] get better."[7]

Even in the best of times, Mickey was never an ideal husband. But it wouldn't be fair to paint him as a one-dimensional monster. Good-looking and slim as a young man, he gave off an intriguing aura of aloofness and vulnerability, which was an appealing combination. He appeared as a tough guy but one with a sensitive side. While his views on women were traditional, expecting Francine to cook, clean, and take care of him, she appeared comfortable in this role, at least in their early years together. His attitude was no different from most of the men she knew. With Mickey, she could laugh and shake off some of her serious nature. There were many times they would go out and have fun together without spending much money, just enjoying each other's company.

In 1970, she became pregnant again. The reconciliation did not last as Mickey reverted back to his violent tirades. Francine moved out taking the children. Mickey came to visit her when the baby was born. As usual, he tried to charm his way back into her life. But Francine was simply too weary. "There had been a radical change deep inside of me as though whatever it was that held me to Mickey had finally snapped. Perhaps I had lost my last illusions about him. . . . I didn't have the strength to take it anymore."[8] Undeterred he would come and go through her house, often using the children as an excuse. The official divorce decree meant nothing. Neither of them realized that an event would take place changing their relationship again. Unbelievably for her, it would make it worse.

Mickey got into a car accident and was critically injured. He had broken bones, suffered from a head injury, and required surgery. The doctors were uncertain whether he would even live, let alone recover from a coma. Francine was with him constantly during his monthlong stay in the hospital. It was apparent that his injuries were not just physical but also mental and emotional. Upon his release, family and friends expected her to be the main caretaker. She could not in good conscience walk away from him while he was so hurt. Mickey moved in with her and the children. She quickly realized that in his eyes, she existed solely for one purpose—to cater to him in every aspect. She knew it was only a matter of time before he would start hitting her again.

When he did, the episode was even more ferocious then before. Police were summoned. Realizing they were dealing with psychotic frenzy, officers had to forcefully drag Mickey off Francine and strap him down in an ambulance. He was taken to a hospital. The whole scene was ugly, brutal, and witnessed by the neighbors. Mickey was released from the hospital the next morning, and it was as if nothing had happened, particularly since Francine did not press charges. She did not want even more retaliation.

The grim situation continued to deteriorate as the years ticked by. Mickey started to hit the children. His constant drinking made him meaner, but it didn't seem to hamper his sexual ability. He expected Francine to service him whether she liked it or not. After sex, she felt dirty.[9] She chose to isolate herself to prevent further public humiliation. There would be days on end when she saw only Mickey and the children. Her despair manifested itself with physical symptoms of dizziness and a sense of suffocation. When she sought help from doctors and mental health experts, they urged her to leave Mickey but offered little practical support. Well-meaning advice couldn't protect her from a raging maniac. Even the police couldn't protect her. All they did was come out, break up the fight, and suggest Mickey be committed to a mental hospital for psychiatric observation. She learned that while a peace bond could send Mickey automatically to jail, it wouldn't take effect until after he beat her up. It seemed that nothing could be done. And her death seemed like a very real possibility. The beatings had increased to two or three times a week. Mickey had choked her, threatened to cut her throat, and attempted to run her off the road. When she went to the Ingram County prosecutor for help after her husband threatened to kill her, she was told to merely contact his probation officer. Ironically, Mickey had been given a suspended sentence for hitting a policeman.

To save her life and to protect the children, she knew she would have to leave Mickey. But this would take money. She decided she needed more education in order to get a better job. Surprisingly, Mickey agreed to her proposal of earning a GED and then going to business college. The routine of school, taking courses that sparked her intellect, and the acceptance of the other students helped her to keep her sanity. Although she never shared the horrific details of her life, a few women sensed trouble and offered their emotional support.

One of her classmates introduced her to George Walkup, a policeman who worked nearby. He was an attractive man going through a divorce. When he asked her out, Francine accepted. George showered her with attention that night. Letting down her guard, she had sex with him. Later in the evening, she learned that George was still emotionally involved with his wife and living at home.[10] The situation could end in heartbreak, let alone what Mickey would do if he found out Francine had seen someone else. She made the decision that it would be their one and only date until complications sorted themselves out.

Francine's life was closing in on her. She was 29 and had endured 13 years of physical and emotional abuse from Mickey. On March 9, 1977, it all came to an end as Francine prepared TV dinners. Faith McNulty's account *The Burning Bed* paints a harrowing picture of the events that transpired.[11] In a drunken rage, Mickey started an argument with Francine about the need to quit school. Punching and choking her, he ordered Francine to burn her textbooks. With tears streaming down her face and blood in her mouth from his blows, she did as she was told.

When he hit her again and threatened to kill her, she had her daughter call the police. Mickey was smart enough to cooperate with them when they arrived. All they could do was try to quiet him down for 20 minutes. After they left, he continued to viciously beat Francine as she tried to serve dinner. He threw the plates on the floor, shoving her face in them. The children were frightened and tried to get him to stop. He told Francine to clean up the mess and bring him something to eat in the bedroom. After eating, he demanded that she have sex with him. She complied. Feeling worse than she ever had before, a new and different thought entered Francine's mind: not only would she finally leave him, this time she would make it so he could never hurt her or the children again.[12] She would burn the house down with Mickey inside it. She would be free. No more beatings, no more pain, no more humiliation, no more degradation. Ann Jones notes in the book *Women Who Kill:*

> Determined to "just drive away," Francine piled the children into the family car. "Let's not come back this time Mommy," they said. She carried a gasoline can to the bedroom, poured the contents around the bed . . . backed out of the room, and set a match to it. . . . Francine Hughes drove immediately to the Ingram County Sheriff's office crying hysterically, "I did it. I did it."[13]

Listening to her story of burning down the house, the police asked if anyone was in it. When she replied that her ex-husband was sleeping upstairs, the interrogation became more intense. She told them all about the years of Mickey's abuse. Her story was familiar to some of the officers, since they were aware of the situation; after all, they had responded to her calls for help over the years. But it was clear to them that a man had been killed while he was sleeping, and she had lit the match that started the fire. She was charged with murder. The maximum penalty for the crime was life in prison.

After a week in jail, she met her court-appointed attorney, Aryon Greydanus. The words tumbled out as she tried to explain the reasons behind what she did. She told Greydanus about the endless physical abuse that started soon after she was married, the emotional degradation. She explained how Mickey's anger was often fueled by his drinking and constant unemployment. She shared her futile attempts to get Mickey out of her life by divorcing him and how he still refused to leave her alone. She described how the accident made him even more violent over the years and how the police failed to do anything that would protect her and the children. She told him every detail about the events of that horrible night when she reached the breaking point. All good defense attorneys are nonjudgmental when comes to their client. Greydanus appeared to be no exception. However, other people were not so open-minded. A neighbor of Francine's was interviewed by the *Chicago Tribune* and acknowledged trying to come to Francine's rescue one day when he saw Mickey hit her. Yet the neighbor stated, "I don't condone women beating but murder is murder and I sure don't condone murder."[14]

A few readers who saw the initial article in the *Lansing State Journal* sent letters to Francine expressing their support. Shortly after the story appeared in the newspaper, a group of feminists and activist groups formed a defense committee to raise money and publicize Francine's plight. Awareness of domestic violence was just beginning to enter into the mainstream. To the defense committee, Francine was the poster child for battered women everywhere. Ann Jones indicates in the book *Women Who Kill*, "During this time frame the FBI estimated that a million women each year, of every race and social class were victims of wife beating while other experts suggested the figure was as high as 28 million."[15] Francine was a poignant symbol of a victim who had tried to reach out to the system for help and had met with repeated failure. When ABC started covering Francine's story on its news broadcasts, both Francine and her lawyer gained national visibility.

Over the course of her seven months in jail, Greydanus set about establishing a strategy that would acquit Francine. Since Mickey had been sleeping and she was not in immediate danger, a plea of self-defense seemed inapplicable.[16] There was no legal precedent that allowed a domestic abuse victim to kill the abuser in a nonconfrontational setting. He decided instead to shape Francine's case around a plea of temporary insanity. Francine had told Greydanus that she was in a trancelike state as she prepared to burn the house and insisted, "I must have been crazy. . . . There is no other way I could have done what I did."[17] To build the case, he gathered evidence showing that Mickey Hughes had indeed physically, emotionally, and psychologically battered Francine over 13 years and that it deeply affected her state of mind. He spoke with the officers who had come to the Hughes house in response to all of Francine's calls for help and reviewed police records. He interviewed neighbors to find out what they had witnessed over the years. He arranged to have experts in legal psychiatry question her at length. Their findings came back suggesting that on the day that Francine had killed Mickey, after years of abuse, Francine did indeed have a psychological breakdown. This breakdown caused her to become totally out of control, and thus not criminally responsible for killing Mickey. If the jury believed that Francine did indeed suffer from temporary insanity, she could get off completely. The prosecution of course was building its case on the hard-line approach that Francine had committed cold-blooded murder. Chief Prosecutor Peter Houk contended, "there was no impending necessity for the action taken by the defendant. Mr. Hughes was asleep when the conflagration occurred."[18]

A few days before the trial began, Greydanus received disturbing news. The prosecutor had letters in his possession that Francine had written to Walkup while she was in jail. She had poured her heart out calling Walkup "sweetheart" and alluded to their brief ill-fated romance. Greydanus was not even aware of the relationship. After discussing the letters with Francine, Greydanus came to the conclusion that they were just a form of naive escapism for her. However, he knew the prosecution would use the letters a proof of a motive for why Francine had killed Mickey—to get him out of the way so she could be with Walkup. The fact that unbeknownst to Francine, Walkup had recently been charged with raping a child and had committed suicide before his trial started just added to the sensationalism of the situation.

Media interest was at a peak by the time Francine's trial started on October 24, 1977. Spectators ranging from reporters, feminists supporters, students who were given extra credit for attending, and curious local people flocked to the trial eager to learn more details of the case. Cynthia Kyle indicates in the article "Curious Spectators Flock to Hughes Murder Trial" that a retired secretary who came to the courtroom noted, "We see so much on television that's exaggerated. I'd like to see what's real and what's being promoted. I want to see if there is a right and wrong."[19] The trial lasted for 8 days while the jury heard 43 witnesses.[20] In the end, it was the testimony of Francine herself that was most compelling. She was able to paint a believable picture of what it was like to live a life of physical and emotional brutality, feeling helpless to leave, and afraid of being killed. The jury acquitted her.

In 1977, the country was angry, and the Women's Movement had just shifted into high gear. That was the year the film *Network*—with its classic line, "I'm mad as hell and I'm not gonna take it anymore"—swept the Academy Awards. Francine became a symbol of an ordinary woman who was mad as hell and who was not going to take it anymore. Media across the country ran articles weighing in over whether or not the verdict was appropriate. Mickey's brother was quoted as saying, "I think this will give a lot of violent women an excuse to go out and commit violent acts. . . . To take their revenge."[21] Shortly after the trial, Francine and her attorney appeared on a TV show hosted by Stanley Siegel, a well-known shock-talk personality. Knowing it would titillate his audience, he turned to Francine and said, "After thirteen years of public humiliation, beatings, kicking the baby . . . I'm going to ask you what you felt when you realized you had to set fire to your husband."[22] Trisha Cofiell indicates in the article "Anatomy of a Murder" that when Francine appeared on *The Phil Donahue Show,* the audience burst into applause as she got to the part of the murder.[23]

In the same year of Francine's verdict, *The Women's Room* by Marilyn French—a story about a submissive young woman's gradual feminist awakening—hit the best-seller list. And only a few short years later, Helen Reddy's Grammy Award-winning song "I Am Woman (Hear Me Roar)" became an anthem for females everywhere. Two fundamental tenets characterized the Women's Movement at that time: (1) women are usually, if not always, right; and (2) at the base of all women's problems was the tyranny of male oppression. Feminists were fuming. And how could anyone blame them?

Men commonly abused their wives or girlfriends, and if the woman tried to defend herself, she faced challenges on every front. The struggle started with the long-standing cultural expectation that "grinning and bearing" a healthy dose of male misbehavior was necessary to sustain a relationship. It continued with the embarrassment and shame of admitting that an abusive incident had occurred, much less reporting it. If a woman did summon the courage to call the police, chances of the authorities taking her seriously were slim to none. And there was little access to safe havens. Women's shelters—scarce and underfunded—were largely ineffectual at keeping victims safe. The final insult? A legal system that couldn't or wouldn't protect them. Women had had enough. A perfect storm had been building for a rethinking and overhaul of the entire system, and the case of Francine Hughes proved to be the catalyst for those changes to finally take place.

Film, television, books, magazines, music, and news reports are the lenses through which we view current events. As such, they define popular culture and play a powerful role in shaping our perceptions, viewpoints, and values. So in order to understand public reaction to the Hughes or any other murder case, it's important to look at how the perpetrator is depicted through these media. Consistent with prevailing social norms in 1977, female killers were depicted in one of two ways: They were either victims or vixens. There was little in between. In light of this simplistic dichotomy, one had no choice but to take sides: Francine Hughes was either warm-hearted or cold-blooded, gallant or cunning, good or evil.

Those who demonized Francine had an indelible picture of Mickey peacefully sleeping, unaware of the smoke and flames hovering around his bed. *Time* magazine's article "The Law: A Killing Excuse" represented Francine as a villain who walked away unpunished after killing someone in the heat of a domestic quarrel.[24] *Newsweek* echoed this portrayal in the essay "Wives Who Battered Back," decrying the new legitimacy for violent retaliation.[25]

But the piece with by far the most powerful and enduring impact on the public psyche was the 1984 TV movie *The Burning Bed*, starring Farrah Fawcett as Francine. Director Robert Greenwald hoped to make a believable and realistic movie that depicted the psychological dynamics of the situation without excusing it.[26] The movie was lauded by critics, earning numerous awards as well as commercial success. It generated the highest ratings for a TV movie that season. According to Greenwald's recollection, more people watched it than the presidential debates that year. *The Burning Bed* was further distinguished as the first television movie to offer victims of domestic abuse help through a nationwide 800 number. According to Charisse Van Horn, in the article "Farrah Fawcett's 'The Burning Bed' Brought Domestic Violence to the Forefront," Fawcett's performance left audiences gripped with raw emotion and caused the Hughes case to become "woven into the fabric of American culture."[27] A few years later, Francine became the subject of a song coauthored by folk singer Lyn Hardy. Entitled "The Ballad of Francine Hughes," it succinctly detailed the horrors of abuse she endured, also documenting her trial and acquittal. It ends on the ominous note that a woman is beaten every 18 seconds, lamenting that every day in court a batterer goes free.[28] Over 3,000 viewers have seen Hardy's performance of the song on YouTube. "The Ballad of Francine Hughes" has also been included in the Smithsonian's collection of folk songs. No question that the Hughes case made an enormous impact on the debate surrounding domestic violence and women who kill their abusers. Hughes became a powerful symbol for battered women.

Before *The Burning Bed,* media depictions of women in volatile domestic situations mostly adhered to the victim/vixen dichotomy. The 1951 film, *A Streetcar Named Desire,* featured two female leads—Stella Kowalski (Kim Hunter), the self-effacing, deferential housewife, and her pretentious, worldly, sexually charged sister, Blanche DuBois (Vivien Leigh). After being raped by Kowalski's husband, Blanche is committed to a mental institution, while Stella loses and never regains her once blissful marital paradise. Both punished further for their troubles. Neither one is a heroine. In the 1976 film, *Carrie,* Sissy Spacek plays an unpopular teenage girl with a troubled home life. Like Francine Hughes, she at last discovers her power in a fiery, deadly mêlée that she alone ignites. Unlike Hughes, Spacek's character gets no sympathy or justice at the end to compensate for her years of suffering and torture.

Many people felt compassion for Francine Hughes, and a jury found her *not guilty* of murder. What traits did this woman possess that made her such a sympathetic character? She came from a *modest* background. She was *sincere* in her desire to make her marriage work. She was *loyal* to her husband and family. And she was *unglamorous.*

Three features of the murder itself are also telling: First, the act was *spontaneous,* not strategic or carefully planned out. Second, it was *brazen,* replete with flames shooting up to the sky and no ready-made alibi. But the brazenness of the killing was tempered by a third feature: *bravery.* With no precedent for a sympathetic verdict, Francine risked the likely consequences of humiliation, shame, condemnation, incarceration, and even death—all in order to save her children and herself. Mixed together, this batch of improbable ingredients gelled into what turned out to be for Francine Hughes a handy recipe for acquittal.

LIYSA NORTHON

Only two people know what really took place on the night of October 8, 2000, at the Shady Campgrounds near the Lostine River in Oregon. One of them, Chris Northon, was found in a mummy bag zipped up over his face, dead from a single bullet through the temple from a short-barreled .38-caliber revolver.[29] The other, his wife Liysa, was charged with murder. The controversy surrounding Liysa Northon centers on what type of man her husband was and whether she was even a battered wife to begin with.

In this situation, we are presented with a scenario in which the character of the respective players is not clear. Was the victim a model of a loving husband or a vicious abuser? This type of ambiguity is often utilized effectively in fiction works to keep the audience guessing, but in a real life case, it only serves to complicate not only the jury's decision process but the public's opinion as well. The prominent true-crime author Ann Rule wrote a best seller regarding the Northon case, *Heart Full of Lies,* which provides an interesting dichotomy between two representations of the same event.[30] Rule's account, which cemented Northon's image in popular culture, has been challenged by Liysa and her supporters in a controversy that continues to this day.

On the surface, Liysa and Chris seemed like a storybook couple. They were an attractive pair—she was pretty, blonde, and petite; he was tall and good-looking. Outdoor sports were important to both: Liysa enjoyed surfing, while Chris pursued mountain biking, skiing, and other athletic endeavors. Each was an accomplished professional: Liysa was a writer and photographer, while Chris was a pilot with Hawaiian Airlines. Both were devoted to their children. They lived a glamorous life shuttling between Kailua, in Oahu, one of the most beautiful beach towns in Hawaii, and the mountain resort town of Bend, Oregon. What went wrong that would cause Liysa to admit to putting a bullet through Chris's head?

Liysa DeWitt came from an affluent middle-class background, spending her formative years in Walla Walla, Washington. While she had a close relationship with her father, who was a well-known and respected community college administrator, her relationship with her mother seemed more problematic. According to Rule's account, Liysa would claim her mother beat her.[31] Whether this parental abuse actually took place, whether it was just overly strict discipline, or whether Liysa fabricated it is open to speculation.

Liysa went off to college in Oregon and married her first husband at 19. Allegations about Liysa's infidelity and her seeming inability to separate fact from fiction caused this "starter marriage" to end in divorce. Her first husband indicated, "She could twist information in the complete opposite direction from reality. She would say *anything* to convince you her story was true."[32] During her ill-fated marriage, Liysa and her husband had moved to Hawaii, a tropical paradise setting where she seemed to find herself. She was the quintessential surfer girl in love with the ocean. She discovered she was good at writing and spent a great deal of time perfecting her craft.

Friends observed an odd trait in Liysa, noting that her storytelling seemed to spill into her personal life. It was hard to tell which parts of her exploits were true and which were false. She often told people multiple versions of an event or contradicted facts they considered to be true based on their own observation. Rule recounts an episode in her book in which Liysa claimed to have amnesia, which lasted for months. Whether the amnesia was real or another example of the dangerous drama she liked to create to manipulate people and block out unpleasant issues she did not want to confront is not certain.

Liysa was a beautiful woman who had no problems attracting men. Her relationships were often filled with intense physical passion and often overlapped, resulting in the chaotic highs and lows associated with complicated situations. She married her second husband in the late 1980s. The marriage started out promising. Her husband was a well-known surf and underwater photographer, allowing him to travel to exotic locations, engage in exciting activities, and experience financial success. Liysa had the opportunity to enjoy these benefits. Under her husband's tutelage, she became an accomplished surf photographer. Her ability behind the camera led to well-paid assignments of her own. The couple also worked together on a successful coffee table book, *Hanauma Bay, an Island Treasure,* which featured stunning photographs of Hawaii accompanied by short narratives addressing historical, social, and ecological issues related to the bay. The book provided her with an outlet to display her creative abilities and enhanced her reputation as a gifted individual. Photography and, particularly, writing would continue to play an important role in her self-definition.

But the talent most important to Liysa was her talent as a mother. At 29, she had a son, who quickly became the center of her life. Liysa went out of her way to provide him with a warm, loving environment that emphasized gentleness and creativity. People often commented on their close bond, and many admired Liysa for her dedicated parenting efforts. If motherhood came easily to Liysa, sustaining a marriage was more problematic. After spending nearly a decade with her husband, Liysa was ready to get out of the relationship. She and her husband had grown apart: they had different goals as well as diverse ideas on what was important, where to spend their money, and how to spend their life together. More significantly, Liysa had met Chris Northon.

Chris had spent most of his formative years growing up on a ranch in Oregon with a close-knit family. Although Chris was a consummate athlete who constantly challenged himself in a variety of sports, he was not a one-dimensional action man. He appreciated music, playing both piano and violin. Reading always interested him. Moreover, Chris had a sensitive side and was not afraid to show emotions or vulnerability.[33] According to Rule, relationships with family were important to him.[34] He was passionate about flying, which represented freedom and adventure—personally significant factors in his lifestyle. To earn a successful living as a pilot takes time, but Chris enjoyed the activities he embarked on over the years in pursuit of his goal. During his stints with chartered airlines, the military, and commercial airlines, he had traveled all around the world. Rule notes in her account of the Northon case that Chris told his father, "I've had a wonderful life. If I died tomorrow, I wouldn't feel as though I'd missed anything."[35]

By the time he met Liysa, Chris was a commercial pilot for Hawaiian Airlines. He was splitting his time between a house in Bend, Oregon, and a bachelor pad he shared on the island of Oahu, just across the street from Liysa and her husband. Liysa was quick to notice her tall, handsome neighbor. Chris had an easygoing charm coupled with a friendly manner. Thanks to his job and his personality, he had a dashing quality. Chris was attracted to Liysa's striking looks that conveyed a sensual aura. Yet, he also noted her depth and creative bent. She was a successful photographer with a career of her own. Both of them shared a strong love for their adopted state, the Hawaiian lifestyle, and the ocean. The fact that she had a husband was problematic, but Chris wasn't looking to get married.[36]

Liysa, however, wanted more. She and her husband had been at an impasse for over a year, by the time she met Chris in 1994. Her husband was happy with the photography business and the investment property they acquired, but Liysa had grander ideas. She talked constantly about acquiring more real estate and moving to Oregon in hopes of developing a range or retreat. Recognizing the marriage had run its course, they agreed to divorce. Now Liysa wanted to be Chris's wife.

Although he wasn't a player by nature, Chris had dated many women over the years and had been in a number of serious relationships, but marriage was not a priority. Pushing 40, he appeared to be a confirmed bachelor. Liysa was undeterred, and set out to make Chris her third husband. She had always been good at expressing herself on the written page, so she embarked on a letter-writing campaign to convince Chris that she was the perfect woman. Using all her talent and skill in persuasion, she painted a glowing picture of how much more fulfilling his life would be if they were married. Chris stalled.

Liysa backed off marriage for a while and they reunited. While some of Chris's friends liked Liysa, others felt she was too moody and manipulative. They weren't sure Chris could be happy with her over the long term, but they also knew that nobody could tell Chris what to do; he had to decide for himself. Professing eternal love, Liysa continued the letter-writing campaign: "I know in my heart that your life would be wonderful if you let me in. I know that there is a bond that is almost a mandate between us. I feel your resistance is almost humorous considering the inevitability, the alchemy, the certainty I feel."[37] Alchemy or no alchemy, Liysa did complain on occasion to her friends about their relationship. When one of them asked why she stayed, she coolly asserted that it was to take advantage of Chris's travel benefits. Despite her disparaging remarks, Liysa continued to make efforts to win Chris over. When he eventually put his reluctance aside in 1996, Liysa acted quickly, possibly to prevent a change of heart.

Their married life started out happily enough as they both appeared to be in love. They enjoyed each other's company. They liked to spend time outdoors engaged in physical activities. Commuting back and forth between Bend and Kailua allowed them to remain close to their families. Each of them took pleasure in socializing with the other's friends. Liysa had wanted more children; her wish was granted when she gave birth to another boy in 1997. Chris became devoted to his son and marveled at the depth of instantaneous love he felt toward the child.[38]

While Chris and Liysa were delighted to be parents, they were having trouble being married partners. As eager as Liysa had been to get Chris to totally commit to a life with her, now that he had, she was constantly finding fault with him. In order to avoid conflict, Chris would often simply walk away. His pattern of withdrawal created issues between the two. Rule would characterize Liysa as a woman who "can make any man do what she wants, for a while."[39] If it is true that Liysa was used to getting what she wanted in a relationship, her inability to control Chris may have contributed to their problems.

For the first but not the last time, Liysa began to make a series of allegations about her husband's behavior. Shortly after their son was born, Liysa joined a postpartum swimming pool therapy group. When the women noticed bruises on Liysa, she indicated that Chris had been abusing her physically.[40] Another friend from Oregon heard about Liysa's fear of physical harm not only to herself but also to the children.[41] Upon hearing these stories, naturally, she was urged to leave Chris. Liysa would contend that no matter where she went, her husband would hunt her down and kill her. They believed her.

In 1997, Liysa called the Honolulu police after she and Chris engaged in a heated argument. She claimed that Chris had beaten her. Although a police account was filed and a statement taken, the report indicated there were apparently no injuries.[42] According to Rule's account, Liysa even went to Jeanne Northon privately and told her Chris had tried to choke her. Jeanne was astounded over the allegations. She could not imagine Chris being capable of any type of violence. "Liysa told me Chris had tried to strangle her. . . . She told me she had marks on her neck. I looked but I could not see anything."[43]

Richard Cockle writes in the article "Eastern Oregon Killer Liysa Northon, Featured in Ann Rule Book, Eyes New Life after Her Release from Prison Next Year" that Liysa characterized Chris as a "drug-addicted 'high-functioning alcoholic' given to rages and violence."[44] If these charges were true, none of Chris's friends seemed to be aware of the situation. People, however, were aware that the couple was spending less time together even though they had been married for just two years. Rule indicates that Chris wanted to salvage the marriage and suggested counseling, but Liysa quit after a few sessions.[45] It's possible that Chris continued therapy in an effort to learn effective ways to diffuse the constant tension between them.

In the early part of 1999, Chris found himself in exactly the type of situation he wanted to avoid. He and Liysa engaged in a bitter quarrel that ended in a physical altercation. According to Rule's version of events, Chris accidentally hit her while he was pushing her away, causing Liysa to hurt her knees badly when she fell to the ground; Liysa punched him, giving him a bloody nose.[46] Subsequently, Liysa went to the hospital for her injuries, telling the doctor she was a victim of abuse. This set in motion a chain of events, resulting in Chris being arrested. The charges were dropped when Liysa failed to show up on the trial date.[47] Richard Swart, a reporter who directly interviewed Liysa (unlike Rule) and was instrumental in challenging Rule's depiction of the Northon marriage, states in the article "Ann Rule's Sloppy Storytelling" that Liysa got a restraining order against Chris after this incident.[48]

Rule notes that after his arrest, "Chris was horribly embarrassed."[49] He may have felt the picture painted by these charges were inaccurate at best, damning at worst. In any event, Chris started to formally explore ways to end the marriage. However, the prenuptial agreement between the couple held him back. In the event of a divorce, Liysa would get full custody of any children. Chris did not want to lose his son.[50] On her part, Liysa also consulted an attorney and continued to feed her friends horrific stories of Chris's abuse. According to Swart's account, Liysa claimed that the beatings occurred as often as two or three times a week.[51] She would also contend that Chris hit her in the face with his fist, smashed her head against the wall, dragged her by the hair, kicked her in the ribs, choked her, and threw her out of a moving car.[52]

While the marriage limped along, the two pursued their own interests. Chris would embark on solitary athletic activities or immerse himself in work. As an airline pilot, it was not uncommon for him to be gone stretches at a time. Liysa would write. Over the years, she had become adept not only in stories and novels, but screenplays as well. Gary Fletcher indicates in the article "Plea Bargain Brings Trial to End" that three of her scripts dealt with an airline pilot whose abused wife purchased life insurance on her spouse and then killed him.[53] Her work reflected a high degree of talent and professionalism. In 1999, she met a successful screenwriter during one of her trips to Hawaii. He offered to work with her on a project in hopes of getting it produced. She spent time working on the script to get it ready. With something to focus on, Liysa's discontent in her marriage seemed to abate. The ever-present animosity she felt toward Chris subsided. He hoped that their marriage had turned a corner.[54]

Unfortunately, the prospective movie deal with Liysa and her partner fell through. The screenplay had represented a golden opportunity to make it big financially. Liysa had often talked about buying a ranch or retreat. Chris had not shown any interest in either idea. An approved deal would have provided money for these and any other dreams she had. To most people, being a Hollywood player is an exciting prospect. It's hard to imagine that Liysa did not share the same aspiration. Yet ever resilient, she decided to work on projects by herself over the next six months. However, Liysa's writing came to a halt during the summer of 2000, when she told Chris that her computer had been stolen.[55] Rule notes that without any backup copies, Liysa was inconsolable.[56]

Liysa's anger and resentment against Chris was taking its toll. She told her father about the alleged abuse. He was so concerned about his daughter's safety that he gave her a .38 revolver to use as protection.[57] Although Chris was ignorant of their conversation, he was very aware of his wife's animosity toward him. According to Rule's account, Chris told a friend, "Liysa's getting psycho—you have no idea how psycho she is."[58] Despite all the tension, or maybe because of it, they decided to go away on a camping trip on October 6, 2000. Their older son would stay with a friend, while the younger son, a three-year-old, would come along.

The Oregon campgrounds near the Lostine River are located in a remote, isolated area. What exactly happened that weekend is unclear. However, what is clear is that on Monday, October 9, 2000, Chris was found dead in his sleeping bag. He had been shot in the head. That very same day, after stopping first at her brother's, then at her friend's to pick up her older son, Liysa went to a hospital to be examined for an alleged domestic assault. The sheriff's department came to investigate. Liysa claimed that during the weekend, Chris drank heavily and took drugs including marijuana. In a night filled with horror, Chris became violent and terrorized her for hours. She fought back fiercely as he tried to choke her and drown her in the river. Eventually, he gave up and went off to sleep. Fearful for her life, she pulled out the gun she carried for protection and shot him as he lay sleeping. Then, she quickly picked up her son and drove off to escape.

After further questioning, Liysa was released from the hospital. The investigation continued. Chris's dead body was found. When Liysa turned herself into authorities, she was arrested for murder. Rule states, "It clearly wasn't what she expected."[59] She was shocked that authorities did not accept her story of self-defense at face value. While her friends and family believed this account, others did not. Certain things were not adding up. According to the deputy who responded to the domestic violence allegation at the hospital, Liysa had a slight black eye, slight shoulder and knee scrapes, and no marks on her neck, noted Gary Fletcher in the article "Defense, State Lay out Cases in Murder Trial."[60] This did not seem congruent with her account of a horrible physical beating that took place over a long period of hours.

Physical evidence from the scene of the crime contradicted Liysa's account of her wildly shooting in Chris's direction. Instead, it looked as if the shots were aimed down directly at his head. As detectives probed into Chris's background, they heard overwhelming denials from his friends and family that he had ever hurt anyone physically, including Liysa. Instead, they shared stories that put Liysa in an unfavorable light. They also denied that Chris was a heavy drinker and drug user. Hawaiian Airlines confirmed that Chris had a clean drug test record. The investigation continued with conflicting testimony and strong emotions coming to the forefront.

Liysa hired one of the top defense attorneys in Oregon. Listed in *Best Lawyers in America*, Pat Birmingham had over 20 years experience dealing with complex charges involving murder, manslaughter, and criminal negligence. He was known for winning his cases. Listening to Liysa's version of events, he developed a strategy based on her claim of self-defense. Her legal team was ready to call 30 witnesses that would support her story of continued spouse abuse.[61] The district attorney, Dan Owsley, prepared to argue that Liysa was a lying ruthless killer who got rid of her husband when she no longer needed him and tried to use the "abuse excuse" to justify her actions. Although the case had not made national or state headlines, Court TV decided to broadcast the trial. Both sides anticipated that it would take weeks. Surprisingly enough, it took just four days.

While Liysa had accused Chris of drinking heavily and using marijuana that night, blood tests entered as evidence by the prosecution showed neither. However, the tests did show heavy doses of sedatives. Gary Fletcher's article, "Murder Victim Heavily Sedated, Toxicologist Says," indicates that according to the testifying forensic toxicologist, the level of sedatives was so high it could have caused a coma or death.[62] A pathologist also testified that Chris's chest had unexplained scratches that were not consistent with Liysa's fingernails. These clinical facts seemed to overshadow emotional testimony provided by Liysa's brother and friend that she indeed shared with them how she was afraid of her life due to Chris's numerous beatings.

Behind the scenes, even more dramatic evidence surfaced. Apparently, Liysa's long-lost computer had been found containing incriminating evidence. Another of Gary Fletcher's articles, "Plea Bargain Brings Trial to End," stated that the computer allegedly had information that showed Liysa had tried to obtain Valium and a stun gun.[63] Liysa told her attorney that while she did own a stun gun to protect her, she had not taken it on the camping trip. Although the stun gun was not submitted into evidence, the fact that a stun gun could have caused the unexplained scratches on Chris's chest did not bode well for her. To make matters worse, according to the prosecutor, the computer contained numerous e-mails from Liysa indicating she had been thinking about this crime or at least anticipating it.[64] The screenplay she wrote about the abused wife who killed her husband could become evidence against her. If the trial continued, it was possible that the jury could conclude that Liysa had deliberately drugged her husband to render him unconscious, used a Taser gun on him while he was asleep, and finally shot him to make sure he was dead; her motive: clear financial gain. Liysa stood to gain $300,000 from Chris's insurance policy since she was the beneficiary, she would have airline pilot widow's benefits that would allow her to fly free, and sole control of the couple's property valued in excess of $1 million.[65]

And what of all her tales of abuse? The jury might conclude that she had made it all up—not only about the night of the killing, but also all the other stories she had told her family and friends over time. In an unexpected move, less than a week into the trial, Liysa accepted a plea bargain of first-degree manslaughter while under the influence of extreme emotional distress. The only words she spoke to the jury were to say, "I did what I had to do to save myself and my children who are the paramount thing in my life. . . . It's just too bad that this is what it takes to protect one's family."[66] She was sentenced to 12½ years in prison and barred from drawing money from Chris's estate or employment benefits.

Except for the initial Court TV coverage during the trial, the story had been relatively low profile. Media coverage consisted of reports from *The Observer,* a local newspaper in Oregon, and a small item that ran in the *Honolulu Star Bulletin,* noting that Chris had been a pilot for Hawaiian Airlines. But public interest in the case changed dramatically in 2003, when noted true-crime author Ann Rule published her book carrying the tagline "A True Story of Desire and Death." A former police officer, Rule burst onto the scene as a prominent author with her first book *The Stranger Beside Me,* an account of serial killer Ted Bundy. Bundy had been her friend and colleague while they worked together on a suicide hotline. Rule became well known for gripping accounts that focused not only on the crime itself, but also on the family histories and backstories of the main characters. Her work provides in-depth personality studies of both the murderer and the victim.

In the Northon case, Rule commented on the split between how the two individuals were perceived, how their actions were interpreted, and what the evidence suggested. During her gathering of research, she found two distinct camps regarding Chris and Liysa. Neither side could agree on much regarding the characteristic makeup of the key individuals. Chris was either a model husband or brutal wife beater. Liysa was either a heroic wife and mother or a cold-blooded killer. The book's afterword offers a summary of the facts and evidence to support Rule's theory that Liysa spent years telling stories of alleged abuse so she could eventually kill him and get away with it.

Like most of Rule's books, her account of the Northon case shot to the best-seller list. More than one million copies were sold, suddenly turning Liysa's case into a high-profile story. In 2004, Liysa, her father, and her brother were so unhappy with the book that they filed a suit against Rule and her publishing company, citing over a hundred separate statements they claimed to be defamatory. In their opinion, the book was not a "true story," as Rule claimed, but one that presented a fictionalized account clearly biased in favor of Chris and the entire Northon family. According to Liysa's brother, Rule had not even attempted to contact him directly although he had been a key witness at the trial. He indicated that he would have been willing and able to corroborate Liysa's contention that Chris had abused her for years.[67]

Liysa engaged in a very visible war of words with Rule. She has her own website, maintained by friends, dedicated to proving her innocence. The site contains a biographical statement, Liysa's personal statement on why she did not leave Chris, and a copy of the Northon versus Rule appellant brief. Using a question-and-answer format, offering pages and pages and pages of detailed analysis, Liysa addresses more than 50 issues she believes were outright lies or distortions from Rule's book.

Liysa may be a convicted killer, but she is determined to get an image makeover in the court of public opinion. She seemed to be on the losing end of this battle when she lost her defamation suit against Rule in January 2011. This setback did not stop her from trying to clear her name. Liysa was back in the media spotlight six months later with the publication of Rick Swart's article, "Ann Rule's Sloppy Storytelling." This article created a controversy not only because the writer supported Liysa's contention of self-defense and disparaged Ann Rule, but also because he deliberately chose not to reveal a critical fact—he and Liysa were romantically involved. Failure to disclose their relationship violated journalistic ethical standards. Supporters and detractors of both Rule and Northon set the blogosphere abuzz as they hotly debated the issues. Even *The Huffington Post* weighed in on the matter. Many people criticized Swart as just another pawn manipulated by Liysa for her own ends, especially when word got around that he became Liysa's fourth husband. He was unfazed by the disapproval and indicated he had no fear of her: "I don't beat women. If I do, she has my permission to shoot me."[68]

In the 23 years between the Francine Hughes and Liysa Northon cases, the Women's Movement quietly redefined itself. Old-style feminism, with its knee-jerk response of blaming men any time a woman behaved questionably, gave way to the precept that we are all responsible for our own actions. While this change represented a major step forward for feminist ideology, it turned out to be a significant detriment for women accused of murdering their spouses.

The laws governing domestic abuse changed: by 2000, most states required doctors to notify the police of any reported case of domestic violence. The police, in turn, were required to investigate and arrest the suspect if they found any positive evidence of battery. This made it easier for a woman to build a case of abuse over time. It also made it possible for someone with an ulterior motive for murdering her husband and to envision, with proper planning, getting away with it. At the same time, restraining orders became less problematic to obtain, and shelters, hotlines, and services for battered women abounded. With so much attention given to the subject of domestic violence, the stigma of admitting and reporting spousal battery had diminished, and women were no longer expected to simply "grin and bear" abuse from their husbands or boyfriends. All good news for battered women in general, but bad news for female murder defendants: It is now harder to justify the type of desperation required to gain a jury's sympathy for the extreme act of taking a life.

Media representations of female killers also evolved over that time period. The film *Thelma & Louise* (1991) told the story of Louise (played by Susan Sarandon), who shot a man she found raping her friend Thelma (Geena Davis), transforming the two women immediately into fugitives and ultimately into martyrs. Audiences cheered Sarandon's character, who claimed justifiable retribution for having been raped herself years before. The film hailed Davis's character for choosing to replace a misguided loyalty to her husband with a well-deserved devotion to her comrade in crime. *The Last Seduction* (1994) continued the trend of glamorizing female killers. In this film, Linda Fiorentino played a sexy *femme fatale* who, through her own cleverness, gets away with murder.

During that decade, images of headline-catching killers exploded on the small screen as well. In 1996, *Medical Detectives,* an engaging true-crime reality show, debuted on the TLC Channel, and in 2000—the year of Northon's trial—the show moved to Court TV and became hugely popular under the name *Forensic Files.* With the proliferation of investigative crime shows like *48 Hour Mystery, Dateline Saturday Night, Primetime,* and *20/20* on network television, so much detailed coverage of complex murder cases served to raise the level of sophistication of the general public regarding the nuances of deadly crimes. The simplistic victim/vixen dichotomy began to recede. Add to this the advent of interactive media, and voila, you've got a public forum that can powerfully influence public opinion. The Internet "democratized" public debate, offering the opportunity for a particular perspective to gather momentum and push public opinion in that direction.

Regarding Liysa Northon, that tipping point came when Ann Rule's 2003 exposé, *Heart Full of Lies,* was published. The huge amount of interest stemming from the book generated lively feedback from readers on various websites dedicated to discussing aspects of the case including Rule's suit. The dialogue on the sites often center around Liysa's motivation, especially in light of the fact that her tangled tale of years of spouse abuse was not compelling enough or verifiable enough to build a legal strategy around. Assuming that the prosecution's depiction and Ann Rule's analysis were correct, Liysa did not kill her husband out of self-defense; her motives were more sinister. She may have been a schemer who killed for monetary gain or she may have wanted to take revenge on a man who no longer loved her the way she felt she was entitled too. Perhaps most frightening of all, she may have just been a sociopath who did not care what the adverse consequences of her actions were. Once Chris stopped making her happy, he became dispensable—it was just a matter of when and where.

Liysa's place in popular culture as a villainess was cemented with the Rule book and fanned by Internet speculation. Responses from readers of the book do not show sympathy for Northon. Rather, they illustrate anger and disgust:

> Northon's lawsuit against Rule is typical of her personality. She is still trying to portray herself as the victim! The way that she used her children as leverage shows that she is not an abused wife. She . . . deserves to be in prison longer than 12 years.—KT
>
> Liysa, why did you plead guilty???? Why didn't you face the jury? No one had a gun to YOUR head.—SMR[69]

Clearly, the public was not buying Northon's story. This was reinforced with comments that showed up on the Internet after people learned of her fourth marriage to the reporter Rick Swart.

Was it just the changing times that accounted for the public's starkly different reactions to Francine Hughes and Liysa Northon? No, there were other fundamental differences: Francine was deemed worthy of compassion because of her lower-class status, her understandable feelings of hopelessness, her admirable loyalty, and her unspectacular appearance. In contrast, Liysa Northon was privileged, talented, successful, capricious, and stunningly attractive.

Hughes acted spontaneously, out of genuine desperation. And despite the brazenness of setting her bedroom aflame, the action she took could be seen as courageous. Northon, try as she might, was unable to paint a convincing picture of herself in this same light. She had no legitimate claim to desperation. The brazenness of shooting Chris as he lay defenseless in his sleeping bag lacked any semblance of courage. For in the newly expanded consciousness of this millennium, *courage* had acquired a more refined meaning: taking responsibility for your part in the situation, affirming your own self-determination, utilizing all available resources, and focusing on building a better life—not on avenging your past. Liysa did none of these things, either at the time of her trial or since then. As a result, she emerges in the public eye not as a heroine, but as a coward.

Francine Hughes became a symbol of female empowerment not because of the brazenness of her act, but because she was perceived as courageous and brave. As we will see in future chapters, only very recently has *brazenness* also become associated with empowerment in pop culture. Unfortunately for Liysa Northon, that association didn't happen soon enough.

Women Who Kill for Revenge

The drive for revenge is one of the most basic of human emotions. So it's not surprising that Betty Broderick and Amy Bishop weren't just mad—they wanted to get even. Their way of getting even was to get a gun. When Betty's marriage of 16 years broke up over another woman and a bitter divorce left her feeling rejected, humiliated, and swindled financially, she killed her ex-husband and his new wife. Showing little remorse, Betty declared she had no regret. After being denied tenure as a biology professor, Amy blasted away at her fellow faculty members. She killed three and wounded three others. Unconcerned about her execution style actions, upon her arrest, she denied that anyone had even been hurt.

The circumstances behind their stories thrust both women into the national spotlight turning them into pop culture celebrities. As the psychiatrist Dr. Edward Hallowell notes, "We love to watch stories of people getting even. It feels so good."[1] Although a jury found Betty guilty, she became the poster child for scorned wives. Amy never was cast as an avenging hero. From the very beginning, tabloids depicted her as a "nutty professor with a heart of stone."[2] When it was revealed that she killed her brother years earlier in a questionable shooting accident and was suspected of being involved in an attempted bombing, it was easy for the public to brand Amy a "psycho scientist." An old Chinese proverb says that one who seeks revenge digs two graves. The backlash from vengeful actions and its collateral damage can take on tragic proportions as these cases illustrate.

BETTY BRODERICK

It's often been said there is a thin line between love and hate. And when that love becomes damaged, murderous hate can rear its ugly head.[3] So when Dan Broderick told his wife Betty that he didn't love her anymore, the news turned her into "an electrified crazy person."[4] He also told her she was old, fat, ugly, boring, and stupid, a comment at odds with Betty's image.[5] A former model as a young woman, she still looked thin and attractive even though she was in her late 30s and had 4 children. All through her marriage, she put her husband first. She worked to support him through medical school and then law school. While he was busy growing his practice, she was the one taking care of the children. She made sure the household ran smoothly. She was the gracious hostess entertaining his friends and clients.

Of course Dan provided quite a good life for Betty. His hard work and talent propelled him into a brilliant legal career that was financially rewarding. He and Betty both had closets full of designer clothes. They drove expensive cars. They owned a beautiful house in one of the best neighborhoods. Together they were well known on the social scene as a power couple. Author Bella Stumbo notes in her account, *Until the Twelfth of Never*, that according to one acquaintance, "They were everything we all wanted to be. . . . They looked about as good as it gets."[6]

Yet underneath the trappings of success, the marriage had gone sour. When Betty accused him of having an affair with his young assistant, Dan denied it and told Betty she was crazy. Years after, when he finally confessed that it was true, Betty was determined to keep the marriage alive. Dan was just as determined to end it. However, as Betty engaged in escalating vindictive actions, he predicted, "It's not going to end until one of us is gone."[7] He was right. It didn't end until Betty snuck into Dan's house and shot him and his new wife, while they were sleeping. On her wedding day, Betty truly thought she and Dan would be together "till death do us part." She didn't realize that someday her actions would give the phrase a sinister meaning.

When 17-year-old Betty Biscegelia met Dan Broderick at a college football game in 1965, she had traditional aspirations that Dan seemed to share. Both were willing to make sacrifices, considered marriage a lifelong partnership, and looked forward to a time when they could enjoy the comforts of the American Dream. At their wedding, they vowed to be married for at least 50 years.[8]

Despite good intentions, the marriage was rocky from the start. According to Bryna Taubman in her book *Hell Hath No Fury*, within weeks, Dan told friends he had made a terrible mistake and Betty talked about getting a divorce even though it was at odds with her strict religious upbringing.[9] Dan turned his attention away from Betty and focused on his studies. He would bury himself in textbooks expecting her to take care of all the domestic duties.

She felt neglected and taken for granted. When they learned Betty had become pregnant on their honeymoon, it came as a shock. The newlyweds were not emotionally or financially prepared to be parents. Betty was still expected to be the primary wage-earner since Dan was in medical school. Needing the money, she worked until the day she went into labor. Betty became pregnant a second time a mere 10 months after their first child was born.

In the middle of his residency, Dan decided he wanted to attend Harvard law school to become a medical attorney. Betty continued to juggle multiple part-time jobs, taking care of an increasing number of children, and taking care of Dan. She remembers "hauling dirty diapers to the laundry in the freezing snow on a bus while he was out at some student activities event or home studying. At the time though, I didn't complain. We were a partnership and that was part of my job."[10]

Upon Dan's graduation in 1973, they decided to accept an offer from a law firm in California. Betty threw herself into activities, befitting the wife of an up-and-coming attorney. She joined charity organizations. She volunteered at the children's school and continued to work. "Dan went out and slew the dragons and provided for us, and I was home and hearth and children, and supported my husband emotionally and through the good times and bad."[11] When Dan decided to open his own one-man medical malpractice firm in 1978, the money started rolling in. But by the early 1980s, the Broderick's were drifting apart. Betty felt Dan was neglecting her and the children. "The guy was just a phantom. And I was a workhorse from five a.m., getting all the kids dressed and all the homework done and everybody off where they're supposed to go . . . he never had anything to do with any of it."[12]

Dan's world was getting bigger and bigger. He was earning more than $1 million a year and became president of the San Diego Bar Association. Betty's world seemed to get smaller and smaller. Amy Wallace states in her article "Till Murder Do Us Part," "Betty's days consisted of shuttling her four children to and from music lessons and soccer games, planning the couple's busy social calendar, and tending to the yard and housework."[13] She accused Dan of making decisions regarding the family's lifestyle without consulting her or taking into consideration her preferences. It appeared that Dan no longer looked at her as an equal partner. In fact, it appeared that Dan no longer looked at her at all. There was a reason for it. Her name was Linda.

Dan first noticed 21-year-old Linda Kolkena in 1983 when she was a receptionist in his building. Tall, blonde, and pretty, she looked like a younger version of Betty. Dan hired Linda to be his assistant, even though she had no legal training or experience in medical malpractice. Betty was immediately suspicious. When Dan told his wife later that summer that he was discontent with his life, Betty asked him if there was another woman. Although he categorically denied it, Betty was worried. Hoping to turn the situation around, she read self-help books, consulted a cosmetic surgeon, and updated her wardrobe. It didn't work. She grew so depressed over the situation that she tried to commit suicide in 1983. Dan reassured her that nothing was going on with Linda. Wanting to believe him, she started seeing a therapist to cope with her fears. She decided to throw a romantic surprise celebration for Dan's 39th birthday and went to his office. He and Linda were already out celebrating. She waited for hours, but they did not return. When she got home, she gathered up his expensive clothes and doused them with gasoline. When he finally arrived that night, Dan still denied having an affair with Linda.

But Dan was having an affair. He continued to lead a double life for two years, juggling his wife and girlfriend. Betty clung to evidence that Dan was happy with her and tried to ignore pieces that didn't fit. Dan accused her of being paranoid and suspicious whenever she questioned him. She later contended this was all part of a plot he designed to drive her insane. In 1985, he told Betty he needed space and moved out. According to her, he still refused to admit that he and Linda were involved with each other.

Betty soon panicked. She dumped the children along with their personal belongings on Dan's doorsteps. Now they were all his responsibility. Betty was banking on the fact that Dan would become overwhelmed with the demands of parenting and come running back to her. Instead, he kept the children and later sought full custody of them. Dan now controlled access to the children as well as access to all their money. He told her she would have to go on a budget and cut back on her lifestyle. Betty's feelings of vulnerability and dependency consumed her with indignation.[14] One day, when she went to visit the children at Dan's house, she decided to get back at him. She found a pie that Linda had baked and smeared it all over the walls. Dan's response to the vandalism was to call the police and get a restraining order.

Despair overcame Betty when she was finally served with divorce papers after 16 years of marriage.[15] Predictably, but unrealistically, Betty had always hoped her errant husband would return to her. But now, after three years of lying, Dan finally admitted that he and Linda were in love; in fact, they had been together all this time. Her plan to just wait it out was futile. She had no idea who to turn to for fair representation. Dan knew all the top lawyers in San Diego. Since no one locally was willing to take her case, she went to a highly recommended Beverly Hills lawyer. It was just the beginning of a five-year battle that turned both Brodericks' lives into hell. Dan's first step in the messy divorce was to file an order to show cause. Whenever Betty ignored the restraining order and committed small acts of vandalism against his property, he would haul Betty into court and ask her to explain why she should not be held in contempt. The vandalism included breaking a bedroom mirror, spray painting wallpaper, smashing a stereo, and tearing off his car antenna. Betty considered this trivial compared to all of his lying over the previous years.

Dan next got a court order to sell their house in La Jolla without Betty's consent. Since their separation, he and Betty had both moved into new places.

Betty agreed in principle, but it was hard for her to let go of the family home. Despite her initial agreement, she sabotaged the transaction on two different occasions. Dan took her to court forcing the sale. When she learned of the ruling, she was livid. She got into her car, drove onto his lawn, and smashed it right through her husband's front door. Dan called the police. Betty was taken away in a straight jacket. She stayed under mental observation for a few days. Joseph Geringer noted in his article "Betty Broderick: Divorce . . . Desperation . . . Death" that Betty had been "a beautiful, intelligent, and talented woman in her own right and by all accounts she worked ceaselessly to create and maintain a near-perfect life for her family, an environment in which her children and ambitious husband could thrive."[16] Now her feelings of betrayal and rage so clouded her judgments that she became known to her friends as "Crazy Betty." She began telling people that she wanted to kill him.

Dan started efforts to use a legal tactic called Epstein credits that later would cost Betty more than half a million dollars in her share of community property. Blithely unaware of this legal manipulation, she refused to pay her Beverly Hills attorney's fees, figuring that Dan would pay them. Not surprisingly, Dan refused. Betty eventually went through three attorneys all the while ignoring their advice. Ultimately, she decided to represent herself. She never expected that Dan would get full custody of the children, that his legal manipulations would take a huge chunk out of her share of community property, that the case would drag on for years, and that at Dan's formal request the court records would be sealed.

As the divorce battles raged on, Betty did try to take control of her life but failed. She could not break away from her obsessive anger toward Dan and Linda. She left dozens of obscene phone messages on Dan's answering machine. The fact that it was Linda's voice on the machine was even more infuriating. She would berate Dan for not paying the bills, yell at him for not checking with her on plans regarding the children, and call Linda a home wrecker. In an effort to stop the messages, Dan devised a fining system that affected her monthly support allowance. According to the article "Till Murder Do Us Part" written by Amy Wallace, "Dan began to withhold $100 for every obscene word she used, $250 each time she set foot on his property, $500 for every entry into his house, and $1,000 every time she took one of the children without his permission."[17]

Dan was tired of hearing Betty complain that he did not support her financially. He wrote to her, "in the twenty months we have been separated, over $450,000 has been spent on you or made available for your use and enjoyment. If you don't have enough money to pay your bills, you only have yourself to blame."[18] Once again Betty was incensed. He was making nearly $2 million a year, thanks in part to her efforts, yet he was threatening to cut her off. She stormed over to his house to berate him and ask how he expected her to live. Dan wasted no time calling the police, since this action violated the restraining order he had taken out. She was arrested, and spent a few hours in jail. On another occasion, she spent six days in jail. From Betty's perspective, the jail time showed just how contemptible Dan was to press charges against the mother of his children.

By the time the divorce and financial settlement came through in 1989, she was awarded $16,000 a month in spousal support and a cash award of $28,000. Meanwhile, Dan got the multimillion-dollar legal practice as well as full custody of the children. She had gone from being Mrs. Dan Broderick to "I wasn't Mrs. Anything."[19] Gaining 60 pounds, she became depressed and reclusive. Former friends who once considered her the perfect wife and mother, now shunned her. In addition to learning from the grapevine all about Betty's self-destructive acts, rumors circulated among them that one of the reasons for the sealed divorce court records was that Betty had been accused of being a child molester. "I thought I would die just right then, when I heard that—I felt like the wind had been knocked out of me."[20] Her once close relationship to her children was strained. As an attempt to punish each other, both of the Brodericks had manipulated the children and put them in the middle of their divorce fight. Not surprisingly, the older children acted out, while the younger ones felt neglected. The close family that had once been so picture perfect no longer existed.

Dan married Linda in April 1989. Betty bitterly noted how close the wedding date was to her own anniversary. Friends of both Brodericks were concerned that Betty would somehow crash the ceremony and do something outrageous. They knew she had recently bought a gun. Linda even asked Dan to wear a bulletproof vest that day. But Betty stayed quietly at home under the watchful eyes of a friend. She managed to emotionally struggle through the rest of that year until early November. Dan's marriage had not put a stop to clashes regarding money or custody of the children. He had recently sent Betty a harsh letter threatening to put her in jail again. Unable to sleep, she got up during the early hours of the morning. She brooded over Dan's last sentence in the letter. He said she was emotionally disturbed and had a mental disorder. She started to write a suicide note, and then decided it would be better to go to his house. "I had one choice: to shoot them or myself. . . . I couldn't let them win."[21] On November 5, 1989, at 5:30 in the morning, she drove to Dan and Linda's home. She broke in, crept upstairs to their bedroom, and five shots went off. Linda died instantly. Dan reportedly said, "OK, OK you got me," then died.[22] Betty yanked the phone cord out of the wall and fled. Hours later she turned herself in. After six long years, the Broderick battles were over.

News of the killings exploded throughout San Diego County. Dan was a high-profile lawyer, and Betty had been prominent on the social scene. People knew that Betty had been replaced with a much younger trophy wife. Here was a case that dealt with sex, money, and murder. Anne Kingston indicates in her book *The Meaning of Wife* that one man joked at a La Jolla cocktail party soon after the killings, "I guess this is 'be nice to the ex-wife' week."[23] *The San Diego Reader* rushed to print an extensive interview conducted with both Brodericks earlier when word of their bitter divorce was making the rounds. Betty depicted herself as a long-suffering wife trying to deal with a husband having midlife crises. While acknowledging that he had not been the perfect husband, Dan tried to tell his side of the story, highlighting Betty's erratic and vindictive behavior. "It's never going to be over for me. . . . She can't let go. . . . She's filled with hatred. . . . She'd like me to be destroyed. . . . She's on a mission from God."[24]

Charged with a double murder, Betty was denied bail and sent to jail. She admitted to the shooting, but told her lawyer she had meant to kill herself when the gun went off. Far from doing poorly in jail, Betty flourished. It provided a haven where she could position herself as the real victim in the case. She gave interviews to anyone who was willing to listen to her tirade against Dan. From her perspective, he had systematically set out to destroy her, and the legal system seemed to punish women unfairly in divorce cases. "He traded me in for a younger model and stole my kids. . . . He sued me to death. . . . My story is relevant to millions of women."[25] Betty became so proficient at telling her side of the story that she began issuing her own press releases that were gobbled up by the media.

The public was fascinated. The unrepentant ex-wife received thousands of letters from women who had been through similar emotional and legal experiences. One stated, "I only wish I had your nerve. . . . THEY lost. YOU won. . . . Your future is not wonderful, but they have none—as they deserve."[26] When TV tabloid *Hard Copy* covered the case right before the trial, Betty's image took on new dimensions. She was no longer just a feminist cause célèbre. To the dismay of Dan and Linda's friends, the Betty phenomenon emerged depicting her as a sympathetic symbol of the scorned woman.

Betty's trial was scheduled for October 1990. Jack Earley, her attorney, told reporters that Betty had suffered enormous psychological abuse from Dan's actions. Betty had shot Dan and Linda by accident while she was in a confused mental state. Prosecutor Kerry Wells described the killings as "a cold-blooded execution motivated by jealousy and hatred."[27] Wells had worked with battered women and was outraged that Betty tried to depict herself as one. She felt that when Betty no longer had access to the privileged lifestyle that being Dan's wife gave her, she wanted him dead.

Reporters and television crews joined the hundreds of spectators. The 2-week trial, featuring a parade of over 30 witnesses, was filled with dramatic moments. Wells enumerated Betty's acts of vandalism. She played clip after clip of Betty's obscene phone messages. Both Broderick daughters testified that Betty had threatened numerous times to kill Dan. The older daughter also indicated that Betty had talked about how rich they would be after they collected on Dan's $1 million life insurance policy, once he was dead. But the star of the trial was Betty herself. Through tears, she recounted all of the emotional suffering Dan had put her through. She didn't remember the killings. She didn't plan them. Dan had told people she was crazy and she went crazy. The jury was unable to reach a decision. They were deadlocked on whether the killings were due to a premeditated intent to kill or merely manslaughter. A mistrial was declared. Although Betty would remain in jail until her next trial, it was a victory. For now, she had escaped conviction on first-degree murder charges.

Betty continued to believe she would eventually get off, especially when she found out that one juror had wondered what had taken her so long to kill Dan.[28] *Mirabella* magazine ran a story with a cover headline asking the same question. *Ladies Home Journal* presented a sympathetic article on her case. Betty's court testimony had shown up on the evening news. One station had even preempted its regularly scheduled soap opera and talk show for her court appearance.[29] The news show *20/20* as well as *People* magazine wanted to interview her. Court TV wanted to telecast her next trial to 6 million viewers coast to coast. Fan mail was now beginning to come from people all over the world.

Aware of the widespread sympathy Betty had generated, Wells decided to focus on a different strategy during the next case. She was determined to spend more time on what happened at the scene of the crime rather than what happened all the years before. Earley also wanted to spend more time at the crime scene. He wanted to show that when Betty entered the room, Dan and Linda were not sleeping but wide-awake. His contention was the gun had gone off accidentally when Betty panicked on hearing Linda say call the police and Dan had responded by lunging for the phone.

Although a host of witnesses were called, again it was Betty who took center stage. Only this time, she was not as convincing. Wells asked specific pointed questions about her actions in the Brodericks bedroom. Betty continually contradicted herself. She was unable to provide an explanation on how or why five shots "accidentally" went off. After Wells blew up a page from her diary for the jurors to see during the closing arguments, Betty knew she had lost the case. The entry said, "There is no better reason in the world for someone to kill than to protect their home, their possessions, and family from attack and destruction. You have attacked and destroyed me, my home, my possessions, and my family. . . . You're the sickest person alive. A law degree does not give you license to kill and destroy, nor does it give you immunity from punishment. No one will ever mourn you."[30] This jury found Betty guilty. She was given a sentence of 32 years to life.

While Betty's lack of repentance may have been what finally convinced the jurors that she was guilty, it was this very quality that propelled her into folkloric status in popular culture. Was this the story of a cold, calculated execution or an example of male power and a biased legal system that could drive an emotionally fragile woman over the edge? Books were written about her. Not one, but two popular television movies were made about her in 1992. *A Woman Scorned* dealt with her life up to the murders, becoming the second highest television movie of the season drawing 39 million viewers.[31] *Her Final Fury: Betty Broderick, the Last Chapter* covered the circus-like media spectacle that surrounded the lead up to her two trials. This movie showed her gleefully opening her fan mail as the prosecution discussed the Betty phenomenon. Amy Wallace in her article "One Angry Betty" reported, "For years Lifetime Television played them so frequently it was impossible to tune in without seeing Betty drive her car into Dan's front door or Dan threaten to take Betty to court."[32] The Court TV trial footage was viewed by so many people it helped establish the network and set the stage for its domination of true crime coverage. Later, an episode of *American Justice* examined the troubling role of the legal system in the sensational divorce and murder case.

While a great deal of people fell in the middle of the spectrum regarding Betty's action, sympathizing with her emotional plight but not condoning her actions, two distinctive highly vocal groups emerged. They were known as the Betty Backers and the Betty Bashers. To the Betty Backers, the movies, media attention, and passage of time seemed to legitimize Betty's anger. Here was a woman who took matters into her own hands. She shattered the image of the injured wife, quietly stepping into the shadows after her husband dumps her. Legions of supporters managed to overlook the double murder and identified with her emotional distress. The Betty Backers sympathized with her plight of being tossed aside for a younger woman. It was easy to relate to her fear of becoming destitute as her husband and his girlfriend lived a life of luxury and ease. Some had firsthand experience of how a woman lost more economically in a divorce than a man. They agreed that Dan's custody suit for the children was "an act of overt emotional terrorism," a phrase used by Betty to describe Dan's controlling actions. Many knew how someone like Dan, with knowledge and influence, could distort the legal system and use it for their own financial gain. In fact, the Alliance for Divorce and Marriage Reform group chose to use her case in its campaign as an illustration for the need of divorce laws that are fairer to women.[33] The Betty Backers considered Betty to be a power figure filled with righteous indignation. She had an understandable desire for revenge.

The Betty Bashers found no redeeming value in her actions. They considered Betty a sick, pathetic symbol of self-centeredness and hate. From their perspective, Dan and Linda had been harassed for years by a vindictive, mentally unstable woman who refused to let go. Betty Bashers had no sympathy for a woman with a boyfriend of her own and alimony close to $200,000 a year. Debra Saunders, author of the article "Read the Right Books and You

Too Can Murder," called the transformation of Betty as the patron saint of victimization the snow job of the century.[34]

Many reacted with irreverence to Betty's deed. She became the punch line in comedy routines.[35] A gag ad appeared for a "Betty Broderick Christmas Album" featuring the songs "Frosting the Old-Man with a .38 Snubnose" and "I'll Be Home for Christmas with an Uzi."[36] One Internet site showed pictures of Dan and Linda's graves. Another featured a trivia game where contestants compared their scores to see just how much they know of Betty's saga.

Was Betty psychotic, or just acting out the fantasies of every jilted woman? Shortly after her second trial, Oprah Winfrey interviewed her in prison. Betty spoke earnestly to Oprah as if they were two friends having a cup of coffee while discussing problems. Betty talked about the "perfect" marriage she and Dan had, full of trust and commitment, until he fell in love with Linda. When Oprah asked her why she brought the gun to Dan and Linda's house if she only wanted to talk, she said, "I brought the gun to make Dan and Linda listen to me. . . . I wanted to keep them from calling the police. It made sense to me then. . . . It makes sense to me now."[37] Her earnest performance was at odds with earlier statements she had made when she said, "the f____ is dead. . . . He's cold to the wind."[38]

Betty was back in the news in 2010 when she appeared before a parole board for the first time. Amy Wallace, a California writer who launched her career with a series of interviews conducted with Betty at the time of her arrest, met up with her again. Betty still had no regrets. "Even if I stay here forever, it's an improvement over the hell I endured."[39] Betty indicated remorse at her parole hearing but continued to blame her actions on Dan and their bitter divorce. Her family's view of the crime mirrored the same dichotomy seen by the public. Two of her children believed she should remain behind bars, while two felt she should be freed. She was denied parole. The Board of Prison Terms commissioner told Betty, "Your heart is still bitter. . . . You show no significant progress in evolving. You are still back 20 years ago in that same mode. You've got to move on."[40] For once, Betty had no comment, but not for long. A month later, she sent out a four-page letter to a television reporter, which blasted the board for their decision. "Once again the law and the truth doesn't seem to matter. I've done my time and have a perfect prison record, yet I got the maximum denial possible!!"[41] Betty has something new to be angry about.

Betty Broderick was not physically abused. No one threatened her life or stalked her as she went about her business. In fact, Dan Broderick wanted as little to do with his ex-wife as possible. He was content to forget that she existed. No, the injustice that Betty suffered comes more under the category of "breach of contract." She and Dan had an agreement, an understanding, a commitment. Betty honored their contract, and when Dan showed that he did not, Betty felt justified in doing whatever it took to get retribution. So strong is her conviction to the unfairness of the situation that to this day she remains unrepentant, believing herself to be genuinely entitled to a suitable payoff for her sacrifice. Judging Betty Broderick requires examining some basic tenets of our society: How much is one person legitimately entitled to expect from another? In this case, more specifically, what is a woman justified in expecting from a man in a relationship? And what is an acceptable course of action if her expectations are never met? One way to answer these questions is to look at how female avengers are portrayed in popular culture.

Over two decades since the murder, media depictions of female acts of revenge have become more numerous, more dramatic, more graphic, and, most would agree, more sympathetic. These trends are consistent with Betty Backers's claims that Betty was warranted in seeking revenge, that even her violent act of reprisal was humanly understandable, and that she is to be revered as the quintessential "scorned woman," a beacon for all angry women to follow. But Betty Bashers, who contend that Betty's actions were over-the-top, can also cite evidence in popular entertainment media to support their position. Either way, it's undeniable that media images in television, books, plays, songs, and films serve to influence, shape, and confirm our opinions of which *motives* for revenge are acceptable, which *traits* of revenge-seekers are admirable, and which vengeful *acts* are appropriate.

Female revenge stories feature women taking charge, overcoming obstacles, and getting things under control. The series *9 to 5* is an early-1980s situation comedy that aired in syndication through most of that decade and has recently been adapted into a musical stage play. It stars three hard-working ladies frustrated at receiving no credit or appreciation for their efforts, ideas, or accomplishments in the workplace. Each suffers a particular brand of discrimination because of her gender. Their boss, Franklin Hart, Jr., is a classically sleazy embodiment of a male chauvinist. In the story, the women don't actually *kill* Hart, but they do share elaborate fantasies about how they *would* do it, and portions of each one's dream scenario are realized when they kidnap their boss and hold him hostage in his own home. During this period, the women make positive changes in the office, ultimately impressing the board chairman. It all ends happily for the three heroines, with the boss shipped off to Brazil, where he is abducted by an Amazon tribe and never heard from again. The series is light-hearted, but its motivational message is clear: Revenge is sweet and well deserved by women who have had to put up with the antics of privileged men.

The Color Purple (1982), the highly acclaimed novel for which Alice Walker won a Pulitzer Prize, has since been popularly adapted to both stage and screen. It tells the story of Celie, a poor, uneducated young black woman living in rural Georgia during the 1930s. After being raped repeatedly by her stepfather, Celie falls into a pattern of allowing herself to be oppressed by men. She bears two of her stepfather's children, both of whom are taken away from her. Eventually, Celie is forced against her will to marry Albert, a man who uses and abuses her. Sofia, the wife of Albert's son, is strong and aggressive, unlike Celie. When her husband tries to dominate and beat her, as Albert does to Celie, Sofia fights back and asserts her independence. Through her interaction with Sofia and other strong women, Celie eventually comes to realize that she is deserving of self-respect, dignity, and the children she bore. In the end, Albert finally does right by Celie, and with Sophia, Celie pursues financial independence by making and selling pants.

The Color Purple and *pants* each denote a motivational theme: *Purple,* the color of bruises, symbolizes suffering and pain. This negative image turns positive when, in the end, standing in a field of purple flowers, Celie realizes that life's beauty is to be embraced. *Pants* represent a departure from the common view of women as simply homemakers. By using her natural creativity to produce this form of apparel, Celie enables women, as well as men, to "wear the pants" and gain control of their lives. Though the book had a particularly profound significance for black women, it has proved to be a powerful, transformative instrument, inspiring women of all races who have suffered at the hands of men to stand up and claim their self-dignity. Celie chose the path of self-sufficiency to escape her abusive situation. Unfortunately, this part of the message was not recognized by Betty Broderick.

In 1988, Jodie Foster won an academy award for her portrayal of rape victim Cheryl Araujo in the film *The Accused*. Foster's character, Sarah Tobias, is gang-raped one night at a bar while a group of drunken male onlookers cheer. Tobias presses charges against the men who raped her, but the rapists are allowed to plea bargain to the lesser charge of reckless endangerment. This angers Tobias, not only because their sentence is light, but also since the arrangement deprives her of the opportunity to tell her story in court. Weeks later, when one of the witnesses to the rape crudely propositions her, Tobias convinces the district attorney to prosecute the men who cheered the rapists on, this time for criminal solicitation. Those three men are found guilty. *The Accused* clearly points to physical violation as a noble motive for female revenge. But in the second trial, the defendants who were found guilty had not actually molested Tobias. Their crime was inciting the act, and the damage to which they were most directly connected and ultimately held accountable for was Tobias's public humiliation. Betty Broderick believed that she had suffered grave humiliation at the hands of her husband. Revenge, she may have reasoned, would be *her* way of getting justice.

These media portrayals—all from the decade leading up to Betty Broderick's episode—depict a variety of acceptable motives for female revenge: *Rewarding hard work and merit, attaining gender equity, ending suffering, seizing self-dignity,* and *avenging injury and humiliation*. And works produced during the years after the Broderick case continue to feature female avengers in a positive light, showcasing in the heroines a number of admirable character traits.

Olivia Goldsmith's best-selling novel *First Wives' Club* (1992) features three middle-aged divorcées whose husbands have abandoned them for younger women. Forming a club with the express purpose of getting revenge, they execute elaborate plans to sabotage their exes' current lives and gain financial rewards for themselves. But the women eventually decide that simple revenge would make them no better than their husbands, so they instead use the situations they've set up to push their men into funding a new organization they create to aid abused women. Each is rewarded for her efforts with a renewed sense of self-worth and the glimmer of a promising new relationship in her future. These women are *clever, industrious,* and a bit *devious, not unlike Betty Broderick.* In the end, they rise to a level of righteousness akin to their noble predecessors in *9 to 5.* There are two messages here: (1) These women triumphantly achieved revenge; and (2) they did so by concentrating their efforts elsewhere. The first message could easily resonate with women like Betty Broderick; the second, not so much. Sometimes we see only what we want to see.

Kill Bill, a graphic and violent two-part film released in 2003 and 2004, broadens the boundaries and raises the stakes of the revenge game. The Bride (played by Uma Thurman) wakes up after a long coma to discover that the baby she was carrying is gone. The situation is similar to that of Celie in *The Color Purple,* in that they both lose their children. But this is not the 1930s, and The Bride is no Celie. She is a professional murderer, and her only thought is to seek revenge against the assassination team that betrayed her—a team she was once part of. Her ultimate target is Bill, her ex-boss and father of the baby. But she takes great pains to extract painful compensation from other unscrupulous adversaries as well, like the hospital orderly that sold sexual access to her body while she was comatose. In the course of her revenge quest, The Bride executes a number of gruesome killings and mutilations that demonstrate intense *single-mindedness,* consummate *prowess,* and an unquestioning sense of *self-righteousness.* She travels the world to execute her revenge plans, mastering incredibly advanced survival skills gleaned from other cultures. And when the young daughter of one of her victims walks into the room to find her mother's lifeless, knife-punctured body, The Bride's only attempt to comfort the girl is to assure her that she, too, will have a chance for revenge when she gets older. Throughout her brutal rampage, The Bride retains audience sympathy because she has suffered the supreme indignity of betrayal by those she trusted and has been forced to make one of the greatest sacrifices imaginable—having her unborn child ripped from her womb. Appalling acts breed iconic martyrs.

A classic pair of time-honored female attributes rounds out the list of traits characterizing sympathetic female avengers: *loyalty* and *devotion. Diary of a*

Mad Black Woman (2005), inspired by the 1991 Donna West play *Fantasy of a Mad Black Woman,* tells the story of Helen McCarter, a woman not unlike Betty Broderick. Everyone envies McCarter and her husband, Charles—their wealth, their success, and their apparent happiness. But this public image belies Charles's growing animosity toward his wife, his unsavory pattern of infidelity, and his secret life as a drug kingpin. One day Helen wakes up to find all of her belongings packed in a U-Haul truck. Charles has kicked her out of the house, in the presence of his young mistress, who happens also to be the mother of his two children. Helen is devastated.

But Helen McCarter has something Betty Broderick did not—a feisty, protective, in-your-face grandmother named Madea. Madea does most of the revenge heavy lifting. It is she, rather than Helen herself, who does dirty work like ramming her car into the security gates of Charles's mansion, taking a chain saw to most of his furniture, and ripping his mistress's clothes to shreds—freeing Helen to lick her wounds and begin to recover emotionally. Helen has not directly dirtied her own hands, so she escapes the negative association with spitefulness, but the fact that another woman is willing to go to violent extremes for her validates the righteousness of her cause. After Charles's divorce attorney bleeds him penniless and shoots him, leaving him broke and paralyzed, Charles's mistress abandons him. Helen takes pity on her husband and returns to take care of him. During this period, she engages in a few benign torture tactics, taking advantage of his disability, but she finally forgives him, divorces him, and moves on, her virtuous image unsullied (thanks to Madea), her integrity preserved, and her dignity intact.

In 2005, Carrie Underwood's sweet country charm, graceful smile, unassuming style, and wholesome demeanor all helped to earn her the title of American Idol in the world's all-time favorite singing competition. A year later, her crossover single "Before He Cheats" made country music history, the video debuting at number one on the charts and staying there for five consecutive weeks. In a 180-degree turnaround from her small-town, girl-next-door American Idol image, a svelte and sultry Underwood exudes a cool, urbane sexuality that augments her seething, righteous anger. "Before He Cheats," named the best video of 2006 by Country Music Television's Top 20 Countdown, lyrically details a young woman's imaginings of her boyfriend's unfaithfulness and graphically depicts her violent and thorough destruction of his prize possession—a shiny new red pickup truck. "I might've saved a little trouble for the next girl," Underwood sings, "'cause the next time that he cheats, you know it won't be on me."

Though all of these stories share the theme of "women done wrong," they differ somewhat in the courses of action they advocate as justifiable retribution. *9 to 5* prescribes that female underdogs kidnap their oppressors, tie them up, and hold them captive. *The Color Purple* encourages victims to leave their abusers and build different and better lives for themselves. *The Accused* advises injured parties to sue their adversaries in court, as many times as necessary. And *First Wives' Club* urges women to unite, organize, conspire, and pool their resources to gain the power they rightfully deserve. In each of these projects, the heroines do their part to improve the lot of womankind for future generations. Their achievements of getting recognition, escaping abuse, achieving justice, and earning success depict them as noble; and since they were each motivated, at least in part, by revenge, it too gains a certain nobility, simply by association. At least it does in the mind of someone looking to *make* that association.

In the postmillennium pieces, "Before He Cheats" glamorizes the cold-hearted annihilation of whatever the betrayer holds near and dear. *Kill Bill* unabashedly exhorts violent murder as the only appropriate recourse for injustice, while *Diary of a Mad Black Woman* points to vicious destruction of property by a third party as the revenge route of choice. Notably, the altruistic feminist theme is gone from the two latter, male-penned works. The other discernable pattern is that acceptable courses of action for female revenge have become more extreme and aggressive over the years.

Not all stories of female revenge, however, portray the avenger in a positive light. The smash-hit film *Fatal Attraction* (1987) recounts the progressively bizarre actions of Alex Forrest (played by Glenn Close), a rage-filled woman who clings relentlessly to a married man, Dan Gallagher (played by Michael Douglas), with whom she has had a one-night stand. Alex does everything in her power to command Gallagher's attention, including a suicide attempt and a claim of pregnancy. When these efforts fail, she realizes that she has been rejected. She seeks revenge for this humiliation through persistent stalking, pouring acid on his car, falsifying her identity to gain access to his home, and killing his daughter's pet rabbit, which she leaves boiling in a pot on the stove in his kitchen. But rather than building a bond of identification with the audience, Alex's actions have the opposite effect. Her eerily chilling statement to Dan, "I will *not* be *ignored*," evokes an unsettling feeling of dread and imminent calamity. In the end, Alex tries to murder Dan's wife, who subsequently shoots and kills her. Alex emerges as an utterly unsympathetic character. The audience can relate neither to her expectation of Dan's committed love nor to her apparent satisfaction from harming his innocent wife and child.

The 1986 novel *The Life and Loves of a She-Devil* by Fay Weldon was later adapted into a popular BBC television series. It is the story of Ruth, a frumpy, overweight housewife and mother who wants desperately to please her husband, Bob. When she first discovers that Bob is having an affair with Mary Fisher, a glamorous and successful romance novelist, Ruth immediately embarks on an extensive makeover that includes radical plastic surgery and even involves breaking and resetting the bones in her legs to make her taller— all in the hope that she will come to resemble Mary Fisher. But neither Ruth's dramatic attempt to transform herself or her continued readiness to be a responsible wife and mother can prevent Bob from leaving her for Mary. When he does, Ruth contrives and successfully executes a systematic, four-part plan of revenge to destroy every aspect of Bob and Mary's lives, ultimately wreaking havoc on their home, family, freedom, and careers.

Ruth is basically a decent woman who has been wronged by an ungrateful and uncaring man. Yet despite our natural inclination to cheer her on in her quest for retribution, we are not moved to do so. Ironically, once Ruth actually transforms herself into a physically attractive woman, she loses a feature that once gained her sympathy. She becomes conniving and manipulative, planning hurtful acts in a most methodical way. To her credit, Ruth aims her venom only at those who deserve it, unlike Alex in *Fatal Attraction*. But one important trait Ruth and Alex share renders them both decidedly unsympathetic: Beneath the surface, driving their acts of aggression is a deep-rooted self-loathing—a core dissatisfaction that negates the natural and healthy human desire to be true to oneself. Although both characters are successful in ruining the lives of their perceived tormentors, neither achieves dignity, self-respect, personal growth, or the gratification of knowing she's made life better for anyone else. Consequently, in contrast to the heroines described earlier, these women's acts of revenge come across as "over-the-top."

So which of these characters does Betty Broderick most resemble? The hard-working, under-appreciated feminist heroines of *9 to 5* and *First Wives' Club*? The loyal but mistreated dignity-seekers in *The Color Purple* and *Diary of a Mad Black Woman*? The angry, trailblazing challenger in *The Accused*? The obsessive mastermind of murder and mayhem in *Kill Bill*? The cool, attractive sexpot bent on destruction in "Before He Cheats"? Or the deranged, self-betraying psychobitches in *Fatal Attraction* and *The Life and Loves of a She-Devil*? The answer is: all of the above.

Broderick has been portrayed in the media as a loyal wife and mother whose "breach of contract" claim was essentially legitimate—a woman who made enormous sacrifices for the benefit of her marriage and was deprived, through no fault of her own, of the rewards she deserved. She was even somewhat successful in painting herself as an underdog who could not get justice because her oppressor was able to use his power, privilege, and societal status to stack the cards against her. On the negative side are depictions of Broderick as a cold-blooded killer whose circumstances did not warrant the drastic measures to which she resorted. A member of the privileged class herself, Broderick doesn't match the common notion of an unfortunate victim of circumstance. Nor has her lack of remorse and refusal to admit wrongdoing helped her gain widespread support. This "mixed bag" of traits explains why media coverage of her case—and the public's subsequent response to her guilty verdict—has been schizophrenically divided.

What, after all, is Betty Broderick's legacy? Broderick was one of the first to justify a dramatic and violent act of revenge on the grounds that she was fundamentally entitled to respect, appreciation, cooperation, and financial reward from her husband. Her posture was that Dan Broderick's "breach of contract" was the sole cause of all subsequent events. As we have seen, post-1989 books, television, plays, films, and song lyrics attest to the fact that Betty's perspective has been an enduring one for women and, in fact, has actually gained credence in our culture, with one important exception.

Fewer of today's scorned and angry women remain fixated on their men. Their implicit belief in themselves precludes the continued *need* for a man and enables them to move on independently. It is for this reason that Betty Broderick ultimately fails as a contemporary role model. In recent decades, female self-reliance has grown to be celebrated in our society. The social perception that women must rely on men for happiness has lost ground. Yet to this day, Betty Broderick remains obsessed with the travesties of her dead husband. She continues to place exclusive blame on Dan for everything that happened. Unlike the sympathetic revenge heroines who earnestly strive to be true to themselves, Betty Broderick *lies* to herself as she continues to disclaim responsibility for her own actions. Alternatively, if she *is* being true to herself, it is to some inner voice that very few of us can relate to.

The practice of romanticizing revenge is alive and growing—not only in romance, but in other types of relationships as well. Enter Amy Bishop, twenty years later. . . .

AMY BISHOP

It was another sad but typical scene of violence that took place on an unsuspecting campus. Three were dead, and three were critically wounded. The motive driving the shooter was revenge. The individual who committed the mass murders neatly exhibited three warning signs identified in a national study as a prelude to school violence: fixation on a grievance, access to weapons, and despondency.[42] Only in a bizarre twist of fate, the perpetrator wasn't the usual angry young male seeking retribution; it was a female university professor in her 40s.

How could this smart scientist, a happily married mother of four who liked taking her children to hockey games and spending date nights with her husband, pull out a shotgun and blast away at her colleagues? Amy Bishop had been expecting tenure. She had played by the rules for six years at the University of Alabama and felt it was owed to her. Her rage led not only to violence, but also professional disgrace and personal destruction.

The region surrounding Boston is home to more than 100 colleges and universities. Nicknamed the "Athens of America," Boston has a reputation

for being a center of education and intellectual life. Growing up in the affluent suburb of Braintree, Amy lived within the shadows of some of the most
prestigious universities in the country. Harvard, MIT, and Tufts were all just
a short drive from her childhood home. The area is filled with academics,
philosophers, artists, scientists, and writers. It's not surprising that with an
IQ of 180, Amy became a brilliant biologist. She was merely following in the
footsteps of her parents, both known for their accomplishments. Her father
was a professor at research-oriented Northeastern University; her mother had
been elected a Braintree Town Meeting member. In high school, Amy and
her brother Seth were both known for being on the shy side and out of the
mainstream.[43]

Unlike most teens that try to conform and fit in, the brother and sister had
decidedly "geek" interests. Both shared a passion for playing the violin and
studying science. Seth had won a number of music awards as well as recognition for his science fair projects.[44] The more talented of the Bishop siblings,
Seth was considered a "genius kid." People tended to take less notice of Amy.
Stephen Smith notes in his article "Ambition Fueled a Smoldering Rage" that
a classmate recalled, "She went to school, she came home and practiced her
music. She lived in her own little world."[45] But the quiet world of a girl who
spent most of her time in the shadows would change dramatically. A terrible
incident occurred that would haunt her for the rest of her life—in more ways
than one. Amy shot and killed her brother.

The shooting took place on December 6, 1986. By this time, 20-year-old
Amy and 18-year-old Seth were college students living with their parents.
When their house had been broken into the previous year, Amy's father had
purchased a 12-gauge shotgun for protection. The gun was kept tucked away
in the parent's bedroom. Mr. Bishop and Seth were members of the Braintree
Firing Range and were familiar with the proper use of the firearm. Amy had
not been trained on how to handle the gun.

On this particular morning, Amy was in her bedroom, Seth was watching television, and Mrs. Bishop was in the kitchen. Mr. Bishop was out shopping. According to Amy's account later given to police, she and her father had
been arguing before he left.[46] For whatever reason, Amy decided that this was
the day to learn how to use the gun. She took it out of its hiding place and
brought it back to her bedroom. Fumbling with the shotgun shells, she
loaded it. The gun accidentally fired, striking a lamp and the wall. Neither
Seth nor her mother heard the shot. Amy covered up the bullet hole to hide
the damage, and then went downstairs.

Seth and his mother were getting ready for lunch. Amy asked for help on
how to take the shells out of the chamber. Mrs. Bishop told her not to point
the gun at anyone. Amy turned and the gun went off a second time. Seth
cried out "Oh God," crumpling to the floor in a pool of blood. The blast
had gone through his chest. A third shot went off hitting the ceiling. Amy

ran out of the house in panic, still carrying the gun. Paramedics took Seth to the hospital but it was too late. He was pronounced dead.

Shortly afterward, Amy was picked up by the police. Her mother was already at the station. Investigating officers asked Amy what happened. She told them it was an accident and that she had not fired the gun at Seth on purpose. Mrs. Bishop corroborated Amy's statement, indicating that the siblings had no animosity between them. Amy was in such an emotional state the police limited the interrogation. She was released into the custody of her parents. The family was questioned in more detail 11 days later. After weighing everyone's description of the event, the investigation officially ruled Seth's death an accident. A short report was compiled by the police and filed away. No charges of any type were brought against Amy.

News of the shooting made its way into the local paper. Most people regarded it as an unfortunate experience. The Bishops tried to move on with their lives. Patricia McCarter notes in the article "What Happened to Amy Bishop's Brother" that Amy was put on medication and under a doctor's care since she was having a difficult time dealing with the death.[47] She dropped out of school, but later returned. One of the individuals who helped her during this period was her boyfriend James Anderson. Amy and James met at a science fiction fan convention when they went to a Dungeon and Dragons event. Both were studying biology at Northeastern and shared many of the same interests—science, writing, reading, and music. James indicated, "I was drawn to her intelligence. She had that combination of looks and intelligence and was fun to be with."[48] They married in 1989.

James had no problem putting his career on hold after Amy decided to go to Harvard in pursuit of a doctorate in genetics. He worked at home and was willing to be the primary caretaker of their four children. James was in awe of his wife's brilliance.[49] But according to colleagues, Amy's brilliance had developed a sharp edge to it. It seems that she was no longer shy and unassuming. Sources indicated that over the years, she had acquired a reputation for being volatile.[50] Amy had accepted a postdoctoral research job in the neurobiology lab at Boston Children's Hospital in 1993. One of her Harvard colleagues at the hospital received a pipe bomb in the mail. Suspicion immediately centered on Amy since the colleague had criticized her work. Associates speculated that Amy had sent the bomb in revenge for his comments. Investigators had reason to believe that Amy and possibly her husband were involved. Although questioned, neither was charged. In 1996, Amy collaborated on a scientific paper with a colleague at Beth Israel Deaconess Medical Center in Boston. When her name was not listed as the first author, a collaborator noted, "She broke down. She was extremely angry with all of us. She exploded into something emotional that we never saw before in our careers."[51]

Amy also had conflicts with her neighbors when she lived in Ipswich, Massachusetts. She found fault with kids playing basketball, the ice cream truck, and her neighbor's basketball hoop. The local police grew used to her complaints. In one of the calls where she objected to children making noise, she reportedly indicated the situation could lead to violence.[52] Neighbors grew tired of hearing her brag about her Harvard degree and how smart she was. Amy's tendency of veering toward self-serving, antisocial behavior came to the forefront during a bizarre incident in 2002. Amy was at the International House of Pancakes (IHOP) restaurant with her children and asked a waitress for a booster seat. None were available since another customer had just received the last one. Amy pitched a tantrum with the waitress. She then went up to the woman who had received the seat, screamed profanities, and punched her in the head, all the while yelling "I am Dr. Amy Bishop."[53] Amy was arrested and charged with assault. She pled guilty and eventually received probation.[54] The judge ordered her to take anger management classes.[55] She never did. Amy was leaving behind a trail of neighbors, colleagues, and acquaintances mystified by her mood swings and volatility.[56]

Although Amy had worked in a number of research jobs, her goal was to be a university professor. If she successfully made it through the tenure process, she would have a lifetime academic position. In 2003, she accepted a tenure track biology position from the University of Alabama in Huntsville. With its eclectic mix of scientists, engineers, inventors, and entrepreneurs, the town seemed a perfect fit for Amy. She appeared to settle in with no difficulty. Her department chair welcomed her to the university and predicted that she would be a great addition. During the next few years, it seemed that Amy was finally living up to all of her potential. Shalia Dewan, Stephanie Saul, and Katie Zezima note in their article "For Professor, Fury Just beneath the Surface" that "at first, colleagues and students said she came across as funny and extroverted, enthusiastic and knowledgeable about campus issues."[57] Her lectures were considered stimulating. She took a leadership position in the faculty senate. The lab she managed attracted bright graduate students eager for her mentorship. She received a grant of $220,000 to research her particular area of interest in genetic therapy. Amy's brilliance came to the forefront with her invention of an automated cell incubator. She and her husband had developed a machine, the InQ, which had the potential of driving scientific advances for the treatment of nerve-related ailments such as Lou Gehrig's disease, Alzheimer's disease, and strokes.[58] A start-up company decided to produce the machine and over $1 million in private investment funds were generated. Amy was featured on the cover of the *Huntsville R&D Report* proudly holding her invention. The headline trumpeted "Prodigy Biosystem's Nifty Device Will Rock the Cell Growth World." While the university owned the invention, Amy had a cut of the profits. She had the potential to reap large financial rewards, making up to 40 percent of net income.[59]

Tenure is usually a seven-year process in which a committee of academic peers rates the individual in the areas of teaching, service, and scholarship.

In early 2009, Amy seemed confident that she would be granted tenure.[60] However, she was denied. While her department chair favored granting her tenure, the majority of committee members opposed it. Beneath the surface of Amy's accomplishments were some troubling issues. Although Amy received favorable comments from standardized student evaluations and had respectable ratings on Rate My Professors.com, a national website that allowed students to provide anonymous feedback, other students were disgruntled. A group had gone to the department chair on numerous occasions complaining about her attitude and behavior in class. Dozens had signed a petition against her.[61] There also seemed to be a high turnover rate among her graduate assistants, which may have been due to her personality.

Colleagues too were finding her behavior unsettling. According to some faculty members, she disrupted meetings with opinionated unrelated comments. Her demeanor was now viewed as arrogant. Most troubling was her lack of publications. Over a five-year period, she had only published six papers. Her most recent one appeared in a little-known journal that was not well respected. The most disturbing part of this particular paper was that Amy had listed four other authors. The authors included her husband and 3 of her 4 children, none of them older than 18.[62]

A person who is not granted tenure still has one year of employment on their contract, a grace year that allows time for appealing the decision and search for another job. Amy started the appeal process immediately. She stopped her colleagues in the hall, badgering them with arguments on why they should support her.[63] She filed a gender bias suit against a member of the tenure committee who had made disparaging remarks regarding her mental health. Neither action served her well. She made little attempt to look for another position. In November 2009, her appeal was rejected.

When a professor does not receive tenure, there is often a stigma attached to it. Katherine van Wormer writes in her article "Amy Bishop and the Trauma of Tenure Denial" that the loss of tenure can be described as the end to one's career, to one's livelihood, sense of personal disgrace, and loss of home, friendships, and community.[64] For Amy, it was not only the blow to her self-esteem but it also had financial implications. As the primary breadwinner of the family, she would no longer have her $66,000 professor's salary. Despite her potentially lucrative invention contract giving her 40 percent of net income, the product sales were still in the infancy stage. She felt the family was on the brink of destitution. She told her husband that she was terrified she would have to drive a bus for a living after losing her job.[65] The perceived injustice of the situation weighed on her for months.

On February 12, 2010, Amy decided to do something about it. She went to her morning class as usual and gave her lecture. At 3 P.M., she attended a routine faculty meeting with 12 colleagues along with her department chair and other tenure committee members. For nearly an hour, Amy sat without saying a word. Suddenly, she stood up and pulled out a 9 mm pistol. One by one, she methodically shot at her colleagues. Chaos ensued. Amy fled the room and dropped the gun into a nearby restroom. Someone called the police. By the time the rampage was over, three individuals were wounded and three were dead. Ironically, Amy had killed the department chair who supported her bid for tenure. When police apprehended her, she was captured on television muttering, "It didn't happen. There's no way . . . they are still alive."[66]

The shooting spree instantly made national news. Women are rarely the shooters in campus killings or mass shootings. The public was astonished over the fact that a Harvard-educated, female professor went ballistic. Interest in Amy jumped exponentially a few days later, when her brother's shooting became general knowledge. New events came to light on the 24-year-old story: details of Seth's death, her subsequent actions when she fled her home, and the results of the investigation.

It turned out that when Amy took off from the kitchen with the gun, she ran to a nearby auto dealership. She startled an employee by brandishing the gun at his chest. She demanded that he give her a car so she could escape from a husband threatening to kill her. Amy looked clearly out of control. The police pulled up and told her to drop the gun, but she refused. A few tense minutes passed as they repeated the order twice. Eventually, she surrendered.

Once at the station, police had started to question Amy. However, at Mrs. Bishop's request, the interrogation had been brought to a halt. Apparently, a phone call was made to a higher up and the request had been approved. Pointed questions were now being raised by the public over two issues: Why had Amy not been charged with assault over the dealership incident and why had the investigation ended so abruptly? There was speculation that since Mrs. Bishop had spoken to the police chief in order to receive preferential treatment for her daughter.[67] Mrs. Bishop was a local politician and had served on the police personnel board. The current Braintree chief of police held a press conference and revealed that the initial police report had been missing for 20 years. He also stated, "I was not on duty at the time of the incident, but I recall how frustrated the members of the department were over the release of Ms. Bishop. . . . It did not sit well with police officers and I can assure you that this would not happen in this day and age."[68]

Howls across the country surfaced suggesting that Amy had deliberately blown away her brother in a jealous fit. It seemed implausible that she had set the gun off "accidently" on three separate occasions in one day. Was it possible that her parents, along with the police, engineered a cover up? A massive media frenzy ensued as television newscasters revealed the pipe bomb and IHOP incidents, cementing the image of Amy as mentally disturbed. Traditional newspaper outlets from *The New York Times* and general interest magazines including *People* and the tabloid *Globe Magazine* churned out reports.

While some comments were sympathetic, many of them suggested Amy was a walking time bomb. *The Wall Street Journal,* a newspaper that typically does not cover true crime, treated its business news watcher to three stories in one week. *The Chronicle of Higher Education,* a newspaper devoted to academics, weighed in with articles covering the shootings, discussions over the tenure process, and dozens of comments from readers with their views on the deadly professor. Bloggers all across the country postulated that Amy's superior intelligence combined with her Harvard background resulted in a lethal mix of entitlement.[69] Amy's husband James appeared on *Good Morning America* to defend his wife. *Dateline* interviewed Amy's colleagues, former classmates, neighbors, and police officers who had crossed her path. TLC aired the investigative special "Killer on Campus" replete with reenactments of the shooting spree and a discussion of Amy's psychological profile. Websites displayed a timeline of her life, high school photos of her and Seth, her curriculum vitae, and the missing police report. Amy had become a twisted icon in popular culture. She was cast as the brilliant but eccentric woman who may have walked a fine line between genius and insanity.

In 2010, Bishop was charged with capital murder, a crime that carries a death penalty sentence. During this time, the furor over Amy's background reopened the case involving her brother as well as the pipe-bomb incident. The June 2010 inquiry into Seth's death led to her being charged with first-degree murder. Two days after Amy heard the news, she attempted suicide. She was cleared of any involvement in the pipe-bomb case in October 2010. By the time the campus shooting trial made its way through the court system, Amy pleaded guilty to avoid the death penalty. She received a life sentence without parole in 2012. The public is still debating why a woman with a violent past and record of erratic behavior got away with so many incidents that ultimately led to a haunting tragedy.

How much is a person reasonably entitled to expect from her colleagues at work? In higher education, where employment policies are generally prescribed rather rigidly, this should be an easy question to answer. But time-honored and exhaustingly discussed concepts like *academic standards* and *institutional policy* are, in the end, interpreted by people with basic human needs, biases, concerns, and fears. Even in committees—the main decision-making structure in higher education—determinations that can make or break a career often boil down to simple relations between people. So was Amy Bishop's expectation of being granted tenure justified? If so, what course of action is understandable if her colleagues do not meet that expectation?

If we look for insight to media images in our culture, we find no shortage of tales about scorned female lovers. Stories of women taking revenge in the workplace, however, are less common, with very little in the specific context of academia. Prominent examples of women in uncomfortable work situations focus either on balancing home and work responsibilities or on sexual discrimination and harassment. These factors may indeed have been in play in Amy Bishop's case. But the dynamics of the Amy Bishop murders cannot be broken down simply to ill-defined parental roles or straightforward gender discrimination. This case involves much more.

In the 1964 Alfred Hitchcock thriller *Marnie,* Tippi Hedren plays a competent, clever, beautiful but troubled secretary who uses her charms to distract a series of male bosses from noticing her pattern of embezzlement from their companies. Marnie is not inherently evil. She is a victim of self-imprisonment due to a traumatic childhood incident. At the end, when Marnie comes to understand her subconscious motivations, she resolves to pour her energies into making her marriage work. Her husband forgives her transgressions, and so do we, knowing that we've all experienced trauma at some point in our lives. Marnie typifies early characterizations of working women, portrayed as talented but emotionally scarred.

The Mary Tyler Moore Show, a groundbreaking, highly acclaimed television sitcom that aired from 1970 to 1977, features Mary Richards, a successful, independent, respected 30-something career woman who works her way up to producer of the Six O'clock News on television station WJM. The character contrasts sharply with the sitcom role Tyler Moore had originally become known for—the mousy, fragile, self-doubting housewife on *The Dick Van Dyke Show.* Far from being a caricature, Mary Richards is a real, mature woman. She has flaws, to be sure—like never being able to sustain a long-term relationship—but she deals with challenging issues, both at work and at home, in a mature and dignified way. The closest she comes to a violent act is to throw her beret up in the air in downtown Minneapolis.

The image of a mature, courageous, and principled working woman advanced further when Henry Leifermann's book *Crystal Lee, a Woman of Inheritance* (later adapted into the film *Norma Rae*) was published in 1975. It tells the story of Crystal Lee Sutton, a minimum-wage cotton mill employee whose working conditions drive her to spearhead a movement to unionize her shop. Sutton's determination and bravery ultimately help her accomplish her goal, but her unionizing efforts take their toll on both her marriage and her livelihood. She loses time with her family, alienates her husband, and gets fired from the mill. Her life takes a different direction when she later finds work as a political activist.

Perhaps the media images of working women who most closely resemble Amy Bishop can be found in the 1997 film *Clockwatchers.* Iris (Toni Collette), Margaret (Parker Posey), Paula (Lisa Kudrow), and Jane (Alanna Ubach) are office temps who try to please their employers in order to get a highly coveted recommendation. They bond with each other as they find themselves in a completely different, and much less fulfilling, world than the permanent hires that surround them. Like the office workers in *9 to 5,* they get no acknowledgment or recognition of their work. But unlike their ancestral cinematic heroines, they lack the power to have any impact on their unjust situation. In desperation, Margaret goes on strike for a day. She gets fired. In the end, the force of corporate oppression is so strong that it poisons the women not only against their privileged coworkers, but also against one another.

Portrayals of female academics are rare, which shows that media decision-makers do not consider this group interesting or worthy of much public attention. The closest facsimiles are females pursuing legal research or advanced education related to law. The *Erin Brockovich Official Website* illustrates the positive end. Brockovich, an unknown legal researcher before the 2000 Julia Roberts film propelled her into fame, used inventiveness, determination, and righteous anger to drive the largest medical settlement lawsuit in history. On the website, her biography begins,

> Say the name Erin Brockovich and you think *strong, tough, stubborn* and *sexy*. Erin is all that and definitely more.

Brockovich complements her feisty posture with an upbeat message encapsulated in the title of her *New York Times Business* best seller "Take It from Me. Life's a Struggle, but You Can Win." While many people may relate to Brockovich's personal struggles, such as being a single mother with limited income, it is her larger struggles that are unmistakably compelling to the general public. Representing small town folks in their fight against the ravages of large corporate polluters is bold, noble, and inspiring. In Amy Bishop's case, it's not clear that her indignation represents anyone but herself. But even assuming that she is fighting for the rights of professors to get the tenure they deserve, this performance plays to a very limited audience.

Less iconic but nevertheless curiously sympathetic is the offbeat, pink-clad, label-defying sorority queen Elle Woods (played by Reese Witherspoon) in the 2001 film *Legally Blonde*. Surrounded by sexism and stereotyping, betrayed by her boyfriend, and foiled by male professors, Elle emerges triumphant when she nails a murderer in court and finishes law school at the top of her class. Her revenge can be heralded by audiences who respect her for remaining true to her quirky self. Who needs a gun, when a simple *bend and snap* can get you what you want with a lot less fuss, and without ruining your nails? But Elle did not shoot her oppressors. For Amy Bishop to glean this type of support, the public would have to believe that murder is what it took for her to be true to herself. Not an easy sell.

Working women are also depicted as being oppressed by female superiors, showing that the demands to "pay your dues" in order to move up professionally can come from many sources. In the 1990 television sitcom *Working Girl*, starring Sandra Bullock, in order to get the recognition she deserves, Bullock's character must find ways to sabotage her antagonistic, bad-tempered immediate boss, Mrs. Newhouse, who continually tries to undermine her. In

The Devil Wears Prada, the best-selling 1993 novel by Lauren Weisberger, Andrea Sachs, an aspiring journalist freshly out of college, works as a personal assistant to powerful fashion magazine editor Miranda Priestly. After enduring all manner of abuse and exploitation, Sachs finally finds the courage to alienate her boss, and in doing so, regains the integrity she lost during the months she worked for her. These are models of sympathetic working women who fought against oppression in the workplace.

Men have always outnumbered women in the sciences. For years, this disparity was attributed to innate gender differences. While the theory that men have more natural aptitude for science and math has essentially been debunked, the underrepresentation of female scientists persists, despite years of outreach programs to help girls overcome their aversions. Dr. Larry Summers has theorized that though men and women might, on average, possess equal mathematical ability, more men may fall in the very highest percentile (i.e., 99.99), since men are more likely than women to fall at the extreme ends of the scale.[70] Dr. Summers has proposed that to be successful, a tenured university professor in the sciences might well need the aptitude, skills, and traits found in such an elite group. This could explain why fewer female scientists are granted tenure at universities.

Dr. Carolyn Porco, a planetary scientist and leader of the Cassini spacecraft imaging team, had this response to Dr. Summers's theory:

> Given an adequate to above-average measure of analytical ability [successful scientific research], next comes down almost entirely to personality.[71]

And Dr. Isis, a physiologist at a major research university who blogs about succeeding as a woman in academia, echoes:

> Scientific knowledge, per se, does not predict one's success as a tenured academic researcher.[72]

Isis goes on to suggest that management skills, communication skills, grant writing ability, as well as teaching and mentoring proficiency all are necessary for a tenured academic researcher.

As both of these women point out, success as a tenured research professor in the sciences requires much more than mere scientific knowledge, or even the ability to publish. The decision to deny Amy Bishop tenure may have been based on committee members' perceptions that she lacked skills not immediately thought of as "essential" to the position. Other traits that tenure committee members may be looking for include being collegial (i.e., willing to share ideas), showing allegiance to the institution, making students a priority, and carrying your weight in the department by taking on extracurricular responsibilities.

Bishop felt strongly that being denied tenure was a travesty of justice. However, she is not the first professional woman to face critics. Many women, including Amy Bishop, may be aware that their academic credentials will not guarantee that they will be treated fairly if they oppose the decisions of those in power. Anita Hill, a respected professor of social policy, law, and women's studies at Brandeis University, was also a former colleague of U.S. Supreme Court Justice Clarence Thomas. In 1991, she gained national exposure when she testified at Thomas's Senate confirmation hearings, alleging that as her supervisor, Thomas had made provocative and harassing sexual statements. Because her accusations—which Thomas denied—were made for the first time at the confirmation hearings, and she could provide no definitive proof, the Senate rejected them, calling her statements politically based. Thomas was confirmed. Hill was brutally maligned by the press. And the assault did not end there. Two years later, a journalist named David Brock published a book entitled *The Real Anita Hill,* which he himself later described as a "character assassination," and in Clarence Thomas's 2007 autobiography, *My Grandfather's Son,* Thomas continued the attack on Hill, claiming she was touchy and apt to overreact and describing her professional work as mediocre. Though Hill has a career history she can be proud of, she has nevertheless been on the defensive for the past two decades.

As the presumptive Democratic nominee in the upcoming 2008 presidential elections, Hillary Clinton was named, as a result of 2007 Gallup polls, the Most Admired Woman in the World.[73] But her detractors used this very popularity against her, attacking her for an attitude of "inevitability" (i.e., viewing the primary process as a ratifying formality rather than genuinely competing for what she felt she was owed). Once this charge took hold, her opponents were able to make others stick, such as labels of "wealthy," "racist," and "establishment."[74] This fall from grace could be interpreted by someone like Amy Bishop in two ways: (1) A strong woman's confidence in herself will always be misinterpreted or (2) be careful about appearing too smug about your chances for success.

Many know Barbara Ehrenreich as a prominent feminist author, columnist, essayist, sociologist, and political activist of the late 20th and early 21st centuries. What most people *don't* know about her is that she earned a B.S. in physics in 1963 and a Ph.D. in cellular biology in 1968. Her senior thesis was entitled *Electrochemical Oscillations of the Silicon Anode.* In her own words, Ehrenreich explains why she left the sciences:

In 1970, the prenatal care I received at a hospital clinic showed me that PhD's were not immune from the vilest forms of sexism. . . . I made the rash decision to quit my teaching job at the State University of NY— where I didn't expect to get tenure anyway—and become a full-time writer.[75]

Ehrenreich's story certainly validates the belief that women in the sciences suffer serious gender discrimination. Her testimony could conceivably be used to feed and justify an act of dramatic revenge against oppressive colleagues. But Ehrenreich is not bitter. She chose a different path, making productive use of her talents in other areas.

Oprah Winfrey grew up poor and lacking a stable home life. As a girl, she was repeatedly molested by male relatives and even refused admission to a juvenile detention home because all the beds were filled. As a young woman, she showed promise as a reporter at a local television station but was denied advancement because she was female, black, and overweight. Yet by the end of the century, she had been dubbed one of the most influential and powerful people in the world by such sources as *USA Today, Life, Time, Vanity Fair, Forbes,* and CNN. Oprah is now an American icon. She is known for her captivating communication style (quite a contrast from Amy), her willingness both to look inward and to speak out for what she believes, her ability to connect with diverse elements of humanity, her effective utilization of her own and others' talents and resources, her unending philanthropy, and her continuous facilitation of others' success and empowerment. Her most urgent message is that you can rise above adversity, as long as you don't let it poison you. She often quotes the English metaphysical poet George Herbert: "Living well is the best revenge."

Models of "wronged women" abound, in both the fictional and real worlds. These women's responses to adverse circumstances run the gamut from bitterness and defeat to transcendence and triumph. Though we can only speculate at this point which if any of these models may have influenced Amy Bishop, we may be fairly certain that when the jury deliberates Bishop's fate, many of these images will come into play when they make their judgments.

So what, after all, is a professional woman entitled to expect from her colleagues? (1) *Empathy, understanding, and compassion.* Like Marnie, whose childhood trauma drove her misguided behavior, we all have deep-seated fears that can sometimes prevent us from actualizing our highest potential. Surely everyone serving on a tenure committee—having gone through the process themselves—should be able to understand and relate to the stress of jumping through all those hoops. (2) *Fair and objective treatment.* Even though there were few female producers at the time, the crew at WJM TV recognized Mary Richard's competence and judged her based on her accomplishments. A tenure committee should do the same. This, after all, is what the tenure review process is supposed to be about. (3) *Unbiased consideration.* Real-life female scientists are unanimous in their view that other sensibilities besides strict analytical skill should be valued and embraced. A tenure applicant should not be penalized for presumed traits that may not conform to conventional standards. (4) *Collegiality.* The expectation that a scholar shows respect, friendliness, good will, and a readiness to share with colleagues is a two-way street. This standard should apply especially to those charged with deciding a colleague's fate.

It is impossible to say for sure whether or not Amy Bishop received the consideration she was entitled to expect, but clearly, in *her* mind, those entitlements were not met. This is where negative media images, like those alluded to earlier, may have come into play to justify Bishop's extreme act of revenge: No matter how hard they worked, the women in *Clockwatchers* could not expect to be treated fairly by their senior associates. No matter how scholarly she demonstrated herself to be, Anita Hill could not expect to receive the respect she deserved. No matter how admirable her achievements, Hillary Clinton could not expect to be supported when attacks were mounted against her. No matter how smart she was, Barbara Ehrenreich could not expect to have a successful or satisfying career in the sciences.

Given that Bishop's committee did not meet what she considered to be fair and reasonable expectations, what types of retaliatory actions are appropriate? Considering the models we have discussed, Bishop had a number of options: (1) *Use the system to fight back.* Erin Brokovich continues to fight the Goliaths of the world—not only for herself, but for all the Davids out there who lack the ability or the resources. (2) *Stay dignified and poised.* Elle Woods successfully got revenge against her male oppressors by simply standing tall and being herself. (3) *Utilize your skills and talents.* Oprah Winfrey has triumphed over her oppressors and detractors through mobilizing her personal resources into transcendent action. (4) *Find or create something better.* Crystal Lee Sutton (Norma Rae) got fired from her mill job but reinvented herself as a community activist.

Judging from the action she did choose, we can only assume that Amy Bishop was either unaware of or unwilling to heed some of the lessons to be learned from pop culture: (1) If you resign yourself to powerlessness and do not change your circumstances—as did the women in *Clockwatchers*—you will turn on those around you, and ultimately on yourself; and (2) behavioral acts void of morality—such as Marnie's series of embezzlements in the Hitchcock movie—result only in self-destruction.

Moreover, society has formed opinions and stereotypes about professors in the "ivory tower of academia," which may cloud their ability to see someone like Amy Bishop as a real human being. We need look no further than the 2008 presidential elections to foresee that being a university professor will render Bishop inherently unsympathetic to the general public. Sarah Palin, the Republican vice-presidential candidate, got enormous traction in her campaign with her constant references to Barack Obama as "the professor"— connoting someone who is part of an elite and privileged group, who has it better than the rest of us, and whose intellectual world is out of sync with the reality of the common person's struggle. Tenure is a concept not well understood by many outside of academia. What it means to most people, if anything, is simply "job security for life." Who among us has that? And especially in these hard economic times, how on earth could anyone have the impudence to *expect* it? The prospect of being banished to the "academic underclass" of adjunct professors hardly seems like a reason to murder three people. And with the high-profile histories of so many other women successfully overcoming career obstacles now engrained in our culture, the choice Bishop made looks demented in comparison.

Although Betty Broderick and Amy Bishop both killed for revenge, a number of significant differences distinguish the two cases: Broderick killed her ex-husband; Bishop murdered her colleagues. Broderick carried a fundamental conception of herself as a wife and mother; Bishop saw herself as a gifted scientist and teacher. Broderick had been violated in a way that many women could relate to; the injustice that Bishop suffered was much more esoteric. Broderick committed her act at a time when female anger was shifting into high gear in our culture; Bishop's act was at a time when models of transcendence were beginning to abound.

Yet, the two cases have much in common: Both Broderick and Bishop suffered what they perceived to be a breach of contract. Both enjoyed a privileged status in society. Both developed a single-minded obsession with revenge. Both had other options that they chose to ignore. In the end, this last similarity is the one that will have the greatest impact on their legacies. In this second decade of the 21st century, Oprah's motto—*Living well is the best revenge*—is beginning to take hold. Both Broderick and Bishop will ultimately be judged in this light.

One final thought on the subject of revenge and living well: When one is betrayed in a committed, romantic relationship, her anguish is deeply personal. Making peace is primarily an inner process. One may find justice and healing by doing inner work, the reward being self-knowledge and self-integrity. It is reasonable to entertain the possibility of making oneself whole without finding a replacement for the lost partner. But when one is betrayed in a work situation, her anguish is likely to be part of the public arena. Making peace, therefore, is both a private *and* public matter. This dynamic could potentially provide for Amy Bishop a route to the common person's sympathies not available to Betty Broderick: If you lose your livelihood, it's not reasonable to expect to be made whole simply by finding inner peace. *You need another job.* But Amy Bishop had a promising future as an inventor. Sadly for her prospect of a judgment in her favor, a more productive form of revenge was well within her reach.

Women Who Kill for Love

3

According to psychologists, poets, and playwrights, love brings out the best in us. But sometimes love can bring out the worst in us. The tainted obsessions of Kristin Rossum and Susan Smith showed how the heady delight of being in love could lead to murder. Kristin was a beautiful and brainy toxicologist who seemed to have a promising future. But her husband threatened to reveal secrets that would shatter her image as the perfect wife and exemplary employee. When he was found dead, Kristin became the center of a sensational murder trial. Speculation ran rampant that she had turned to a popular movie for inspiration on how to get rid of him.

Susan Smith's image was also at odds with her inner self. On the surface, she seemed like the ideal young mother. Yet, Susan was willing to destroy her children when her boyfriend told her he was not interested in being a father. For nine days, Susan tricked the nation into believing the boys were missing; in reality, they were dead at the bottom of a lake. Both cases exemplify the public's fascination with women who risk everything to be with their lover.

KRISTIN ROSSUM

The state of California is the setting for one of the darkest and most famous film noir movies featuring a femme fatale. *Double Indemnity* centers on a beautiful married woman who plots with her lover to get rid of an unwanted husband. The perfect murder is almost committed, but as one of the main characters says in the film, "Murder is never perfect. It always comes apart sooner or later. When two people are involved, it's usually sooner."[1]

In the true-life case of Kristin Rossum, a beautiful young wife from California was charged with committing almost the perfect murder, but it too fell apart. Kristin's husband was found dead of an apparent suicide. Rose petals were strewn around the lifeless body eerily reminiscent of a scene in the film *American Beauty*. Kristin told the police that her husband had been depressed over their disintegrating marriage. At first, they believed her. Until they learned she had a lover and decided to take a second look. Kristin told those around her, "No matter what you hear about me, I'm not a bad person."[2] When the case was over and the facts came out, the reality was quite different. Her standing went from innocent victim to deadly femme fatale.

While growing up, Kristin expected great things from herself. "I wanted to be the best in everything I did. I wanted to be perfect."[3] Smart, talented, and pretty, Kristin appeared to be the perfect teenage daughter. But in 1993, her parents learned to their dismay that she was using drugs. A hysterical scene ensued, filled with accusations and screaming. It ended when a distraught Kristin ran off to slash her wrists in a suicide attempt. Realizing their daughter needed help, the Rossums enrolled her in a 12-step program.

Any relief felt when Kristin finished the program was short-lived. She went back to using drugs during her senior year. Another family confrontation ensued, this time ending with a call to the police and Kristin being arrested. Luckily for her, the arrest never went to court. Possibly hoping to put her troubled past behind her, Kristin chose to enroll in college early. She moved into the student dorms at the University of Redlands, where she met new friends and immersed herself in study. She reassured her family that she was doing well. Throughout 1994, it looked like Kristin had indeed overcome her habit.

Unfortunately, Kristin's recovery had been an illusion. The 18-year-old had been kicked out of school for her drug use. By now, she was smoking methamphetamine on a daily basis. Unwilling to tell her parents about this distressing turn of events, she simply vanished around Christmas time. One particular day, Kristin decided to go down to Tijuana, Mexico, a town offering easy access to drugs and alcohol with no questions asked. Crossing the border, she met 21-year-old Greg de Villers. Greg was the man who became her knight in shining armor, her rescuer, and her doomed husband.

While Kristin had grown up in a traditional family with a privileged background, Greg had a more chaotic upbringing. His parent's marriage ended in a bitter divorce. As the oldest of three boys, Greg assumed the responsibility for being the head of the household. His father was often absent not only physically, but also emotionally and financially. Always close to his mother, Greg made a point of looking after his brothers Jerome and Bertrand. Not surprisingly, the siblings had a tight bond. According to author Caitlin Rother in the book *Poisoned Love,* these experiences trained Greg early and often to be the protector, advisor, and caretaker.[4] In spite of these duties, Greg seemed good-natured and optimistic. His interest in science led him to the University of California in San Diego. Jerome admired his older brother and followed in his footsteps by attending the same college. The two shared an apartment together along with another roommate.

In December 1994, Greg rounded up his two brothers and a friend to have some fun in Tijuana. He and Kristin met when they literally bumped into each other at the border. Greg was attracted to Kristin and suggested she come along. After spending the day and evening together, he invited her home. As it turned out, Kristin didn't just spend the night; she moved in permanently.

The account provided by John Glatt, *Deadly American Beauty*, notes that while Greg was happy with this turn of events, his brother and roommate had reservations.[5] After all, Kristin had moved in within a week, did not have any money to pay rent, and seemed to have no plans for her life. When Kristin's drug pipe was discovered and some items went missing from the apartment, they wanted to evict her. Coming to his girlfriend's defense, Greg said that he still loved Kristin and would help her give up drugs once and for all.[6] Caitlin Rother noted in *Poisoned Love*, Jerome continued to have reservations about the whole situation, especially since Greg had always been so intolerant of drugs, rarely using them for medical reasons and never for recreational purposes.[7]

Greg became her "angel," and Kristin would credit him with helping her overcome her addiction.[8] Kristin finally phoned her parents to inform them she was safe. When she arranged a meeting, her mother and father welcomed the young man who appeared to have such a positive influence on their daughter. By the time Kristin and Greg announced plans to marry later that summer, the Rossums credited him with getting Kristin to kick drugs. Kristin and Greg got their own apartment, postponing wedding plans to complete their degrees. Always a gifted student, Kristin won an academic award in her junior year. Her professors considered her uncommonly bright and talented. By now, she was interested in forensic pathology. This branch of medical science uses medical knowledge for legal purposes such as providing evidence to convict murders.[9] In 1997, Kristin applied for a student internship with the San Diego Medical Examiner's Office. She was not asked about her arrest and did not mention her addiction problems. If she had, she never would have been hired. She was considered an outstanding employee with a promising future.

As Kristin's graduation grew near, Greg was making plans for their wedding to finally take place. The couple had been together for nearly five years. Kristin, however, was having doubts about the relationship.[10] Perhaps, this was the reason she would flirt provocatively with the men in her class. According to Rother's account, in *Poisoned Love*, a fellow student commented, "she's sure hot to trot for someone who is engaged."[11] Greg of course knew nothing about her misgivings; nor did her parents who were happily planning a big wedding. Kristin worried that she loved Greg out of a sense of obligation, writing in her journal, "If I had been given the family support I desperately needed . . . I wouldn't have Greg in my life."[12] She finally shared her reservations with her parents. Although her father assured her that she could cancel the wedding, her mother treated it as normal jitters. In any event, Kristin decided to go through with it. Their wedding took place in June 1999. Greg toasted his bride saying, "Kristin is the most wonderful person I ever met. . . . She's incredible in so many ways . . . so kind and sharing and caring. . . . I just can't wait to spend my whole life with her."[13]

The marriage appeared to get off to a positive start. However, Kristin's dissatisfaction quickly resurfaced. She made an attempt to say she was unhappy, but she failed to mention the dilemma her job placed her in and the relationship she had with her new boss.

Kristin became a full-time toxicologist at the San Diego Medical Examiner's Office in March 2000. Once again, she was not asked about a criminal record or drug use. Nor did she volunteer any information. It seemed like the perfect job for her. She had enjoyed her internship experience and had great personal interest in the field. The position had another allure: She had access to illegal drugs often found at accidental death sites, including methamphetamine and various. She later said, "I fell in love with the job. . . . It was something I really loved because it was something I was really close to. Close, probably too close."[14]

As it turned out, Kristin was not only in love with her job, but also in love with her boss. Michael Robertson was the chief toxicologist at the Medical Examiner's Office. Originally from Australia, he was an authority on date-rape drugs. Michael had published numerous articles and served as an expert witness in high-profile cases. Highly respected on a professional level, employees noted his friendly manner and management skills. While his professional life was stable and fulfilling, his personal life was chaotic. Michael was a handsome man with a very flirtatious manner. Despite being married, he fooled around a lot, often with coworkers. One friend said, "Michael is a player of women's emotions. . . . He has been since a young age. I think he is driven by the need for everyone to like him, and will compromise everything and everyone to achieve this."[15]

The attraction between Michael and Kristin was immediate. They spent a great deal of time hovering around each other at work, causing coworkers to speculate about their relationship. An intense romance developed. Passionate e-mails were sent back and forth. At one point, Kristin wrote, "Thank you for giving my week such a lovely start. I can smell you all around me and it's wonderful. You light up my life. I love you with all my heart."[16] Michael told Kristin, "My dreams were sweeter . . . full of you. Your smiles, dancing, laughing. I'll keep dreaming them with the hope that soon my dreams will be our reality."[17] They took to hiding gifts for each other around the office. Later, they would leave roses on each other's desk. Kristin was fascinated by the symbolism of the flower, long associated as a sign of love throughout many cultures. She often commented on how much she liked the film *American Beauty,* which featured a prominent scene with rose petals.

Office gossip continued to swirl. Michael was especially vulnerable to the whispers, since it was inappropriate to have a personal relationship with a subordinate. When a senior manager asked them about the rumors, both Michael and Kristin denied everything. They toned down their behavior. However, it was still obvious that something was going on between them. But while Kristin's coworkers may have known about her secret affair, they didn't know about her secret drug use. Kristin had started smoking crystal methamphetamine again. It's quite possible she was stealing it from her work-place, since she had access to methamphetamines that had been impounded at death scenes.[18] Kristin concealed her habit by minimizing its effect on her appearance and behavior. For now, no one knew, not even Michael. Although she had confessed her previous use to him, she maintained it was strictly in the past.

Kristin officially graduated from college in May 2000, earning a number of scholastic distinctions. It was a proud moment for the beautiful, smart 23-year-old. Kristin and Greg celebrated their first wedding anniversary in June. Greg had recently accepted a job at a start-up company, working under his former boss. With promising jobs after college, Greg and Kristin seemed to have ideal future prospects. Moreover, at Michael's suggestion, Kristin was scheduled to make a formal presentation at an important toxicology confer-ence, which would not only increase her professional visibility, but also give her another chance to spend time with Michael.

By now, Kristin was complaining to her family about unhappiness in her marriage. Her litany of complaints included Greg's neediness and how re-stricted she felt in the relationship. She neglected to mention her involvement with her married boss. Greg found out about Michael when he discovered one of his love letters to Kristin. Confronted with this evidence, she admitted the attraction but denied having an affair. Greg called Michael and demanded an end to the relationship. Michael's wife, who had been vaguely suspicious of her husband's behavior, realized there was something much more serious taking place.

Although Kristin and Michael continued to minimize the extent of their relationship to their respective spouses, they persisted in making plans for the future. Michael told her, "You are my love, my perfect match, the one I see beside me at the altar, at home, holding my children, walking beside me in the morning, and kissing good night."[19] The excitement of the affair, Michael's notes of passion, and their secret trysts may all have contributed to Kristin's willingness to take whatever action was necessary to get Greg out of her life. Something else may also have fueled her willingness to take risks: The emotional residue from Greg's discovery upped Kristin's drug use. She was making secret trips to Mexico to buy narcotics.

Kristin and Michael made plans to attend the conference together in October. They spent a great deal of time developing her presentation, which dealt with the investigation of a poison case. Aware of the ongoing rumors, a superior once again asked Michael about the relationship. Michael remained steadfast in his denial. By now, Greg had learned about the conference. He made it very clear that he did not want Kristin to go. Kristin turned Greg's anger against him, using it as another example of his controlling nature. Her justification for attending the conference was twofold: It would provide an excellent opportunity for networking, and making a presentation would enhance her professional reputation. Not wanting to stand in the way of her career, Greg relented. Kristin eagerly joined Michael for a week at the conference. Together, she and Michael attended a number of presentations including one featuring a discussion on fentanyl, a drug that can play a role in accidental deaths and suicides. While at the conference, Kristin and Michael indicated to a few friends they were now officially a couple.

Upon returning home, Kristin told her husband she wanted a trial separation. According to her, "He was devastated. There was a period where he basically went to bed for a couple of days and would not talk to me, not to anyone."[20] Their marriage limped along for a few weeks. They continued to live together, socialize with friends, and spend time with family members. Kristin celebrated her 24th birthday in October 2000. Meanwhile, Michael wrote a letter to her suggesting that while he loved her and wanted to be with her, he was getting tired of waiting.

On November 2, 2000, Greg caught Kristin reading one of Michael's letters. A bitter argument erupted. It ended with Kristin shredding the note. According to Kristin's account, Greg spent hours trying to piece it back together, possibly as evidence of an affair.[21] During the ensuing days, Greg continued to accuse his wife of having a sexual relationship with Michael. He also started to accuse her of using drugs again. Kristin denied both claims. Greg was livid when he found pills in her purse. According to Kristin, he gave her an ultimatum—he would go to the Medical Examiner's Office and expose her affair and her drug use unless she stopped both.[22] Kristin told Michael about Greg's threat when she went to work the next day. Privately, Michael had been wondering if Kristin was using again. He had noticed her erratic performance at work, her mood swings, and the changes in her physical appearance. Michael found a hidden stash of drugs in her desk later that week, keeping the discovery to himself.

The couple continued to argue during the ensuing days. Everything came to a head on November 6, 2000. According to Kristin's version of the day, Greg awoke that morning indicating he was sick with a cold. She left a message with his office, informing them he would not be in. As it turned out, the message was left on Greg's voice mail; no one received it. Concerned over his unexplained absences, coworkers tried phoning him at home to see if he was all right.

Throughout the day, Kristin left work to touch base with her sick husband. One of these visits occurred at lunch. She stopped at the store to buy some soup and prepared it for him. In Kristin's account, Greg was glad to see her although he indicated that he was very tired. Finding her old prescriptions of oxycodone and clonazepam, he took them in order to get some rest. Kristin returned to work. Greg was still sleeping when she got home that evening. The phone rang. It was one of Greg's coworkers checking up on him. Kristin explained that Greg had been ill, but would be at work the next day. Kristin ate dinner alone, and then went out shopping. She returned home around 8:00. Checking on Greg, she found him asleep. He appeared fine. At 9:22 P.M., she made a fateful call to the paramedics saying that she discovered her husband cold to the touch and not breathing.

Kristin seemed to be upset and in hysterics. The dispatcher tried to talk her through administering CPR. Paramedics soon appeared. Walking into the bedroom, they found Greg's lifeless body sprinkled with rose petals. The couple's wedding picture was nearby. Kim Zetter notes in the article "The Husband, the Wife and the Lover" that Kristin's diary was opened to an entry stating that she had made a mistake in marrying Greg.[23] At first glance, the paramedics thought it was a suicide. This seemed to be confirmed when Kristin told them about their arguments and Greg's despondency over their marital problems. She mentioned that he stayed home sick that day. Needing to rest, he had taken some of her old prescription drugs. Kristin wondered aloud if he could have overdosed by mistake on some combination of the pills and cough medicine. Greg was taken to the emergency room.

As doctors tried to revive Greg, Kristin called Michael, asking him to meet her at the hospital.[24] She also called her father to tell him of the situation. Within 12 minutes of arrival, Greg was pronounced dead. Michael was present when Kristin received the news. Death brings with it procedures to be followed and paperwork to be filled out. Kristin was questioned once again about what happened and told the same story she had shared with the paramedics. She thought Greg had taken some of her old pills. This time, she added that the five-year-old pills were originally purchased to help her overcome an old drug habit. She quickly agreed to donate Greg's organs. However, she was taken aback when told that an autopsy would be performed. The hospital staff informed her that this was customary after someone had an unexplained, unexpected death. Michael told them that he was the chief toxicologist from the Medical Examiner's Office. He would make sure someone took care of it.

The news of Greg's unexpected death came as devastating shock to his family. The story they initially heard was Greg might have suffered an allergic reaction to some cough syrup. It didn't make any sense to them. How could a healthy 26-year-old die from that? It seemed even more improbable when they were told that Greg may have killed himself with some pills in an accidental overdose or a suicide attempt. Greg's brother Jerome totally rejected this claim. He knew how much Greg was against drugs; it was highly unlikely that Greg would use them for any reason. Jerome was also adamant that Greg had not been depressed. As far as Jerome knew, Greg had no reason to kill himself. The conflicting stories made Jerome wonder what was going on. He was also confused as to why Kristin asked for an immediate cremation. Everything was moving too quickly for his comfort. When Jerome met with Kristin, he immediately recognized the scabs on Kristin's face and body as signs of drug use. All of these factors led him to conclude that somehow Kristin was involved in the death.

Others also began to wonder if Kristin was involved. It's not unusual in a case involving an unexpected death to suspect the spouse. Detectives as well as an investigator from the Medical Examiner's Office had gone to Greg and Kristin's apartment. They saw the rose petals, the wedding picture, the torn love letter, and Kristin's journal. While it was exactly as Kristin described, there was something unsettling. The rose petals seemed an odd gesture for a man to make. Kristin said she didn't know where they came from. There was no sign of drug containers lying around. There was no suicide note. Although Kristin's story was possible, it just did not seem likely. How could Kristin have checked on her husband at 8 P.M., finding him fine, then one hour later discover him in a life-threatening situation? There seemed to be too many unanswered questions.

An autopsy is designed to address some of those unanswered questions. In a move that surprised both Kristin and Michael, the autopsy and toxicology tests were sent to a private lab. When the tests came back, they carried stunning news. Greg's body contained oxycodone and clonazepam, just as Kristin mentioned. However, the body also contained lethal doses of the powerful pain killer fentanyl, a highly regulated drug. Investigators learned that fentanyl patches from the Medical Examiner's Office were missing. Kristin had been responsible for logging in the patches. Michael was the last person known to have handled them.

As detectives learned the results of the autopsy report, they also heard from Jerome who shared his suspicions that Kristin was using drugs again and might somehow be involved in his brother's death. It seemed completely out of character for Greg to accidentally or deliberately kill himself. Greg's coworkers had written a note to investigators stating that Greg had not shown any suicidal tendencies. They were concerned that foul play was involved. Some employees at the Medical Examiner's Office had the same concern. One told detectives of the rumors surrounding Kristin and Michael's relationship. Another sent a copy of a love letter to Kristin found on Michael's desk. Investigators soon realized they had a motive.

They went to Kristin first. Confronted with the letter, she admitted having an affair. She also owned up to recently using drugs. But she vehemently denied having anything to do with Greg's death. Michael was interviewed a short time later. He too spent most of the time denying everything. Eventually, he came clean about the relationship and conceded he was aware of Kristin's addiction. Investigators passed along the information regarding Kristin's drug use to the Medical Examiner's Office. Kristin was terminated. Michael was also let go. His failure to report a subordinate's drug use was a major violation that could not be tolerated.

Detectives now had enough information to consider Greg's death a possible murder. Kristin was stunned and outraged that she was a suspect. As far as she was concerned, she had suffered a tragic loss. She had written in her journal, "My dearest Greggie . . . I lost you, your precious life so unfairly cut short."[25] In other entries, she described her unbearable heartbreak at losing her best friend, lover, and future father of her children.[26] Police weren't buying it. On January 4, 2001, they had a search warrant for both Kristin's and Michael's apartments. Kristin was on meth when they arrived. Investigators confiscated her stash of drugs, an article about fentanyl, her journals, and her computer. She was arrested for being on narcotics, but was released the next day. The police grilled Michael about his actions as they searched his place. He admitted that he and Kristin spent a great deal of time together at work the day Greg died. They even went to one of their favorite rendezvous places later in the afternoon. Supposedly, the two were discussing his discovery of Kristin's drug cache—not plotting Greg's murder. According to Michael, the relationship was over. "I've lost my job. I've lost my profession. I'm losing my wife. . . . I don't want to be part of this. . . . This isn't where I envisioned my life in 2001—in the middle of a homicide investigation—and I want it over and done with."[27] He left for Australia in May 2001, claiming he needed to be with his dying mother.

Upon her release from the drug charge, Kristin tried piecing together a semblance of her old life. She stopped using meth. She found a job, working at another biotech company. She spent time with her parents. Detectives remained on the case gathering more evidence. In June 2001, Kristin was arrested for murder under special circumstances. When an individual is murdered by poison, California law requires that the convicted murderer be given the death penalty or life without parole. Michael was still considered a suspect, but no charges were filed. The investigation against him remained open for years.

The sensational nature of the case attracted widespread attention. Here was a beautiful young woman charged with murdering her husband: throw in drugs, a steamy love affair with the boss, the mysterious rose petals, and possible poison. Kristin and her parents decided to do what they could to publicize her side of the story. Her father, a well-known professor, told reporters,

"You are making a victim of our daughter, who lost a husband. She does not have it in her to commit these charges."[28] In a bid for sympathy, he indicated that his daughter would use a public defender. This would allow the family to apply their resources toward the $1.25 million bail. Kristin's mother had a strong marketing background from her corporate days and knew the power of the media in shaping public opinion. In an exclusive interview by Joanna Powell with *Good Housekeeping,* she loudly proclaimed, "My Daughter is Innocent." According to Mrs. Rossum, Greg was not a young man with a bright future ahead of him; he was in debt over his head and depressed. Although she had no proof, she stated that Greg was a fentanyl user. As far as she was concerned, Kristin had no motive for killing her husband. "Kristin may have made some moral slips, but that doesn't make her a murderess."[29]

Kristin's cover girl looks, coupled with her image as a sexy, brainy scientist did not go unnoticed. There was immediate talk of a book and movie deal. According to John Glatt's account in *Deadly American Beauty,* the lawyers working on Kristin's behalf found themselves spending more time on media requests than working on her defense.[30] *Good Morning America* and *Inside Edition* featured segments on the story. But the biggest boost in public attention came from the airing of *48 Hours,* shortly before the trial started. It featured a tearful Kristin talking about what a nightmare her life had become. After the show aired, Alex Roth, a reporter covering the case for the *Union Tribune,* noted that the judge on the case criticized "the insatiable appetite" of the press and stated he was afraid of "further poisoning" an already polluted jury pool.[31] The judge sealed pretrial documents, placing a gag order on authorities as well as potential witnesses. By this time, not only had the Rossum family been quoted in interviews, so had members of the de Villers family, coworkers of Kristin's and Greg's, friends of the couple, and a former professor of Kristin's. Michael had even been tracked down in Australia. In interviews to reporters, he denied deserting his lover and skipping out of the country to avoid prosecution. "I stayed there (in San Diego) for many months after this happened to facilitate the investigation as much as I could. To say I fled is not the case."[32]

The trial finally started in October 2002. Prosecutors felt they had a strong case against Kristin but knew the jury might perceive her as a sympathetic figure. They anticipated that the defense strategy would rely on Kristin's image as a beautiful young widow trapped by circumstantial evidence. Given this, they chose not to seek the death penalty. They also chose not to extradite Michael as a witness or suspect at this time. Nevertheless, he was referred to as an "unindicted coconspirator" throughout the trial. The prosecution argued that Kristin plotted with Michael to get rid of her husband by using fentanyl, anticipating that the Medical Examiner's Office would conduct the autopsy and not routinely check for the drug. The defense conceded that fentanyl had killed Greg. Their job was to create reasonable doubt on how it got into his body. Testimony centered on whether Greg had indeed been suicidal or whether Kristin had deliberately used her position in the toxicologist's office to poison Greg and then cover it up. As could be expected, two distinct and conflicting points of view were presented. Jerome testified that his brother Greg was not suicidal. Kristin and her parents maintained that he was.

Facts from the investigation were put forward to support the prosecutor's contention that Kristin was a habitually lying drug addict who would say and do anything. It was noted that she had started the day of Greg's death by contacting her dealer in Mexico. The prosecution theorized that she was making arrangements to ensure that she had enough supply of meth to get her through a day, which she knew in advance would be grisly. They claimed that she gave Greg the clonazepam purchased years ago, knowing this date-rape drug would make him drowsy and unconscious. She then used the fentanyl she had stolen from work to murder him. The defense pointed out that while Kristin did have access to fentanyl, security was so lax in the lab that anyone of the employees could have stolen it. Medical experts were called in to discuss the level of drugs found in Greg's body. Given the high dosage and its side effects, witnesses debated how likely it was that he could have taken the drugs, and then physically taken the time to hide the evidence. Police officers who arrived on the scene pointed out that no syringes, patches, or needles had been found near his corpse.

Kristin's testimony regarding the timeline of her actions on the day of Greg's death contradicted what she had told the police earlier. Experts testified that Greg was comatose for 6–12 hours before his death, making lunch with her improbable.[33] However, the defining moment in the trial came when it was revealed by the prosecution that on the day of the murder, Kristin had gone to the grocery store and bought a single rose. Kristin had always denied knowing where the rose petals that were found on Greg's body had come from. She now admitted buying the flower. However, she maintained that she'd given it to Michael later in the day. The rose petals that were found around Greg were from a different flower. The jury didn't believe her. She was found guilty and sentenced to life without parole. Kristin vowed to appeal.

The case of beautiful people, a love triangle, sex, poison, conspiracy, and betrayal was a murder story that fascinated the public.[34] When *Cosmopolitan* ran an article about Kristin prior to the trial, readers where invited to write in regarding their opinion. They responded in droves, with 68 percent considering her guilty, while 32 percent considered her innocent.[35] Apparently, Kristin was not a "Cosmo Girl." Her notoriety didn't seem to bother men. Kristin had attracted a large contingent of male fans during the trial. Caitlin Rother notes in *Poisoned Love* that some came to the courthouse to show their support, and others joked about wanting to date her.[36] The day after her verdict, a cartoon appeared in a local San Diego newspaper showing a guard leading Kristin to her cell. The path was strewn with rose petals. Her image as a scheming sexy murderer became seared into the public's mind along with a tie into *American Beauty.*

Hollywood approached both families to buy rights to their stories. Media interest in depicting her as the "forensic femme fatale" didn't stop once Kristin was sentenced. Although true-crime shows had been a staple of television for years, the show *Snapped* was unique. It burst onto the scene in 2004. The show's narrative focused on women who had committed murder or been accused of murder; no men were allowed. Kristin's story was featured in the first season. The case fit perfectly with its breathless profiles of women who purportedly reached their breaking point and ended up paying for the price of their crime. In 2005, *E! True Hollywood Story Investigates* aired the episode "Women Who Kill." It featured Kristin Rossum as one of the most publicized murder cases in American history. The television show *Deadly Women,* another that focused on female killers, featured an episode devoted to Kristin.

Kristin's legal issues also continued to receive coverage in the media. After the guilty verdict, Greg's family filed a civil wrongful death suit against Kristin. One of their concerns was that Kristin might profit from Greg's death. The "Son of Sam" law, which required convicted criminals to give all money earned from book, movie, or other deals to their victims or the state, was struck down in 2002.[37] One of the marketing experts testifying for the case noted that since Kristin was a "notorious" criminal, she could sell the rights to her story for $2.5 million or more with unlimited future earning potential.[38] Kristin was ordered to pay $4.5 million in compensatory damages and another $100 million in punitive damages to prevent her from profiting off the rights to her story. Although punitive damages were later reduced to $10 million, Kristin filed for bankruptcy to avoid paying anything.

Kristin became a hot topic once again in 2010 after being behind bars for eight years. Her appeals in the past had gone nowhere. However, her most recent one was different. Posted on the Internet for the whole world to see, the habeas corpus stated that her attorneys had committed a grave error. They should not have so readily agreed to the contention that Greg had died from an overdose of fentanyl. Instead, the appeal stated that the attorneys should have conducted additional drug tests. The tests would have determined whether Greg had in fact ingested fentanyl or whether fentanyl found in the samples was a product of laboratory contamination subsequent to his death.[39] Was it possible that someone at the San Diego Medical Examiner's Office or at the outside lab that conducted Greg's autopsy had tampered with the evidence? The court initially ruled in favor of conducting an appeal. However, in 2011, they reversed their decision ending her hopes of another trial.

And what of Michael, the lover Kristin was so desperate to be with? He certainly had the medical knowledge to ensure that Greg would get the appropriate dose of drugs rendering him unconscious and ultimately ending his life. After all, Michael was a well-known expert on date-rape drugs such as clonazepam. Was it just a coincidence that the police discovered 37 different articles related to fentanyl in his possession? What about all the PowerPoint presentations they found, including one with a slide called "The Crooked Criminologist" talking about a corrupt toxicologist who had stolen some fentanyl patches?[40] It was quite possible that Michael had not only colluded with Kristin but had even been the mastermind. His departure to Australia could have been a desperate attempt to avoid arrest. There was speculation that Kristin had turned down a plea bargain in exchange for implicating her lover. Without her cooperation, although not impossible, it would have been difficult to prosecute Michael. This may have been why he was never arrested. When Michael heard about Kristin's verdict, he continued to say he believed in her innocence. Yet, he commented, "If she did do it, then she should be punished."[41] He has never returned to the United States. How Kristin viewed Michael's departure to Australia is unknown. But given the life sentence she received, if Kristin did indeed turn down a plea bargain to protect Michael, she may be the ultimate example of a smart woman who made foolish choices for love.

Our society promotes the axiom that love conquers all. It's not surprising that Kristin wanted to believe this. The classic, tried-and-true message has been a staple of storytelling since anyone can remember. The basic theme comes in a number of variations: As long as you have love, everything will turn out right. True love justifies any action. Being willing to do anything for your lover, shows the depth of your love. Taking dangerous risks for love is a noble thing. Like all maxims, "love conquers all" has a ring of truth at its core. Its appeal may be especially strong for women—particularly young women—and most notably for those whose personal insecurities drive them to seek to be "completed" by another person. Kristin found out too late that the message is not always accurate.

Before the 1960s, idealized images of romantic love permeated pop culture. Love was depicted as a supremely empowering, hope sustaining, all-inclusive justification for just about any action. By the 1970s, romantic love had begun to get knocked down a peg. The ideal of finding romantic love was being replaced with the imperative of "being yourself," no matter what the cost. The divorce rate soared. In books, television, and films, many protagonists survived—even thrived—without the security of a long-term relationship. By the mid-1980s, the old model of romantic love had started to creep back into fashion, but this time with some adaptations to a new era: Few people were "saving themselves" for a committed relationship. True love was no longer limited to married couples. And it didn't necessarily happen "magically." Lovers were permitted assistance such as support groups and couples counseling to help them along.

The 1990s saw a major resurgence in the ethos of romantic love. Celebrity weddings like Jane Fonda and Ted Turner, Cindy Crawford and Richard

Gere, and Jennifer Aniston and Brad Pitt captured the public's heart and imagination. The media successfully revived the once heroic message that love conquers all. But, as we shall see, this basic theme became subtly but commonly coupled with other, less noble messages. By 2000, the year Kristin Rossum killed her husband, the ideal of romantic love had morphed into much more complex variations.

In *The Andy Griffith Show,* an early television sitcom running from 1960 to 1968, Andy Taylor, the sheriff of Mayberry, and Helen Crump, a spinster teacher, carry on an innocent, slow-moving courtship for the entire length of the series. In this small-town setting, we assume that Andy and Helen are chaste, though this is never made explicitly clear. Helen only occasionally broaches the subject of marriage, promoting the innocuous message that having the patience to build a stable, wholesome relationship will bring its own rewards. Several decades later, the theme of friendship building slowly into lasting romance was embodied once again in the characters Chandler Bing and Monica Geller on the tremendously successful 1990s sitcom *Friends.* This time, we know exactly when Chandler and Monica first sleep together, which makes it even easier to follow the couple to their eventual wedding vows and restore faith that love will find a way in the end.

While these characterizations of love mildly fulfilled our need to believe in the virtues of romance, other media images glorified the power of love more dramatically. In the 1967 film *The Graduate,* Benjamin Braddock (played by Dustin Hoffman) is seduced by Mrs. Robinson (played by Anne Bancroft), the wife of his father's business partner. During the course of this affair, Braddock falls in love with Robinson's engaged daughter, Elaine. He eventually barges in on Elaine's wedding ceremony to declare his undying love for her. Despite her knowledge of Benjamin's affair with her mother and angry protests and threats from her parents, Elaine chooses Benjamin, again reaffirming that love will win in the end, no matter the hurdles. This theme, echoed more than two decades later in Celine Dion's 1992 hit "Love Can Move Mountains," shows its staying power:

> *Ain't a dream that don't have a chance to come true now . . .*
> *Long as we got our love to light the way.*[42]

At the same time, television continues to reinforce the message in programs like the highly acclaimed sitcom *Mad about You* (1992–1999), where young newlyweds Paul and Jamie Buchman deal with everything from silly and mundane daily matters to major life struggles. Over the course of the series' seven-year run, Paul and Jamie brave uncomfortable in-law relations, challenging sibling rivalries, and the dissolution of their best friends' long-term marriage. Through it all, their love triumphs.

The love triangle—in which a woman or man struggles with making a choice between two different and distinctive romantic partners—has also been an enduring theme in entertainment media. In *Peyton Place*, the quintessential 1960s prime-time soap opera, Allison McKenzie (played by Mia Farrow) falls in love with Rodney, the older brother of a classmate. Despite Rodney's feelings for Allison, he marries his girlfriend, Betty, whom he believes is pregnant with his child. But Allison, the sexy "bad girl," holds too much allure for Rodney. He winds up divorcing Betty. The only thing preventing Rodney from finally marrying Allison is the unfortunate exit of Mia Farrow from the series. In the 1987 film *Moonstruck*, Loretta Castorini (played by Cher) breaks off her engagement to milquetoast Johnny Cammareri (played by Danny Aiello) in order to marry his wild and passionate brother Ronny (played by Nicolas Cage). A decade later, *L.A. Law* attorney Grace Van Owen (Susan Dey) is torn between her doting boyfriend, Michael Kuzak (Harry Hamlin) and tall, dark, and dangerous newcomer, Victor Sifuentes (Jimmy Smits). Grace dumps Michael for Victor. Who wouldn't choose excitement over predictability? Kristin Rossum made a similar choice. She opted for a handsome, exciting, risk-taking boyfriend over a staid and predictably devoted husband. But although the public may have found this choice palatable for some film and television characters, Kristin Rossum gained no public sympathy.

One of the principles that render love conquers all a noble concept is the presumption that a lover's motives are grounded in more than just her or his own self-interest. In his classic novel *The French Lieutenant's Woman*, published in 1969 and later adapted to film, John Fowles explores the relationship between love and selfishness. Set in a late 19th-century English coastal town, the novel features Sarah Woodruff as a disgraced woman, abandoned by her supposed lover—a French naval officer who, unknown to her, was married to another woman. When Charles, an English gentleman, and his fiancée Ernestina see Sarah standing on a cliff looking out to sea, Ernestina relates what she has heard is Sarah's story, and Charles develops a fascination with Sarah, ultimately pursuing and becoming intimate with her. Throughout the novel, Fowles depicts Sarah ambiguously. The reader is unsure whether Sarah is a manipulating character, feigning self-pity in order to exploit Charles, or a genuine victim of upper-middle class gender prejudice prevalent at the time. This same type of ambiguity surrounded Kristin: some felt she was trapped in circumstantial evidence, and others felt she was a conniving plotter who ruthlessly killed her husband.

Forty years later, the interplay between love and selfishness remains a popular theme. In the 2009 romantic comedy spy thriller *Duplicity*, Ray Koval (played by Clive Owen) and Claire Stenwick (played by Julia Roberts) are corporate secret agents with an uncertain romantic history who collaborate to execute a complicated con. The problem is that they don't trust one another and with good reason. They each appear to be out for their own selfish interests. After catching each other in repeated lies throughout the film, Claire finally confesses that she loves Ray. They're cut from the same mold, she observes, and for this reason, they are each the only person who could ever understand the other. If, in the mind of the public, love and selfishness can peacefully coexist as it did in this film, then Kristin Rossum may yet have a chance of gaining public sympathy.

The idea of enduring love has also been harmoniously blended with darker, more sinister themes. *Twilight,* Stephenie Meyer's tremendously successful series of four fantasy romance novels, features Bella Swan, a teenage girl who falls in love with Edward Cullen, a 104-year-old vampire. Together, Bella and Edward overcome sadistic plots against Bella's life, outside rivalry for her affection, internal conflicts between Bella's human shortcomings and Edward's supernatural powers, and a nearly fatal pregnancy. Meyer considers her books as "romance more than anything else," and describes the stories as being about "love, not lust."[43] She adds that each book in the series was inspired by and loosely based on a different literary classic: *Twilight* on Jane Austen's *Pride and Prejudice, New Moon* on Shakespeare's *Romeo and Juliet, Eclipse* on Emily Brontë's *Wuthering Heights,* and *Breaking Dawn* on a second Shakespeare play, *A Midsummer Night's Dream.*[44] Thus, the most archetypal love stories in history have been reinvented and popularized to include nonhuman heroes who supplement their undying love with a similarly undying body. If even these blood-sucking characters can be viewed sympathetically, when motivated by love, why can't Kristin Rossum?

Bonnie and Clyde, the 1967 film about a notorious bank-robbing, antihero couple, introduced a new, hybrid genre—the stylish, mostly light-hearted crime drama/romance. This film broke new ground with its combination of a carefree, folksy feeling and graphic scenes of bloody violence. It tells the story of handsome, gun-toting, amoral drifter Clyde (played by Warren Beatty) who rescues beautiful dreamer Bonnie (played by Faye Dunaway) from her drab existence by regaling her with colorful tales of the outlaw life. Because of the film's romanticized portrayal of criminals, audiences can't help but cheer Bonnie and Clyde as they watch them wreak havoc on society. For an hour and half, we're a part of their private, excitement-filled world—not the mundane world of law-abiding folks. Bonnie and Clyde get sprayed with bullets at the end, but we walk away identifying with them anyway, because love conquers all.

Another unlikely protagonist is the kind-hearted bank robber Sonny (played by Al Pacino) in the 1975 film *Dog Day Afternoon.* Oh sure, "technically" he is a criminal. Well yes, he does threaten the lives of a dozen or so people at the bank. And okay, he's more devoted to his gay lover than he is to his wife and children. But he never really hurts anyone, and when we discover that he's only trying to get some cash in order to pay for his lover's gender reassignment surgery, we excuse all of his other shortcomings. Why? Because love conquers all.

More than two decades later, Dharma and Greg, two extreme opposites, carry on an unlikely romantic relationship in a television sitcom of the same name. Dharma, a free-spirited, eccentric hippie-type, and Greg, a conservative, straight-laced, traditional guy, marry on their first date and remain devoted to each other, despite societal pressures that threaten to destroy them at every turn. Both characters are so extreme that they're truly difficult for most of us to relate to personally, yet this award-winning show captured the public's imagination and interest for five years. It was just the evidence we needed to sustain the belief that love conquers all, regardless of what society thinks.

Can love justify professional misbehavior? If one of television's most popular medical drama series is any indication, the answer quite often is yes. Though many of the doctors on *Grey's Anatomy* are romantic partners, the most enduring relationship is between the two main stars, Meredith Grey and Derek Shepherd (a.k.a. Dr. McDreamy). From the beginning, their relationship poses professional difficulties, since Derek is Meredith's supervisor and mentor, not unlike the relationship between Kristin and her boss, Michael.

Throughout the *Grey's Anatomy* series, which started in 2005 and is still going strong in 2012, Meredith and Derek continually face situations that pit their professional responsibilities against their relationship: having to defend the partner's misdiagnosis of a patient, for example, or withholding information about the partner that might help the hospital but adversely affect the partner's career. Both characters must struggle with each situation as it arises, which usually entails crossing professional boundaries at some point in the story. These decisions pose such compelling moral dilemmas that in 2009, the producers created a video game allowing fans to navigate through the characters' psychological and emotional states in order to personalize their own decisions. Is love conquers all a more powerful imperative than the code of professional medical conduct? You decide. Since the *Grey's Anatomy* game had not yet been invented in 2000, Kristin had no other choice but to play out her decision in real life.

We've seen now that the originally pure message "love conquers all" has since evolved in a number of directions, having been combined with images of selfishness, the underworld, disregard for society, and professional misbehavior. It's not hard to imagine how these images could be perceived by someone of questionable integrity as the validation of a less-than-righteous act, as long as it was committed in the name of love.

Twelve years after committing her crime, Kristin is still trying to win over the public. But her chances of gaining popular support are slim, for reasons we shall see as we review the next case.

SUSAN SMITH

Tom Findlay was everything a woman dreamed of: handsome, smart, young, and rich. It's reasonable to assume that Susan Smith considered herself a pretty lucky woman when Tom Findlay had asked for a date. The boss's son had noticed her. Even though the relationship had a low profile, Susan was happy. Tom took her out, paid attention to her, and made her feel special. At long last, life seemed to be looking up. She could close the door on her failed marriage. She could forget about the husband who cheated on her. She no longer had to tolerate dead end jobs. If everything worked out, she would soon be living in a nice house with nice things. Susan wanted to become Tom's wife.

Their whirlwind romance certainly had the potential for a fairy-tale ending. Prince Charming had come along to sweep Susan off her feet, shower her with riches, and allow her to live happily ever after. But real life and fairy tales are often two different things. Tom had sent Susan a letter telling her he did not want to be in a serious relationship. Although he liked her two young boys, he wasn't ready to have a built-in family. This news prompted her to take drastic action to keep his interest.

Susan loved her children and was considered a "good mother." But in 1995, she decided she loved Tom more. Perhaps in her mind, the only choice was to drive her car into a lake with her two sons strapped inside. Susan spread the story on national television that a black man had abducted the boys after a carjacking. When the world found out it was all lies, she went down in popular culture as the personification of maternal evil.

The very name of Susan's birthplace, Union, South Carolina, has the ring of small town folksiness. It evokes the impression of friendly neighbors, lazy summer days, and rural simplicity. So naturally, one would expect Susan to have an idyllic time growing up there in the 1970s. While Susan did enjoy some early carefree years, there was always shadows hanging over her childhood memories. Like many people in the area, Susan's parents had wed young: Her mother was a teenager, her father not even 21. Although they stayed together for 17 years, the marriage was not happy. There were tears and fights, drunken nights, and accusations. Susan was shielded from a great deal of the drama. Life was all about playing outside, going to school, and having fun with friends. Many daughters want to be daddy's little girl, and Susan was no exception. The two spent a great deal of time together, apparently enjoying each other's company.

While Susan was able to block out domestic turmoil at home, her mother was not. Trapped in a marriage as the best years of her life slipped by, she wanted an exit. Susan was barely seven when her parents got divorced. Dissolution of a marriage often causes great anxiety between parents and children. Susan may have wondered how she would be able to see her father, spend time with him, and let him know how much she loved him.

Shortly after the marriage officially ended in 1978, her father shot himself. Most of the town knew he had been in a deep depression. Whether it was a deliberate attempt at suicide or a failed cry for attention is uncertain. At seven years old, the reason was unimportant to Susan. Her beloved father was gone forever. The loss was overwhelming. According to Andrea Peyser's book, *Mother Love, Deadly Love,* "It was a shock from which friends and family, with the benefit of hindsight, now believe she never recovered."[45]

Susan's mother remarried. Her second husband was a prosperous local businessman connected to conservative politicians. His success allowed him to provide a better standard of living for the family. Susan now lived in a big house in a nicer part of Union. She observed firsthand the benefits of moving up on the social scale. While it was unlikely that she was class conscious, Susan could readily appreciate the benefits her stepfather's money brought. Having money allowed options, especially when you lived in a small town. On the surface, Susan spent her teen years as the typical all-American girl. Engaging and popular, her life was filled with activity. She participated in high-school clubs, became a volunteer, enjoyed dating, and devoted herself to getting good grades. But two incidents marred this idyllic picture.

The first occurred when Susan tried to kill herself at 13. Whatever reasons led her to this action, an overdramatic case of teenage angst, genuine depression, a sad attempt to emulate her father, or a combination of all three, Susan's actions indicated that she was clearly unhappy with her life. More turmoil was evident when Susan turned 17. In 1988, she confessed to a school counselor as well as her mother that her stepfather was sexually abusing her. After an investigation, her stepfather moved out, acknowledging that he did have sex with Susan. A revelation like this can split families apart. A startled wife often feels betrayal. Relatives might wonder if the relationship was somehow consensual. The victim may be afraid of retaliation for bringing the secret out in the open. Whatever the dynamics, the situation is dysfunctional. But families can be notorious for choosing to turn a blind eye on problems. Author Maria Eftimiades notes in the account *Sins of the Mother* that court records were sealed when Susan and her mother chose not to pursue the matter further.[46] Susan's stepfather moved back into the house. The family acted as if nothing happened.

Given the tumult in Susan's life, she may have looked to David Smith as someone who could rescue her. The two originally met in high school. They got to know each other better at the local Winn-Dixie grocery store, where Susan was a cashier and David was a manager. Since Susan was outgoing and vivacious, it was no surprise that David noticed her. He also heard rumors about her involvement with other coworkers, including a married man. When one of these romances ended badly for Susan, she made her second suicide attempt at 18. Despite David having a fiancée, or maybe because of it, the two started to see each other. The relationship brought an element of excitement to their lives. Unexpectedly, Susan learned she was pregnant. David was engaged to marry another woman; Susan wanted to go to college. Now these specific plans were in jeopardy. The two of them discussed their options, and a shotgun wedding took place in 1991. Susan was still a teenager just like her mother had been. David was not quite 21, the same age her father was when he married Susan's mother.

Money was tight for the newlyweds. Susan never had the opportunity to show off her engagement ring; David couldn't afford to buy one. The first night of their honeymoon was spent at a Day's Inn. Upon their return, they lived with David's grandmother since Susan had refused to move into the house David had been building for his previous fiancée. This house was much smaller and more modest than the one she grew up in. Thanks to her stepfather's largesse, Susan had enjoyed a more affluent lifestyle. In all probability, she may have hoped to marry up, not down. Despite these problems, the couple looked forward to the new baby. David Smith writes in the book *Beyond All Reason* that when Michael was born in October 1991, Susan was overjoyed and he was deliriously happy.[47]

They were less thrilled with each other as their marriage disintegrated. Money continued to be a source of contention between the two. David tried to live within their means; Susan did not. Her continued financial requests to her parents made David feel insecure about his ability to provide for his family.[48] Privacy was another issue between the couple, since Susan had a tendency to complain to her mother about marital issues. When their sex life stopped after the baby was born, David was shut out physically and emotionally. On her part, Susan found it difficult to accept when David treated her as just another employee at the store. As their unhappiness with each other grew, arguments escalated. The lowest point came when one of their fights turned physical and they hit each other. It's not surprising that Susan went home to her mother shortly after her first anniversary. She told David she wanted a break from the relationship.

The separation lasted only a short while. David was shaken when Susan walked out, especially when he learned she was dating other men. He wanted his wife to return, pleading, "I promise if you come back I will never, ever take you for granted again."[49] Agreeing to reconciliation, she accepted his contrition. Whatever their good intentions, each of them still blamed the other for their difficulties. It seemed the only thing they had in common was their love for their son Michael. Susan spent a great deal of time chronicling his milestones in a scrapbook. Shortly after the baby's birth, she had written, "It was truly the most wonderful experience of my life. . . . I was so happy."[50] But the two continued to have problems with their relationship. Now it was David who chose to leave.

At first, Susan didn't seem to care. Upon learning that David lost little time in selecting a coworker as his girlfriend, jealousy entered the picture.

Even though she too was dating, Susan made a public scene at work, berating David for infidelity. The two argued over which one was being more unfaithful and disrespectful of their marriage vows. Although Susan and David could never seem to live with each other, they also couldn't seem to live without each other. They continued to date one another and sleep together. When Susan found out she was pregnant a second time, she was willing to give the marriage another chance. "We've got to make this work. We have two kids involved in it now," she told him.[51] They scraped together enough money to move into their own home for their growing family.

Their reunion continued to be problematic. Susan grew more distant, causing David to feel lonely and isolated.[52] Giving into loneliness, he started a relationship with another young woman from work. Susan learned of the affair while she was pregnant. At times, she treated the situation with indifference; on other occasions, she would storm into Winn-Dixie to create public scenes. The Smiths' second son, Alex, was born in 1993. By this time, the marriage was heading toward total collapse.

The couple made feeble attempts to patch things up throughout the next year only to separate yet again. Friends couldn't keep up on the status of their relationship. Despite their marital mismatch, both were devoted parents. According to David's account, Michael was a thoughtful toddler who felt enormous love and responsibility toward his younger brother. Alex was a happy baby who smiled a lot, taking great delight in the new world around him. David took care to spend time with the children even when living apart from them. He often came to the house to do odd chores, babysit, or take the boys on outings. The young father was always willing to provide financially for his sons. Susan showered both boys with affection. Family and friends considered her an exemplary parent by all standards. She never seemed to get impatient with the children. She enjoyed taking them places as she went about her errands in town. She was always eager to show off their latest pictures. According to Eftimiades in *Sins of the Mother,* one acquaintance that often observed Susan with the boys noted, "They loved her and she loved them back."[53]

Despite the joys of motherhood, Susan decided to go back to work. A job would expand her horizons and put her in a stronger financial position given the uncertainty of her marriage. Conso Products Company had a secretary position open. Although the pay was only $17,000 a year, the job was more upscale than her former cashier's position at Winn-Dixie. She would be in an office environment doing clerical work. The president of the company would be her direct boss. She wouldn't have to see David and his girlfriend together. Her coworkers wouldn't know all the details of her floundering marriage. She might even be able to move up the ladder, gaining more responsibility and earning more money.

The Conoco position also provided an unexpected benefit when she met Tom Findlay, the boss's son. As a college graduate, Tom was more educated and more sophisticated than the majority of men Susan knew. His family was affluent, making him one of the small town's most eligible bachelors. Women of all ages responded to his smooth manner and good looks. In fact, his nickname was the "The Catch." Being asked out on a date by Tom Findlay immediately bestowed a social cachet on the recipient. It didn't take Tom long to notice his father's secretary. He learned that Susan was married with children. This news did not stop him from asking her out in January 1994. He enjoyed playing the field and wasn't looking for a serious relationship. Susan appeared to be someone he could have a good time with, no strings attached. The two began dating.

Susan, however, seemed to see things quite differently. Although they were not officially a couple, she started to fall in love. Tom's attentiveness provided a huge boost of confidence. It appeared that he really understood her as a person. He seemed to care about her feelings and encouraged her to have dreams. Of course, there was also the fact that Tom was a wealthy young man. Susan had observed that in "marrying up" with her second husband, her mother had been able to ensure a better life for herself and the children. This same path appeared in Susan's reach. Her disappointing relationship with David paled in comparison. Even though Susan periodically made efforts to salvage her marriage that past year, it didn't seem worth it. In the summer of 1994, she told her husband she wanted a divorce. Tired of all the Sturm und Drang in their relationship, he agreed.

The divorce paperwork was filed in September 1994. While the couple had agreed to settle things amicably, Susan publically charged her husband with adultery. David Smith writes in *Beyond All Reason* that he was angry over the violation of their agreement and felt Susan was being hypocritical given her involvement with others.[54] Even so, he went along with the practical details and financial arrangements that were negotiated. Susan asked for full custody of the boys. Michael was now 3 years old and Alex 14 months. David consented but made it clear he wanted to remain an active participant in their lives. He generously complied with Susan's child support demands to ensure that his children were well cared for. In an effort to provide security and stability for the boys, he even agreed to let Susan own the house, providing she continued to make the payments. As the divorce moved toward reality, it seemed as if Susan's world was ready to take off in wonderful new directions. Her happiness lasted barely a month.

On October 17, 1994, she received a letter from Tom indicating that he wanted to break up. He had written,

> You are intelligent, beautiful, sensitive, understanding, and possess many other wonderful qualities that I and many other men appreciate. You will without a doubt, make some man a great wife. But unfortunately it won't be me.[55]

The letter went on to enumerate the differences Tom saw between them that prevented an ongoing relationship. Their backgrounds were too different. He was not interested in a long-term relationship. And most chilling of all, "I am speaking about your children. I am sure your kids are good kids, but it really wouldn't matter how good they may be. The fact is I just don't want children. . . . And I don't want to be responsible for anyone else's children, either."[56] This turn of events was shattering. The man Susan had pinned all of her hopes on had rejected her. Aside from crushed romantic dreams, Susan was facing overwhelming pressure. Even with David's financial generosity, she was in a precarious financial position. Her monthly paycheck did not cover her household bills, let alone anything extra she might want. Any aspirations for the finer things in life must have seemed like unrealistic pipe dreams. The situation worsened when she saw Tom at a local bar with coworkers on the evening of October 24, 1994. He made no attempt to sit by her or include her in the conversation.

On October 25, 1994, Susan was feeling utterly distraught.[57] Somehow she had to persuade Tom to take her back. In his letter, Tom had commented on her flirtatious behavior at a party they both attended, where she had kissed a married man. It occurred to her that Tom might be jealous. She decided she would see him to explain the situation meant nothing. Tom heard Susan's argument but wasn't interested. His relationship with her had merely been a diversion, nothing more. Although he appeared sincere in wishing her the best, he didn't want anything beyond friendship. He told her once again the relationship was over. She was filled with self-pity. Brooding throughout the day, she considered her options. That night, she bundled her sons into the car and drove aimlessly around. Lulled by the motion of the automobile, the boys fell asleep. Shortly before 9 P.M., she reached the John D. Long Lake. According to her account, she decided that she had nothing more to live for. She would commit suicide and take the boys along with her. But she didn't commit suicide. Instead, she let the car roll into the lake with the two sleeping boys strapped inside their safety seats. She watched the car for a few minutes as it slowly sunk into the dark water, and then she ran.

She reached a house not far from the lake. Pounding on its door hysterically, she told the woman who answered it a frightening tale: A black man had taken her car and abducted her children. The police were called immediately. Struggling to compose herself through her tears, Susan elaborated on the details. She had stopped at a red light when a black man brandished a gun and jumped into her car. He ordered her to drive around for a while. She begged him to take the vehicle and let her and the children go. Refusing her entreaty, he ordered her out and slid into the driver's seat. She pleaded once again to let her take the children. Instead, he drove away leaving her abandoned on the road. The police sprung into action sending out an all-points bulletin upon hearing the details. Susan called her estranged husband to give him the crushing news. David left work immediately. Despite their differences, he and Susan still had children together. Now their precious sons were missing. He would stick by Susan and support her in whatever way possible until the boys were safely found.

Susan left to go to her parent's house with David following. By this time, word of the carjacking went out over the wires. A local newspaper photographer heard the news and met up with the police near the lake. Afterward, he went over to Susan's parents hoping to get additional information. He spent half an hour with the young couple learning more of the tragic story. They gave him a photo of the boys to print in the newspaper: 3-year-old Michael was smiling straight at the camera, while 14-month-old Alex had his hand on his big brother's leg. The heartbreaking tale and picture were featured as the top story in the Union newspaper the next morning. It was the start of a nine-day ordeal played out in the national media.

Union County's Sherriff Howard Wells was in charge of the investigation. Wells had known Susan and her family personally for years. He offered assurances that he would do everything in his power to bring the children back safely. But in the back of his mind, there may have been a disconcerting thought. Law enforcement authorities knew from sad experience that parents were often the culprits in cases like this. Was it possible that Susan was somehow behind the children's disappearance? Wells focused on the task at hand. It was important to get the word out as fast and as far as possible in order to recover the two Smith boys. Highway patrol officers and helicopters were dispatched to cover the area for clues. Law enforcement agencies around the country were notified of the abduction. Wells held a press conference in hope that leads might come from increased public awareness.

The focus was on the 22-year-old mother who had been the victim of a carjacking. Looking fragile and worn out, Susan told the reporters how she had been forced to get out of the car despite her pleas to take the children with her. The press was sympathetic when she told them how much she missed her boys. "I can't even describe what I am going through. I mean my heart is— it just aches so bad I can't sleep. I can't eat. I can't do anything but think about them."[58] Later in an interview with the local paper, she shared how her last words were a tearful "I love y'all," as a stranger drove into the darkness with her two screaming children.[59]

The story galvanized the citizens of Union. Volunteer search parties were quickly organized to comb the area around the lake. Homemade flyers were posted all over town. News of the carjacking quickly spread throughout the state as well as the country. By the next day, October 27, 1994, CNN picked up the story. People were transfixed by the plight of two innocent children snatched from their young mother in a small town in the middle of rural America. Representatives from the Adam Walsh Center, an organization founded to get the word out about missing children, visited Susan and David, offering to help spread the search nationwide. The center quickly produced a public service announcement featuring a video of the boys celebrating Alex's first birthday party to generate leads. Sheriff Wells appeared on *The Today Show* and *Larry King Live* to publicize the case. Articles featuring interviews with both of the Smiths continued in the press.

Unfortunately, the leads that poured in didn't supply any useful information. Law enforcement officials were beginning to have misgivings about Susan's story: certain elements didn't seem to add up. How could a black man with two white children mysteriously disappear so completely given all the public attention? Others noted that Susan's demeanor often seemed peculiar. While David was emotional in his interviews, Susan was oddly dry-eyed. Investigators had questioned both parents extensively. While David passed a polygraph test unequivocally, Susan's results were inconclusive. More troubling was that Susan seemed to remember additional details about the actual incident with each telling of the story. Yet, the account of her activities throughout the day was nebulous at best and often faulty when efforts were made to corroborate them.

Suspicions among media members were also beginning to appear. While David became more visible in seeking help from the public regarding any possible information, Susan had retreated into the shadows. Was her withdrawal due to the ordeal she had gone through? Or was she deliberately staying in the background because she had something to hide? This suspicion was spreading throughout Union. In Gary Henderson's account, *Nine Days in Union,* a resident said, "It's a hoax. . . . I think the mother knows something about it all and I think that's the way about 95% of people down here think."[60]

Susan did make a public appearance later that week after a promising lead about finding an abandoned baby with a motel attendant turned out to be false. She went before national television cameras and implored, "I would like to say that whoever has my children, that they please, that they please bring 'em home to us, where they belong . . . whoever has them I pray every day that you are taking care of 'em and know that we would do anything, anything to help you get 'em home back to us."[61] While Susan spoke a bit more emotionally this time, once again her delivery was suspect. It seemed odd that a mother whose children had been missing for over a week shed no tears. The next day, November 3, 1994, Susan along with David once again appeared on national television. They gave interviews to both *This Morning* and *Today* shows. Susan was aware that certain reporters were now referring to the situation as an "alleged kidnapping." Looking straight into the cameras, she steadfastly denied having anything to do with the abduction. "I don't think that any parent could love their children more than I do, and I would never even think about anything that would harm them. It's very painful to have the finger pointed at you when it's your children involved."[62] David staunchly defended his wife and proclaimed that he believed completely in her innocence.

By this time, certain events were pointing to the conclusion that Susan was lying. Nothing she said to authorities concerning her activities just prior to the abduction or the particular facts she remembered about the abduction could be corroborated. Even more damning for her was that Tom Findlay had come forward with details of their breakup. His letter provided a simple motive—Tom wasn't interested in having children, so perhaps conveniently Susan got rid of them. On November 3, 1994, Sheriff Wells called Susan for a private meeting. He outlined all the discrepancies in her story and threatened to share them with the media. Finally, giving in to mounting pressure, Susan admitted that she had gone to the John D. Long Lake and killed her sons in a moment of despair and confusion. She wrote in her confession,

> I didn't want to live anymore. . . . I felt I couldn't be a good mom any-more, but I didn't want my children to grow up without a mom. I felt I had to end our lives to protect us from grief or harm. . . . I had never felt so lonely and sad in my entire life. I was in love with someone very much but he didn't love me and never would. . . . I don't think I will ever be able to forgive myself for what I have done.[63]

Officials went to the lake. Dredging the water, they found Susan's automobile. The dead boys were strapped inside their car seats. On November 3, 1994, Susan was arrested and charged with the murder of her sons.

The news spread like wildfire. David learned of Susan's confession when he heard it reported on television. In his account, *Beyond All Reason,* he described being overcome with blackness, sorrow, and rage.[64] An outpouring of grief over the death of the little boys swept the country. The John D. Long Lake turned into a memorial site. People came to look at its dark waters, perhaps imagining the horror of Michael and Alex slowly drowning, while their mother stood by doing nothing. Flowers and cards were left nearby in quiet tribute. The yellow ribbons that had been put up by townspeople were now replaced by blue and white bows—blue representing the boys, white representing their innocence.[65] Reporters from every national television network came to the children's funeral to cover the sad event. President Clinton sent his condolences. South Carolina was in an official day of mourning.

The mood of the general public now toward Susan was a deep sense of betrayal.[66] Originally, the young mother had been a sympathetic figure. Her soft-spoken manner and tearful pleas in her southern drawl to return the missing boys had touched many hearts. Susan's confession turned her into one of the most hated women in America. A neighbor publically called for her execution; another denounced her saying she should be strung up on Main Street as an example.[67] Talk show callers were outraged over her actions and demanded the death penalty. Kathie Lee Gifford and Oprah Winfrey both used their national television shows to talk about the heinous nature of the crime. Everyone wanted to know why she did it. The trial attempted to answer that question as well as determine how she should be punished.

In *Crime and the Media,* the account provided by Roslyn Muraskin and Shelly Feuer Domash, the prosecution asserted that Susan wanted to free herself of the children and demands of being a mother, so she could be with her rich boyfriend.[68] Throughout the trial, Susan was depicted as a selfish, cold-hearted killer who deserved the death penalty. In this version of events, she not only murdered her two sons, but also blatantly misled the police and the public. For nine days, she had knowingly deceived the entire country on national television. Their contention was that if Susan no longer felt like she could be a good mother, as she said in her confession, why not let David take full custody of the children: He had always been a willing, caring partner. To the prosecution, the fact that she had not even considered this alternative clearly showed her total disregard for her sons.

Susan's reputation suffered further when evidence from the trial indicated that she had time to save the boys, but chose not to: It took over six minutes for the car to disappear into the lake. Moreover, it may have taken an additional 40 minutes for the automobile to completely sink to the bottom, meaning the boys were alive for some length of time. The diver who found the bodies testified that he saw a small hand pressing against the window. When the public learned about this detail as well as how long the boys may have suffered, Susan was condemned even more harshly.

Susan's lawyers faced an uphill battle in not only trying to defend their client, but also in trying to save her from the death penalty. The account by George Rekers in *Susan Smith Victim or Murderer* reports that the defense strategy centered on painting a picture of her as a victim of mental illness with an abusive past to gain sympathy, even though they could not contend that she was insane at the time of the boys' death.[69] Citing Susan's confession in which she claimed she wanted to kill herself, defense attorneys tried to prove that the horrible event was not a planned murder, but a desperate suicide attempt that failed. To support this argument, it was imperative to prove that Susan had suffered from a serious mental illness caused by depression. Building on the fact that suicide as well as depression can run in families, one expert witness testified that Susan's grandmother, aunt, and brother had tried to commit suicide. Another expert discussed in detail the emotional trauma Susan felt from her father's untimely death. He theorized that while she may have been able to conceal her misery through most part of her life, it was always present, lurking in the background. When Tom rejected her, this depression came forward once again to cloud her judgment.

A prominent psychiatrist who had extensively interviewed Susan discussed the torment of her stepfather's abuse as well as the disastrous Smith marriage that had been filled with unfaithfulness on both sides. His testimony revealed the details of Susan's bizarrely tangled sex life. In the few months leading up to the murders, she had been sleeping with both David and Tom. Moreover, she told the psychiatrist of being pressured by her stepfather to secretly continue their relationship—a relationship extending throughout her marriage. Tom Findlay also testified on Susan's behalf, indicating that on the fateful day of the murders, Susan had seen him not once, but three times to reconsider the breakup. When he refused, she lashed out that she had been sleeping with his father. Although she later recanted, the statement presumably showed how troubled Susan's mind was.

By focusing on tales of abuse and despair during the weeklong trial, the defense hoped the jury could at least understand why Susan did what she did. It was the only way to save Susan from a death sentence. One of the agents present at Susan's confession depicted her as a sorrowful figure filled with gut-wrenching remorse. Susan's stepfather publically apologized for his role in her troubled background, acknowledging that he too shared some guilt in this tragedy. Her supporters advocated that she needed prayer, not punishment. In July 1995, the jury agreed: Taking the route of compassion, they choose not to give Susan the death penalty, instead giving her a life sentence. Upon serving 30 years in prison, she would be eligible for parole in 2025.

While the jury bought into the picture of Susan as an emotionally troubled woman who snapped under mounting emotional pressure, the vast majority of the public did not. Lurid details of the case with its sexual abuse, infidelity, suicide attempts, and double infanticide seemed to epitomize a Southern Gothic tale of misguided love.[70] In her case, this love blasted away stereotypes about the sanctity of motherhood. Popular culture tends to reinforce the notion of mothers who will protect their children at all costs. Susan was vilified in the media for shattering this myth. She also failed to live up to the image of a self-sacrificing mother willing to submerge her own personal needs. The fact that she not only killed her two children so she could be with her boyfriend, but also then concocted a story about their abduction, lying about it for nine days on national television, left the country with a sense of sadness and disillusionment. *Time* put her on the cover, with a headline asking, "How Could She Do It?" *People* also ran a cover story on the case posing the question, "Does She Deserve to Die?" Even Newt Gingrich, a prominent conservative Republican espousing family values weighed in, arguing that Susan's crime was a sign of how sick American society was becoming.[71] On television shows, in newspaper editorials, and magazine articles, Susan Smith became the very embodiment of a woman corrupted by love.

Susan's search for love continued to generate attention throughout the years. In 2000, two prison guards admitted to having sex with her. She surfaced in the news again when she posted an online personal ad in 2003, indicating that she was hoping to receive letters from those who are not judgmental and are sincere.[72] Although she received responses, the ad was pulled after it received sensational media coverage.

All murders are distasteful, but few acts have the power to evoke as strong a revulsion as a mother killing her children. And the most horrifying of all is when it is premeditated. We believe as a society that a mother's most basic function is to *protect* her children. This is true not only among humans, but across the entire animal kingdom. It is almost unfathomable to imagine how a woman could justify the physical act of ending the lives of the innocent, defenseless souls whom she herself brought into the world—dependents relying on her for their very survival. For a mother to consciously make this decision and effectively execute it must require the strongest of rationalizations. How could Susan Smith have gotten to a point where she could excuse such an act in her own mind? Could she have had help along the way?

The historic glamorization of romantic love is so embedded in American popular culture that it is virtually impossible to escape, despite the highly questionable validity of some thematic messages. Certain ones represent plain old wishful thinking, like the lyrics of the 1964 Beach Boys song, "Don't Worry Baby":

She looks in my eyes and makes me realize . . .
She says, "Don't worry baby. Everything will turn out alright."[73]

Others—like the infamous quote "Love means never having to say you're sorry" taken from the 1970 best-selling novel *Love Story* by Erich Segal— simply make no sense at all, as Ali MacGraw and Ryan O'Neal, the stars of the film adaptation, confessed in an interview with Oprah Winfrey.[74] Yet, these quotes are memorable, and they can certainly serve the purpose of a person who wants to believe that love can justify any action. In Segal's novel, the love of the two main characters—Oliver, a "preppie" from a wealthy upper-class family, and Jenny, the irreverent daughter of a lowly blue-collar worker—triumphs over their different economic and social backgrounds. When Jenny is diagnosed with a terminal illness, she tries to console Oliver by demanding that he stop blaming himself. "It's not your fault," she assures him. "It's nobody's fault." For one looking to rationalize murder, the interpretation could be that when love is involved, all bets are off regarding personal responsibility.

In the 1987 film *Dirty Dancing*, 17-year-old "Baby" Houseman (played by Jennifer Grey) defends her love interest Johnny Castle (played by Patrick Swayze), inspiring him to realize that "there are people willing to stand up for other people, no matter what it costs them." At the end of the film, Johnny responds in kind by standing up to Baby's oppressive father, telling him, "Nobody puts Baby in a corner." Then Johnny and Baby dazzle the audience with a stunning dance performance to the theme song "The Time of My Life," as the room is transformed into a majestic place where everyone dances happily together. Viewers are left to digest the message that when two lovers stand up for each other, any wrong can be righted.

Romeo and Juliet, William Shakespeare's classic tale of two ill-fated young lovers, was the inspiration for the award-winning 1961 musical *West Side Story.* In the modern version, as two rival teenaged gangs rumble for turf on the streets of New York City, star-crossed lovers Tony and Maria—from opposing sides—conduct a passionate courtship. Though it ends in tragedy, the dream of love traversing societal bounds lives on to fuel the romantic fantasies of teenage girls for years to come.

Nearly 50 years later, the embattled relationship between Justin Walker and Rebecca Harper, idealistic and devoted young lovers on the popular primetime TV drama series *Brothers and Sisters,* catapulted them into romantic icon status in the eyes of the show's millions of viewers. During the years of the long-running series, Justin and Rebecca faced nearly every taboo imaginable. When they first fell in love, they were believed to be half-siblings, Rebecca being the daughter of Justin's father's longtime mistress. Justin suffered from posttraumatic stress disorder, which fed his propensity for drugs, while Rebecca is tempted at every turn by ex-lovers, unscrupulous in-laws, and deep-rooted secrets from her past. Although their love affair ends during the last season of the series, it survived—year after year—despite a thwarted wedding, an unplanned pregnancy resulting in miscarriage, and a series of bitter, ongoing family feuds that pit the two against one another.

But what if the barrier is that one lover has children and the other doesn't want them? Finding support for the idea that children constitute little more than an inconvenient nuisance to adult relationships may be hard to find, but it's certainly not impossible. This situation is exemplified in the dynamics around the character of Angus T. Jones in the television sitcom *Two and a Half Men.* Between 2003 and 2011, audiences watched Angus's character, Jake, grow up in a household that consists only of him, his divorced father, Alan, and his freewheeling uncle, Charlie. The primary preoccupation of both adults is gaining female companionship. Though mostly tongue-in-cheek, the majority of Charlie's references to Jake are derogatory, insinuating, if not overtly stating, that the precocious boy is cramping his style by simply being alive under the same roof. While Alan makes half-hearted attempts to attend to Jake's needs, it's clear that he, too, would happily dump the kid if given half the opportunity.

It's inconceivable that Susan Smith was not aware of the inevitable difficulties her children would pose for her desired relationship. The perspective that children's lives don't really count is a precursor to the attitudes of the adults on *Two and a Half Men.* In one episode, Charlie explains to his nephew, Jake, how life works: "It's not that I don't care what you want," he tells the 10-year-old, "it's just that . . . you're a kid. What you want doesn't count."[75]

Like Kristin Rossum, Susan Smith found the man she would kill for to be much more exciting than the one she had married. Did she make a conscious choice to do whatever had to be done in order to win his love? A choice for which she should be held responsible? This is debatable, according to the wisdom of Bailey, a main character on *Party of Five,* one of TV's most popular drama series of the 1990s:

> You don't get to choose. You just fall in love and you get this person who is all wrong and all right at the same time. And you know you love them so much, except sometimes they just drive you completely insane and no one can explain it.[76]

If love is so powerful that it can "drive you completely insane," this dynamic could call into question Susan Smith's responsibility for her actions.

Although both Kristin Rossum and Susan Smith murdered for love, their cases differ in several ways. Rossum, an attractive *femme fatale,* killed her husband, while Smith, a plain, ordinary-looking woman, killed her children. While the behavior of both shatters stereotypes, Rossum does so by demonstrating that she lacks the integrity we expect from a professional scientist, and Smith belies an image of women more fundamental to our universal psyches by showing no sign of the natural protective instinct we expect of all mothers. Yet, Rossum and Smith also share a number of important traits. At the time of the murders, they were young, both romantic idealists. Both regretted their choices of spouses and craved more exciting partners. Both have proven to be unsympathetic to a public that found them to be characters they "love to hate." Both committed their crimes in pursuit of what they hoped or believed to be "real love," and both convinced themselves that getting that prize justified any act.

So when all is said and done, in what instances is love truly a motive noble enough to justify murder? The answer, of course, is that it never is. Despite a dizzying barrage of media messages regarding the ethics, morals, and predilections of love, most people still know the difference between right and wrong. Most of us have the capacity to sort out the reasonable from the fantastic. We realize that there *are,* in fact, times when saying you're sorry may actually be an appropriate thing for someone in love to do. We also understand that simply having somebody who loves you doesn't necessarily make all of the world's problems go away. We acknowledge that when one relationship dissolves, it may not be possible to set the stage optimally for the next one. We admit that love is not an utterly irresistible force that automatically absolves us from responsibility for our own actions. But if an unstable person seeks to find refuge under the protective umbrella of "love" from the stormy consequences of their misguided deeds, pop culture can certainly point them in that direction.

Murder for love is just one example of a classic, essentially truthful message—in this case, the idea *love conquers all*—becoming blurred, twisted, and merged with other, less gallant themes. The progression over the years has been gradual and sometimes quite subtle, yet it has steadily occurred in our most popular forms of communication and entertainment. This trend suggests that it may not be a bad idea for us to become more vigilant about examining the messages we consume from media sources. What other culturally esteemed truisms, one might ask, could right now be on the path to becoming similarly tainted?

Women Who Kill for Money

In a quote attributed to Woody Allen, money is better than poverty, if only for financial reasons.[1] Money can bring wealth, status, power, and choices. So it's not surprising that whether the form has been shells, cattle, rice, gold, coin, or paper, throughout history people have been interested in money. But what happens when the pursuit of money turns into one of the deadly sin with an emphasis on deadly?

The next two cases show how money can be a prime motivation for inciting someone to commit murder. Olga Rutterschmidt and Helen Golay, two elderly women, concocted an elaborate scheme that ensnared men in hopes of getting a big payoff. Ann Woodward chose to take the more traditional route of marrying for money and then knocking off her husband. While the circumstances between the cases seem very different, in actuality, all of the women knew that it was more important to be a player than to be played. Their love of the almighty dollar led them to commit murder for profit.

OLGA RUTTERSCHMIDT AND HELEN GOLAY

When Kenneth McDavid met Olga Rutterschmidt and Helen Golay in 2003, his life was finally taking a turn for the better. He had been homeless and living on the brink. Olga and Helen had rescued him from the Hollywood Presbyterian Church soup kitchen and treated him like a family member: buying him clothes, setting him up in an apartment, taking care of his rent, purchasing his groceries, and paying for all of his living expenses. But Kenneth didn't know he was part of a long con scheme the two deadly women had cooked up years before. Kenneth was just one in an extensive line of potential victims that the two women had selected for their nefarious plot that would put them on easy street. It took a chance conversation between two police officers to connect Kenneth's untimely death in a hit-and-run accident with another unsolved crime in a cold case file.[2] By the time the connection was finally made, Olga and Helen, both spry septuagenarians, had illegally collected nearly $3 million in insurance money and were the prime suspects in two murder cases. Headlines around the world compared them to the dotty Brewster sisters in *Arsenic and Old Lace*. But to investigators working on the case, their bizarre behavior epitomized true evil. And in the end, after the two women turned on each other, the "killer grannies" were locked up for life.

When Olga Rutterschmidt and Helen Golay met in the late 1980s while they were living in Los Angeles, the two recognized each other as kindred spirits—both of them wanted money and lots of it. Olga had the more traumatic background having lived through the hardships of World War II in Hungary. According to Jeanne King's book *Signed in Blood,* as a young child, Olga experienced the terror of exploding bombs and the insecurity of seeing people she knew either die or disappear.[3] The effects of the ordeal remained with her long after the war ended.[4] She developed a cold combative demeanor that many found disconcerting. Although she had once been married, Olga had few close relationships aside from her friendship with Helen. She never pursued a career. Consequently, her financial situation was precarious. As she grew older, she had to watch her money carefully and waited each month for her social security check. Her government housing allowance subsidized the small Hollywood apartment she lived in for 25 years. It seemed that the American Dream had passed her by.

According to the account in Jeanne King's book, *Signed in Blood,* although Helen's background had also been filled with uncertainty while she was growing up, life had dealt her a better hand.[5] An attractive vivacious person, Helen had been married twice. An unlikely romantic conquest in her later years turned out to be her daughter Kecia's former boyfriend. But Helen's focus wasn't primarily on men; it was on money. She spent over a decade and a half working as a real-estate agent in Los Angeles. When her boss died, Helen had power of attorney over his assets, allowing her to become wealthy.[6] His daughter contested Helen's actions, claiming Helen had swindled her father: "I feel cheated. She was stealing something that wasn't hers."[7]

Olga and Helen met as middle-aged women in their 50s. In Karl Vick's article "In LA a Case Straight out of 'Arsenic and Old Lace,'" he wrote that the two had similar interests, including as one relative stated, "a common interest in fleecing people."[8] The two would sit for hours concocting schemes on how to scam unsuspecting dupes. Their first step was to make themselves look glamorous. Helen liked to wear sexy miniskirts, towering high heels, and big hair—regardless of how age inappropriate it was.[9] Olga had a trim body, a charming Eastern European accent that made her sound chicly cosmopolitan, and bleached blonde hair giving her a youthful appearance.[10] Reporters Paul Pringle and Hemmy So state in their article "An Unlikely Friendship that Finally Unraveled" that there were allegations that the pair often paraded around the health club or hotel pools, keeping their eye on unattended purses and wallets with credit cards.[11]

After a while, they realized they could go for bigger stakes. Pringle and So state that an acquaintance heard Olga talking about ripping off credit card companies.[12] Helen involved herself in dubious real-estate transactions over her dead employer's property. But what filled most of their time were the dozens and dozens of lawsuits they engaged in. Anything they could sue over, they did. Paul Pringle and Hemmy So's article "Portrait Emerges of a Baffling Pair" indicates "Helen filed the bulk of the lawsuits—more than 30 since the 1980's—against tenants, real estate partners, banks, health clubs, restaurants and neighbors."[13] Helen even filed a suit against her own daughter. She claimed that Kecia assaulted her, causing Kecia to declare her mother exhibited "thirty years of psychopathic behavior."[14] The two eventually made up. Olga filed suit against a grocery store as well as a coffee shop, claiming she had been injured.

While it's unclear how many of the lawsuits paid out, it didn't matter. The suits filled the two women's days with activity, giving them a sense of deviant purpose. Helen seemed to take delight in her twisted behavior. She told her hairdresser, "I am evil. You have no idea how evil I am."[15] Somewhere along the way in the late 1990s, the two friends came up with their most brazen and diabolical idea—an insurance fraud racket. Life insurance is a financial product that provides protection to the estate or beneficiary of the policy when someone passes away. An individual enters into a contract with an insurance company to pay monthly premiums in return for a settlement upon their death. Their plan was to befriend someone, get that person to take out life insurance naming one of the women as the beneficiary, and then collect the settlement when the person died.

The key to the plan hinged on a number of factors. Typically, a beneficiary has to have some type of close relationship with the insured. They would have to find someone who was willing to designate them as the recipient. Plus, it would make sense to ingratiate themselves to someone not close to their own family. Helen had already learned the hard way through her real-estate lawsuit that a disgruntled relative could make trouble. They would need to make sure the settlement was large enough. Since a person can have more than one life insurance policy, it's possible for a beneficiary to get a substantial monetary windfall through coverage by multiple policies. There is no centralized database that keeps track of how much insurance a person has purchased, so red flags would not be raised. Helen and Olga wanted to cash in big: each policy would have to be large enough to provide hundreds of thousands of dollars in death benefits. An added bonus was that beneficiaries are not taxed on death benefits, so the government couldn't get their hands on any of it.

Finally, they wanted to make sure their scheme went undetected. Because millions of claims are submitted every year, insurance companies typically don't investigate each one. They don't have the manpower to do so. Moreover, the women found out through a little research that the state of California makes any policy incontestable once it has been in effect for two years and the premiums have been paid.[16] Their victim would have to stay alive during this period, and then he or she could conveniently die. And to make sure the victim conveniently died according to their timetable, *they* would do the killing. After going over all the angles, they decided it was time to put their plan in action. In the late 1990s, they started trolling for victims. They hit upon the idea of going for a homeless man. Like every large urban metropolis, Los Angeles had its fair share of people living on the streets. On any given night, you could find 82,000 inhabitants of the city without a roof over their head.[17] Olga and Helen needed just one.

Over 100 years old, the Hollywood Presbyterian Church is a well-known institution within the community known for its social welfare programs to assist less-fortunate individuals. It utilizes volunteers to serve meals to the homeless and provide general resources to those in need. When Olga and Helen started showing up, they blended in easily with the other helpers. Their professed desire to do something to make the world a better place was appreciated by the minister in charge of the community programs. According to Pastor Suhayda, "They seemed like such nice ladies. They were like grandmothers."[18] The two women, who by this time were in their late 60s, chatted with other members, making an effort to get to know some of the homeless people that attended both the services and events.

In 1997, they selected Paul Vados as the ideal candidate for their brazen plot. He and Olga connected over their shared Hungarian background. Now in his 70s, Paul was living on the streets, battling an alcohol problem. His three children had lost contact with him and were unaware of how transient his life had become. Olga told Paul that she would help him find an apartment and pay for it while he got back on his feet. She used Helen's money to pay for Paul's rent, food, and electricity. The arrangement lasted for two years, allowing them to keep track of their intended victim. During this time, the two women took out more than half a dozen life insurance policies in his name, totaling nearly $900,000. They listed themselves as either relatives or a fiancée. In most instances, Paul's signature was affixed with the use of a rubber stamp that the two had ingeniously purchased from a stationary store.

On November 8, 1999, Paul was found dead in a Hollywood alley. His twisted body, which was covered in grease, looked as if a car had crushed it. The scene appeared to be a hit-and-run collision. On November 17, 1999, claiming to be related to Paul, the two women called the police station and filed a missing persons report. They were told of the accident. The Vados death was put into the cold case file as an unsolved fatality.

Olga and Helen wasted little time in notifying the insurance companies of Paul's death so they could collect the settlement. When Mutual of Omaha appeared to be taking its time, Helen called demanding to know when the claim would be settled. The company was taking a cautious approach since there had been no witnesses to the accident—a red flag for possible fraud. Helen demanded that her money be sent immediately. If not, she would sue. The company quickly paid up. Monumental Life Insurance Company was also concerned about possible fraud when the two women filed for $188,000 in death benefits. In this instance, a suit actually went to court. The insurance company had no proof—only suspicions. Luckily for the two women, they won the suit. Eventually, they made off with nearly $600,000.

Emboldened by their efforts, Olga and Helen were ready to build upon what seemed like a foolproof scam. The two spent time researching which insurance companies paid out the quickest with no hassle or investigation. By 2002, they were ready to put their plan back into action. This time they be-friended Kenneth McDavid. Now in his early 50s, Kenneth was down on his luck—unemployed and living on the streets. He had not spoken to his family in over six years. Like Paul Vados, Kenneth was a regular who accepted free hot meals and solace from the Lord's Lighthouse Ministry Program at the Hollywood Presbyterian Church.

The quiet middle-aged man responded to Olga and Helen's overtures of friendship. Their offer of free room and board was a lifeline in helping him get back on his feet. He quickly accepted. Kenneth complied when they asked him to sign a $500,000 insurance policy listing them as beneficiaries. After all, they would pay the premiums and it was a show of good faith on his part. Unbeknownst to him, Olga and Helen didn't stop at just one policy. They applied for and paid premiums on 16 policies. These policies weren't just typical policies either; some were "key man" policies, designed to protect a company from loss when a critical member of a business dies. To secure this type of policy, Olga and Helen claimed they were partners of Kenneth. According to them, Kenneth was a gifted and profitable writer who had written a movie script worth millions. Since Los Angeles is the movie capital of the world and home to successful screenwriters, this seemed possible. They claimed on other policies that he was a successful businessman earning a six-figure salary. The fact that Kenneth's income was below poverty level was irrelevant to the two women. All they cared about was that they would be able to collect nearly $6 million when Kenneth died.

During September 2002, Olga set Kenneth up in a studio apartment in Hollywood. She paid the $875 rent, plus utilities, groceries, and insurance premiums, with Helen's money. The monthly outlay was almost $3,000. But the partners in crime looked at it as an investment. The arrangement went along smoothly until Kenneth invited four other homeless people to live with him toward the end of 2004. When Olga found out, she was livid. This was not part of the plan. She swooped down on Kenneth one afternoon while he was at the apartment, belligerently telling him that he had to get rid of his friends. When he stalled, she tried getting the complex manager to evict the other occupants. Later, she enlisted an armed security guard to evict Kenneth's friends and to ensure they would not have access to the apartment. Kenneth quickly moved out. He gathered up his few personal belongings and put them on a bicycle he had. Once again he was homeless. The two women were anxious not to lose their prey. Over the next five months, they paid for him to live in cheap motels in the Hollywood area.

On June 21, 2005, Kenneth was found dead in an alley next to his bicycle. Although his body was bloody, there was no broken glass at the scene or any skid marks. According to evidence presented in "People vs. Rutterschmidt," his neck and shoulders were crushed, while cuts ran across two parallel tracks on his body.[19] Security tapes monitoring the area's activity showed that a silver 1999 Mercury Sable had entered the alley, backed up, turned off its headlights, and then left the scene.[20] Unfortunately, the license plate on the Sable was not visible. It looked as if another hit-and-run accident had sadly taken place.

Kenneth's body was taken to the coroner's office and an autopsy was conducted. Helen later showed up at the coroner's office and claimed the body, saying she was a relative. The women wasted no time filing the insurance claims: They were able to collect $2.2 million. The police conducted an investigation around the neighborhood hoping to discover witnesses. No one had seen or heard anything. The detective in charge was beginning to feel the hit and run accident would remain an unsolved mystery. Although he did not know the amount of insurance involved, he knew that Olga and Helen had started to collect. Three months after the accident took place, he happened to be discussing the case with another colleague. As the detective told the story about the accident involving a homeless victim and two women collecting insurance, the colleague mentioned that he too had been involved in a similar case in 1999. They compared their reports and saw Olga and Helen's name in both of them. The connection seemed too unlikely to be a coincidence. The men instantly deduced that foul play was going on and reported their suspicions. Authorities sprang into action. By September 2005, a 50-member task force of police officers, detectives, and insurance specialists started probing into the two cases, tracking down applications by the two women and surreptitiously monitoring their activities. The team was quickly convinced that the two women were involved—not only in insurance fraud, but in murder as well. They did not want another homeless man to be the next victim.

As it turned out, Olga and Helen had already picked out a succession of victims. In 2002, James Covington had been plucked off the streets and made an offer he couldn't refuse. Olga had lured the 45-year-old homeless man with the tried-and-tested promise of a place to stay and paid living expenses. He could temporarily camp out in an office space she had access to while she looked for more permanent housing for him. All she asked in return was that he provide her with information for claims she would file on his behalf, entitling him to certain benefits. Believing that Olga was some sort of professional do-gooder, he complied. Olga kept badgering him for more and more personal facts that seemed irrelevant to typical social welfare paperwork. He left after she became menacing when he was no longer forthcoming. This arrangement was over. He was unaware that Olga had used the information to take out an $800,000 insurance policy on him. In 2005, when police learned out about the policy, they spent months tracking him down to alert him of the potential danger.

During this time period, the police also spent a great deal of effort shadowing the two women as they went about their day-to-day activities. They were interested in seeing who they met with on a regular basis. It turns out that another potential victim lucky to get away with his life was Josef Gabor, a blind man in his mid-70s. Olga had befriended Josef and was seen spending time with him at the bank on numerous occasions. She was observed helping him fill out paperwork. Detectives later found that Olga had taken out a credit card using his name. When investigators alerted him to the potential danger involved in his friendship with the two women, Josef quickly dropped all contact with them.

Olga and Helen were oblivious to the intense investigations going on around them. The police had found out about the signature stamps the women purchased, pieced together all of the insurance applications they had applied for, and traced their insurance payment proceeds. Between them, they had over $1 million in cash sitting in their bank accounts. Most damning of all was that AAA roadside service had confirmed that on June 21, 2005, the night of Kenneth's murder, Helen had requested towing roadside service in the exact vicinity where his body had been found. When the tow truck driver arrived, the car to be towed was a silver 1999 Mercury Sable—the exact type of car seen on the surveillance tapes in the alley where Kenneth had been hit. A vehicle check showed that Olga had bought the car. The car showed evidence of an accident and later DNA tests revealed Kenneth's blood on it.

On May 18, 2006, Olga and Helen were arrested. The police told them they were being charged with mail fraud and were under suspicion of murder. Hoping to get incriminating evidence from them, police put them in the same holding room and secretly recorded their conversation. Olga was beside herself. She placed the blame squarely on Helen, charging her with total stupidity. "You cannot make that many insurances. . . . You were greedy. That's the problem."[21] Helen spent most of the time telling Olga to keep quiet and not admit anything. She was worried that Olga's angry rants would link them to the homicides. As far as Helen was concerned, there was no proof of anything larcenous or deadly that could be pinned on them. By the end of the conversation, the finger pointing between the two became ludicrous. Moreover, they were still arguing over whether or not it was possible to sue the insurance companies that had been slow to respond to their claims. The two were sent to jail and placed in separate cells. Three months later, they were formally charged with the murder of Paul Vados and Kenneth McDavid.

Being arrested was quite traumatic for both women.[22] It became worse when they were kept in jail and denied bail. In addition to loudly proclaiming their innocence to whomever listened, they continually complained about conditions. The elderly women were told they were unable to wear makeup, color their hair, or wear their own clothing; not being able to carry a cell phone, limited television viewing hours, and bad food were also issues that filled them with indignation. [23] They ended up cooling their heels behind bars for nearly two years as the case made its way through the criminal justice system.

When the media learned about the case, it became an overnight sensation. Dubbed "The Black Widows," Olga and Helen captured public attention because of the incongruent nature of their crime relevant to their age. One of the big questions on everyone's mind was whether or not the two women would face the death penalty. Since both were now in their mid-70s and the appeals process could take years, prosecution lawyers decided not to pursue it. They knew that Olga and Helen had a good chance of dying in prison before the appeal was even considered. Moreover, the prosecution was also concerned that the jury would be reluctant to consider the death penalty for two little old ladies. By the time the trial started in March 2008, after years in prison, neither woman looked like her former glamorous self. Both of them appeared frail, haggard, and gray haired.

Although much of the evidence against the two women was circumstantial and the insurance aspects were rather complex, the case moved along at a clipped pace, lasting just four weeks. Olga's lawyers maintained that Helen had duped her; Helen was the mastermind behind the killings, and Olga was merely an innocent bystander who had genuinely cared for both men. Helen's lawyers indicated that she was entirely blameless; in fact, it was Kecia Golay, Helen's daughter who had driven the car that killed Kenneth McDavid.[24] By this time, the two old friends had viciously turned on each other and were filled with mutual distrust.[25]

Thanks to diligent efforts of the 50-person investigation, prosecution provided a meticulous overview covering how many policies the two women took out, how they were able to commit fraud, and how the car used to kill the victims became a murder weapon. At their disposal were 90 potential witnesses who could provide testimony against the two women.[26] James Covington told of his fleeting weeklong encounter with the women. Sandra Salman, the sister of Kenneth McDavid, indicated that neither of the women was related to the victim, nor was she aware that her brother ever had a fiancée. Helen's call to AAA for the towing of a Mercury Sable and the DNA findings on its undercarriage were discussed. One of the more gruesome aspects of the case came to light when autopsy results for Kenneth McDavid were revealed. His broken body showed positive signs of Ambien and Vicodin, two drugs that had been found in Helen's apartment during her arrest.[27] The expert witness indicated that these drugs had rendered him unconscious for hours before the time of death. The implication was that Kenneth had not been killed by a hit-and-run accident. Instead, he was forcibly made unconscious, his body tossed into the dark alley alongside his bike, and then deliberately run over. The videotape of the two women in custody—bickering with each other and showing no remorse for their greed and betrayal—sealed their fate. Both were found guilty of murder and conspiracy. They were sentenced to life without parole.

Public reaction was immediate in condemning the two. California's state insurance commissioner accused them of knowing how to manipulate the system for their heartless scam. When everything was added up from a financial perspective, Olga and Helen had spent $64,000 over the years on rent, food, and insurance premiums in order to support their victims. They had hoped to collect nearly $6 million in life insurance. In the end, they made off with over $2 million. Their fierce chase for a dollar at the expense of homeless men made international headlines and received global attention. Most people were horrified by the callous nature of the crime. Yet, its very bizarre nature and the age of the murderers made an intriguing story. CNBC featured an episode of the case on *American Greed,* a prime time show devoted to "scams, schemes, and broken dreams."[28] Not surprisingly, the tale sparked Hollywood's interest. In 2007, Shirley MacLaine and Olympia Dukakis had committed to star in the feature film *Poor Things* about two aging con artists who befriend and then murder homeless men.

The most common and enduring love triangle involves neither two women and a man nor two men and a woman. It is the relationship between a woman, a man, and money. Stereotypically, money represents a desirable commodity that men (particularly older men) are valued for their ability to provide, the same way as sex is perceived in regard to women (particularly younger women). American society tolerates and even encourages men to engage in some morally questionable behaviors in pursuit of sex—"sweet talking" women, buying them expensive gifts, making them promises they are hard-pressed to keep. In the same way, certain dubious tactics are socially sanctioned for women in order to land men who can provide them with the finer things in life. Capitalizing on one's looks in order to gain access to a man's financial assets—even if it means hiding or stretching the truth—is a cardinal appeal tactic for advertisers of cosmetics, hair products, weight loss programs, designer fashions, and match-making services. There are even websites that enumerate rules for gold digging. But where does it end? Does society set any parameters regarding the ambitions of materialistic women? If it's okay to go for the gold, is it okay to *deceive* for the gold? Is it okay to *kill* for the gold?

There's no denying that American culture, based as it is on capitalism, glamorizes being wealthy. Nowhere is this more evident than on the popular television series *Lifestyles of the Rich and Famous* (1984–1995), which profiled extravagant celebrities, revealing how they obtained their wealth and showing how they currently use it. Robin Leach, the show's narrator, ended each episode with the sign-off phrase, "champagne wishes and caviar dreams." Many of the show's featured guests were contemporaries of Olga Rutterschmidt and Helen Golay, offering women their age romanticized models of success to which they could compare and contrast their own lives. Many had capitalized on their earlier status as sex symbols. Their stories showed that each one had an interesting relationship with both men and money.

Zsa Zsa Gabor made no secret of her unending love for jewelry and furs, but her love for men proved to be somewhat less enduring. She was married nine times. Lana Turner had a reputation as a glamorous femme fatale. Her husbands numbered eight, exactly the same as Liz Taylor, the renowned actress and beauty queen. For these women, men were disposable, money was not. Other wealthy beauties grew up poor, but became successful through their associations with men who had something to offer. Sophia Loren, chosen in 1991 by *People* magazine as one of the 50 Most Beautiful People in the world, owed her rise from poverty to Carlo Ponti, some 22 years her senior, whom she eventually married. Bettie Page, the quintessential "pinup girl" of the 1950s, came from a poor area of Nashville. At 28, she met photographer Irving Klaw, who cut her hair, posed her in spiked heels, and gained her a reputation as "Queen of Bondage."

Others had less happy results with men and money. Actress, singer, and dancer Debbie Reynolds learned not to trust men when her first husband Eddie Fisher left her for Liz Taylor, causing a very public scandal. Her second marriage, to millionaire businessman Harry Karl, ended in financial difficulty because of Karl's gambling and bad investments. Her third marriage, to real-estate developer Richard Hamlett, yielded no better results. He proved to be a disappointing partner, both in love and in business. Though Reynolds was a successful entertainer, when she finally left Hamlett after 12 years of marriage, she found that she had waited too long. She was forced to declare bankruptcy. Reynolds's story—consistent with the societal trend of women becoming successful through careful planning and strategic choices—may very well have influenced Olga and Helen.

On the heels of *Lifestyles of the Rich and Famous* came VH1's *The Fabulous Life Of...*, which debuted in 2003 and is still going strong as one of the channel's most popular shows ever. The show mimics *Lifestyles* in its fascination with those who are independently wealthy. In addition to episodes focusing on individual celebrities like Britney Spears, Pamela Anderson, Oprah Winfrey, and Martha Stewart, some episodes group successful people into categories. Some of these episodes—such as "Celebrity Wives," "World's Hottest Heiresses," "Rags to Riches," and "Who Got What"—include women who owe their fortunes to their associations with men. One categorical episode that may have particular significance to Olga and Helen is "The Fabulous Life Of... Hollywood 'It' Girls."

The term "*It* Girl" was initially created by English romance novelist Elinor Glyn, who explained in the introduction to a 1927 film starring Clara Bow that "*It*" is a quality that defies strict definition, but represents a quality that attracts others with its magnetic force. "*It* Girls" are featured in *The Fabulous Life Of...* series because they clearly get what they want. And since the magnetism they use to accomplish this feat is so elusive and indefinable, well a girl can pretty much fill in the blanks for herself, can't she? "What has Clara Bow got that I haven't got?" one could ask herself.

In 2005, the huge success of the television comedy-drama series *Desperate Housewives* inspired the producers of *The Fabulous Life Of...* to do a categorical episode on the show's popular female stars. It was a perfect marriage, since the characters on *Housewives* exhibit many of the same traits that real-life characters on *Fabulous Life* demonstrate: They are materialistic, strategic, glamorous, a bit naughty, and not averse to bending the rules for a payoff. On the show, the housewives are constantly seen plotting, conniving, lying, bribing, tricking, misleading, and generally compromising their integrity to get whatever they want or need at the time. Gabby, for example, offers her teenage lover a bribe not to tell her husband about their affair. When Bree discovers that her daughter is pregnant, she creates an elaborate hoax to convince everyone that the daughter has gone off to school and that she herself is the pregnant one. Susan tries to arrange two separate sham marriages in order to get health insurance for an operation. And Lynette undermines her husband by convincing his boss not to give him a promotion. Notably, it is the *women* on the show who remain constant. Their husbands, boyfriends, lovers, and children seem to appear only to serve some purpose in the ongoing drama of the women's lives. The show's prescription to be calculating and its message that men are incidental, both illustrate growing societal trends that Olga and Helen's actions reflect as well.

It's important to point out that none of the housewives actually commit murder. Okay, Susan does. She kills two people while driving, but it was an accident. And well, there *is* that incident where Bree's son runs over and kills an elderly woman, and Bree covers it up. Oh, yes and the time when Mary Alice, the deceased matriarch of Wisteria Lane who narrates the entire series from her grave, reveals why she took her own life. It seems she happened to have bought a baby from a heroin addict before moving to the suburbs to start a new life. So when the birth mother returned, sober and wanting to reclaim her child, Mary Alice, understandably, had little choice but to stab her, chop up the body, and bury it under their pool in the back yard. These examples of conniving behavior may not only affect the way society views women, but may also have an effect on the way some women actually act.

Olga Rutterschmidt and Helen Golay may have *wished* that they were as glamorous as the women on *Desperate Housewives,* but the age difference between them and the housewives cannot be ignored. Older women face additional obstacles that they must overcome in order to get what they want, so if they desire to pattern themselves after younger female models, they need to be inventive in adapting their strategies to their own situation. One type of inventiveness could involve the murder weapon, as depicted in the short story "Lamb to the Slaughter" by Roald Dahl, published in 1953 in *Harper's Magazine.* In the story, Mary Maloney bludgeons her husband to death with a frozen leg of lamb, then cooks the lamb and feeds it to the officers who come to investigate the crime. With the evidence gone, Maloney is not charged. While Olga and Helen tried to compensate for their ages by showing a certain type of inventiveness, their attempts to get away with murder were far less successful.

Older age is less of a problem for men than it is for women. In men, grey hair is a sign of distinction; in women, it is deemed unattractive. When an older man is seen with a younger woman, his status is elevated for having grasped such a prize. An older woman on the arm of a younger man is viewed as a predatory "cougar." The assumption that the younger partner is with the older one because of money does not reflect as poorly on the older man as it does on the older woman. Is there any way for an older woman to overcome this double standard? Perhaps even capitalize on her age? A few prominent entertainers have done it successfully, finding professional success and popularity in their later years.

Like a bottle of fine wine, comedian Phyllis Diller always seemed to get better with age. Her self-deprecating humor served her well as she grew older, since every year brought more fodder for her routines. The same is true for Joan Rivers, whose funniest jokes as of late have to do with her dozens of plastic surgeries; and Betty White, whose cameo appearances in TV and films as a quirky, racy, sometimes foul-mouthed grandmother type, earned her an invitation to host *Saturday Night Live,* giving her the distinction of being the oldest person ever to do so. Each of these women has masterfully used negatively perceived traits to her advantage by honestly embracing universal truths about the tribulations of female aging, while at the same time appearing youthful. Their approach of looking young while incorporating their age into their personae marked a societal trend that Olga and Helen appeared to have followed as well.

Early depictions of older women reflected the general "victim/vixen" dichotomy, but in more specifically defined subsets. One dual categorization, which can be described as "kind/wicked," counterposes the sweet, gentle, benevolent older lady with the evil, cackling witch. The best examples of these are the classic Thanksgiving song "Over the River and Through the Wood," which celebrates freshly baked pudding and pumpkin pie at grandma's house, and the covetous, green-faced Evil Witch of the West in L. Frank Baum's classic tale *The Wonderful Wizard of Oz*. A second duality pits wisdom—exemplified by the carefree, life-affirming 79-year-old savant in the 1971 novel *Harold and Maude*—against foolish absentmindedness, personified by the perpetually confused, nasal-voiced Edith Bunker in the 1970s TV series *All in the Family*.

Older women have often been depicted as desperate, undesirable, and even pathetic, as in the Academy Award–winning 1950 film noir *Sunset Boulevard*. Gloria Swanson plays over-the-hill silent film star Norma Desmond. Her unforgettable line, "I'm ready for my close-up, Mr. DeMille," which ends the film, attests to her tenuous grip on reality. Ten years later, Harry Farrell's novel *What Ever Happened to Baby Jane?* features aging child star Blanche Hudson, in grotesque, caked-on makeup, dressed as if she were still 10 years old. No self-respecting woman would want to end up like either of these characters. The mounting societal pressure not to become a pathetic old woman was embodied in these caricatures, which may well have had an impact on Olga and Helen's aspirations.

In the mid-1980s, the image of older women got a huge boost from the premiere of the groundbreaking television sitcom *The Golden Girls* (1985–1992). The four main characters—all women over 60—were each portrayed as dignified, independent, desirable, and multifaceted, giving this segment of the population a new set of role models to look up to. It appeared now that older women could actually lead respectable lives and that much of what life has to offer could actually be within their reach. This theme—with a much more sinister edge—was brought home by a character in one of the longest-running, never-to-be-forgotten TV dramas of that same period.

Dynasty—a melodramatic, larger-than-life saga about a wealthy oil family, the Carringtons—debuted in 1981, but it was not until 1982 that the show took off. That was the year Joan Collins became a prominent cast member. In her role as Alexis Colby, Blake Carrington's conniving and manipulative ex-wife, Collins gives new meaning to the term "evil bitch." She is not the only female character on the show that is greedy and unscrupulous, but she is the most glamorous. And she is the best at it. That's why her character spawned so many imitations in competing prime-time soaps—and why Collins was purportedly earning $120K an episode by the end of the series. The vice-chairman for Spelling Entertainment, the company that produced *Dynasty,* observed that "the actress herself, her personality, brought something to that role which I don't think anybody else could have done."[29] So when viewers watched the actions and demeanor of Alexis Colby, they saw a character whose realism was not hard to imagine.

Throughout the series, Alexis schemes to destroy her ex-husband, undermine his new marriage, and thwart his wife's supplanting of her status as matriarch of the Carrington household. To accomplish her goals, she engages in the basest forms of psychological, verbal, and even physical warfare. She accuses Blake of illegal weapons dealings in order to ruin his financial empire. She tracks down Blake's estranged brother and plots with him to steal Blake's fortune. When Blake gets amnesia, she exploits it by convincing him that they are still married. And when Blake's wife gets in the way, she's not averse to a little hair-pulling or even some physical mudslinging. Her unscrupulous behavior is shocking and revolting, but audiences tuned in every week for eight years to see the urbane, stylish, middle-aged beauty do her outlandish dirty work.

Make no mistake about it, Alexis is resilient. She returns to Denver, after being exiled by the all-powerful Blake, to testify against him. She survives being locked inside a cabin that is set ablaze by an arsonist attempting to kill her. She manages to get exonerated at her trial for murdering Mark Jennings, the second of her husbands to die while married to her. From the first one, who wed her as he lay on his deathbed, she acquired a major oil company. As Alexis's cousin Sable remarks, "With Alexis, death is always a simpler solution than divorce." Though Alexis is not totally incapable of having feelings for others, her main regard is clearly for herself. *Dynasty* features only rich and powerful characters, so Alexis never has to deal with the disenfranchised. The complete invisibility of this segment of society makes the silent but profound statement that the lives of the less fortunate don't really matter.

It's easy to see how Alexis Colby could have personified the image Olga and Helen wanted for themselves: clever, cunning, glamorous, desirable, and self-assured. Alexis was a throwback to the femme fatale archetype prevalent in film noir. Sure, she did some questionable things, but she did them with style and got away with them. And for that, you had to love her or at least love to hate her. But try as they might to be glamorous and cunning, Olga and Helen could not create for themselves a real-life narrative even remotely resembling the fictional plotlines of *Dynasty.*

The concept of elderly women profiting from men's deaths is not new. *Arsenic and Old Lace,* Joseph Kesselring's hugely successful 1939 play, features two eccentric spinsters, Abby and Martha Brewster, who murder lonely old men for their pensions by poisoning them with a concoction of homemade wine laced with a few fatal chemicals. The play works as a black comedy because it takes the traditional image of the sweet, if slightly dotty, old grandmother and turns it on its head. Quietly, but methodically, these women accomplish their perverted goals by capitalizing on common gender and age stereotypes, showing that older ladies are not as dumb as they may lead you to believe.

This theme is reiterated in the 1981 film *Deathtrap*, in which a young male playwright Clifford Anderson (played by Christopher Reeve) pens a play that his teacher, mentor, and lover Sidney Bruhl (played by Michael Caine) tries to lay claim to. After orchestrating the death of Bruhl's sickly wife for the insurance money, Anderson and Bruhl engage in a protracted power struggle that is veiled at first but grows to become blatant and physical. During this period, an elderly psychic, Helga Ten Dorp, moves in next door. Ten Dorp is a dotty, comical character, not taken seriously until the end, after an incident where she walks in to discover the two men in a dramatic scuffle. They are wrestling on the floor, various weapons lying around them, trying to kill each other. A lightning storm causes a black out. A gun goes off. The final scene shows opening night of the Broadway play *Deathtrap*, which is received by the audience with a standing ovation. Helga Ten Dorp, credited with being the author, takes a bow.

With 264 episodes aired between 1984 and 1996, *Murder, She Wrote* earned the distinction of being the longest-running mystery show on television. Veteran actress Angela Lansbury stars as Jessica Fletcher, a murder mystery novelist whose keen intuition and savvy detective work enables her to solve crimes with predictable regularity. One episode, "Mr. Penroy's Vacation," appears to be derived from *Arsenic and Old Lace*. The plot points to two aged spinsters as the likely murderers of an elderly man, whose body they have buried in their yard to fertilize their chrysanthemums. But Jessica has other suspicions and eventually unmasks the real culprit, showing that eccentric old ladies are sometimes just eccentric old ladies. In another episode, "Smooth Operators," a homeless man found dead in an alley is assumed to have succumbed to alcoholism. Jessica follows her instinct about a missing shoe on the man's body, leading to the discovery that a group of disreputable doctors were actually responsible. These plotlines, planted in the collective consciousness of American society, may have helped prime the public to expect the unexpected, in cases where murder and stereotypes were both involved.

The long-running show certainly taught us that murder is a phenomenon older women do not necessarily shy away from. Not only was Jessica Fletcher comfortable at murder scenes, but she was also able to use her considerable life experience to identify clues, understand the implications of evidence, and distinguish reality from illusion. Despite these assets, Jessica Fletcher's expertise was constantly underestimated by those around her. Olga and Helen were also initially underestimated, both by their victims and by authorities. But perhaps due to the growing awareness that age and gender stereotypes can be misleading, they were eventually identified as killers.

What genuine traits of the two women may have negatively influenced public sentiment and contributed the jury's decision to convict them? Looking at those traits may give us some insight into elements of their lawyers' defense strategies.

Olga and Helen were *greedy*. Helen owned valuable properties in Santa Monica. And together, they had enough money not only to provide for their own needs, but also to support their victims for two years. Yet, their relative financial stability could also be used to *obscure* the greed motive. They were not desperate women needing a man's monetary assets to lift themselves up from poverty. Olga Rutterschmidt is no Bettie Page. Helen Golay is no Sophia Loren.

Olga and Helen were *conniving*. They plotted their strategies. They targeted their victims. Once caught, Golay even tried to place blame for the killings on her own daughter. Part of their defense was to portray themselves as incapable of masterminding such an elaborate scheme. Rutterschmidt's attorney went out of his way to depict his client as dim-witted. She couldn't have done it. Olga Rutterschmidt was no Mary Maloney or Helga Ten Dorp.

Olga and Helen were desperately *unfulfilled*. Unable to accept their station in life as unremarkable older women, they went to great pains to try to look young and sexy—coloring and perming their hair, wearing layers of makeup, and dressing inappropriately for their ages. They craved financial independence, seeing it as a way to make themselves attractive, like older *men* so commonly do. After they were indicted, they appeared in court looking quite different. Gone were the coiffed hair, heavy makeup, and racy clothing. These women were not to be mistaken for the materialistic vixens of *Desperate Housewives*.

Olga and Helen were deluded into believing they were capable of pulling off their crime. They were unrealistically *self-confident*. They may not have been "*It* Girls," to whom all good things gravitated without any effort on their part, but they did prove themselves to be able predators who could lure their victims into a fatal web of deceit. They believed they had the shrewdness, the wherewithal, and the capacity to get the job done when they pulled off the first murder and began gainfully collecting the insurance payoffs. So they did it again. But at their trial, they were strategically portrayed as weak and timid. Helen's attorney painted a picture of her as frail, unable to summon sufficient resources, and incapable of violence. This legal strategy sought to downplay Golay's similarities to Alexis Colby—that she was conniving and overconfident—and distance her from that character by displaying her as unglamorous. Helen Golay, he essentially argued, was no Alexis Colby.

Possibly the most damning trait that characterized the two women was their *brazenness*. Olga, having grown impatient with the slow pace of the insurance investigation, actually called the police to check on the status of the vehicle that had run over her victim—a car they were ultimately able to trace back to *her*. Helen, not content to collect just one single prize for her efforts, took out multiple policies on the homeless men. Yet, even these actions presented an opportunity to pose reasonable doubt. With the *Arsenic and Old Lace* theme so firmly planted in the public psyche, the defense could argue that the modus operandi for murderous little old ladies was *surreptitious* behavior. The defendants did not fit this profile. Olga Rutterschmidt and Helen Golay, they claimed, were no Abby and Martha Brewster.

These defense strategies, of course, were unsuccessful. By now, everyone knew from pop culture that women commonly seek to exploit men for financial gain, that elderly women can be quite comfortable with murder, that little old ladies were rarely as innocent as they might appear to be, and that female septuagenarians can be masters at using self-deprecation as a clever act to capture an audience's hearts and minds.

Unlike fathers, who encourage their sons to pursue their desires forcefully and in an aggressive, straightforward manner, mothers have traditionally taught their daughters the art of using indirect or disguised means to get what they want: subtle persuasion, implied coercion, and sophisticated trickery. Only recently has a more brazen approach become fashionable for women. One need look no further than recent music videos to see that female brazenness is pretty cool, whether it's Lady Gaga and Beyonce dancing half-naked over the dead bodies of the people they've just poisoned or Pink, shopping for a guitar, smashing one on the floor, and beating up the salesman. If a female caller to popular talk show host Dr. Laura mentions that she lives with her boyfriend, the good doctor is quick to restate the situation in her own brazen rhetoric: "So he's doin' you for free," she insists. And in her 2009 book *My Horizontal Life: A Collection of One-Night Stands,* Chelsea Handler writes: "I think we can all agree that sleeping around is a great way to meet people."[30] Yes, brazenness is cool, especially since it is easily associated with sex. And there's the kicker: If you're brazen and sexy, you're cool. If you're over 70, you're not sexy. So if you're over 70 and brazen, you're just brazen.

As 70-something murder defendants, Olga Rutterschmidt and Helen Golay were handicapped at both ends of the female image spectrum. By 2008, the year of their trial, the well-worn rendering of the dotty, lovable, eccentric, but harmless old lady was no longer believable, yet society was not yet ready to apply the concept of "brazen chic" to the more advanced stages of life. These two women—guilty as they may have been—were essentially doomed to be convicted. With the pop-culture cards stacked against them, they had little actual chance of gaining the public's sympathy.

Now let's transport ourselves to a different place and time, where a woman has killed for money, but with the realistic hope of a more promising outcome.

ANN WOODWARD

When Ann Woodward married Billy Woodward in 1943, she was not good enough: not good enough for his friends, not good enough for his relatives, and most of all, not good enough for her husband. Billy was the only son of an established New York family with old money. Ann was a nobody from Kansas. At 22, she had left the drab surroundings of the Midwest to escape from a background filled with poverty and uncertainty. The move was the beginning of a lifelong quest in transforming herself. She became a part-time model, chorus girl, and bit actress. Like many beautiful young women in these types of jobs, Ann was not afraid to use her sex appeal to get what she wanted. She wanted to get noticed by the right person. Should the right person have lots of money, even better.

Billy Woodward fit the ticket perfectly. He was good-looking, charming, sensitive, and filthy rich. She did love Billy. But she also knew that as Mrs. William Woodward, she would have access to the very best. For 12 years, Ann enjoyed all the perks of the upper crust. Big houses, fancy clothes, expensive jewels, exotic trips, and entry to the most exclusive parties were at her disposal. On the surface, her life seemed like a glittering success. However, the marriage that made it all possible was a sordid fiasco. It disintegrated into a sham of lies, accusations, infidelity, and physical altercations. Ann knew that Billy and his set would never forget or accept where she came from. Without Billy's money, she had nothing. She was nothing. When her husband died from a gunshot wound that she inflicted, an event *Life* called the "shooting of the century," her fate was sealed.[31] Ann Woodward was known as the ultimate gold digger, and a deadly one at that.

Ann Woodward spent her entire adult life driven by the need to improve herself. Her raw determination stemmed from a childhood beset by an absent father, an ambitious mother, and lack of money. Ann was born in 1913 to parents who were sorely mismatched. When they eventually divorced, she spent time with her mother, traveling from one small town to another. According to Susan Braudy, in her book *This Crazy Thing Called Love*, money was an endless source of worry.[32] The constant upheaval made a solitary life for the young girl. Ann retreated into a world of fantasy, dreaming of the day when she would become a famous actress adored by millions. Since Ann inherited her mother's good looks, people often commented on how pretty she was. During the 1920s and 1930s, Hollywood fan magazines churned out breathless stories of beautiful young girls making it big despite their small-town origins. Ann told herself that she too could become a star. At 22, she decided to leave Kansas City to seek fame and fortune in New York.

The depression had devastated the country with its stock market crash, massive unemployment, soup kitchens, and breadlines. But in 1937, the year Ann arrived, New York City was beginning to slowly recover. Manhattan's Art Deco architectural masterpieces dazzled millions of young newcomers. The city offered Times Square with the Cotton Club, Broadway and 42nd Street, entertainment by Frank Sinatra in nightclubs, and a world of glamorous parties to those well connected.[33] Ann was in heaven. She decided to approach the John Robert Powers agency, since she had done some modeling back home. Ann mastered the simple logistics related to taking alluring head shots, compiling a portfolio, going on a test shoot, and what to do to impress a client. Advertisers started to request her. She won a small role in a Broadway production. Of course, it helped that she had her nose reshaped, took acting lessons, and was not afraid to flirt with the right people. Ann spent a great deal of time at the El Morocco, a popular nightclub frequented by celebrities. One of her conquests from the club was the film star Franchot Tone. Tone was a sophisticated actor known for his cultured manner. Unlike many stars of the era with lower-class backgrounds, he came from a socially and politically prominent family in New York. Highly educated, Franchot had gone to Cornell and became a Phi Beta Kappa member. His career in Hollywood led him to a costarring role opposite Joan Crawford. The two stars fell in love and eventually married. Throughout the four-year marriage, Tone was a mentor to Crawford, teaching her how to soften her hard edges. He played the same role in Ann's life. He encouraged Ann to not only improve herself physically, but also grow intellectually. He supported her efforts to develop her vocabulary, while suggesting books for her to read. On a practical level, he helped her get a job as a dancer in a Noel Coward review. Ann was disappointed when the affair ended, but she gamely moved on.

During the next few years, she kept busy doing radio work and appearing in chorus lines. She continued to audition for plays. Although she willingly made a number of screen tests, none of them ever resulted in film offers. At 27, Ann was smart enough to realize that while she had a small amount of talent, it wasn't enough to make people immediately sit up and take notice. Consequently, she was not afraid to use her sexuality to get the roles she desired. She told a friend half jokingly, "I'd sleep with anybody if it would help my career."[34] It was not unusual for men to be attracted to the vivacious showgirl exuding sex appeal. One evening in 1941, while she was performing in a nightclub act, William Woodward Sr. and his son Billy noticed her. Woodward Sr. discretely asked Ann out. She accepted and engaged in a brief relationship with him.[35] The relationship had run its course by 1942. Apparently unaware of their involvement, Billy invited Ann to dinner.

Twenty-two-year-old Billy Woodward was one of the most eligible single men in New York. Not only was he young and handsome, but was also rich enough to turn the head of any female. Billy had grown up in the shadow of his formidable parents. William Woodward Sr., in possession of a large banking fortune, was able to do exactly what he wanted, when he wanted. Most of his attention was focused on racehorses and other women. Billy's mother, Elsie Woodward, enjoyed a reputation as a grand dame of high society.[36] The Woodward's value system was entrenched with that of the old guard, a group who put a premium on appearances, background, and social standing. Billy grew up with his sisters in a six-story mansion near Manhattan's Millionaire's Row. Butlers, footmen, and maids went out their way to make every aspect of his life comfortable. Sadly, neither his mother nor father took much interest in him. Susan Braudy's account *This Crazy Thing Called Love* indicates that William was disappointed his son was not more like him, while Elsie was open about her dislike of children.[37] Given these attitudes, one can imagine how Billy felt disconnected from his family. Although he was attending Harvard, Billy was drifting through life with little ambition. It seemed the only thing that interested him was having a good time.

Billy and Ann's romance seemed to meet the psychological needs each of them had. Billy was used to well-bred debutantes with backgrounds similar to his own. In contrast, Ann was like a rare exotic creature. She had broken away from her family to establish an independent life. Although she did not tell the whole truth about her background, Ann was willing to share some of her struggles with him. He sensed the vulnerability behind her glamour girl persona.

Ann liked the way Billy showered her with attention. Dinner and champagne at the best restaurants blocked out bad memories of growing up poor. It also eased the anxiety she felt over her future. Being publically linked with one of the country's most socially prominent bachelors might lead to interesting prospects. The payoff personally as well as professionally could be remarkable. She quickly arranged her time so that it revolved around Billy. It was important to always be available to him in order to keep his interest. Five months after their first date, Billy invited her to spend a day at the races with his family. She was demure when she saw his father again. William treated her cordially making no reference to their past. Elsie was gracious, but secretly appalled that her son's new girlfriend was a vulgar upstart. "One look and I knew the whole story," she later told her friends.[38] Ann sensed her disapproval, but hoped it was temporary.

Elsie wasted no time in showing her son the findings of a private investigative report she had commissioned to dig into Ann's past. Billy didn't care about the results. William also tried to dissuade Billy from his relationship with Ann, although he never admitted to being involved with her. Billy brushed aside his reservations in the same way he had brushed aside his mother's. He was serious about Ann no matter what his parent's thought. In all likelihood, their disapproval probably added to her appeal. He knew their threats to cut him off from his inheritance were empty.

Billy had joined the Naval Reserve while he was at Harvard. After the attack on Pearl Harbor, he formally enlisted. Not wanting to lose him, either because of his family or the war, Ann pushed for marriage. Billy acquiesced. Ann became Mrs. William Woodward Jr. on March 10, 1943. Billy's father was the only member of his family to attend. Ann told Billy that she had no relatives, failing to mention her estranged father or her aunts living in Kansas City. From her perspective, the less Billy knew about her lowly family the better. Since Billy was stationed in Tacoma, Washington, Ann packed her bags to join him, and tried to remake herself so she could fit in better with Billy's world. In an effort to understand business principles, she took an accounting class. After all, Billy's family had made their millions with the Hanover National Bank. Billy wasn't interested in discussing with his wife how or why his family made money—that's why they had advisors. When Ann read books to learn more about culture, Billy accused her of being pretentious. On the other hand, it was important to him that Ann looked the part of a Woodward wife. He bought her jewelry from Harry Winston, so she could literally outshine other women at military dinner parties. Yet, when officers paid too much attention to Ann, Billy grew jealous and resentful. He was critical of how she looked, what she wore, and how she acted. The constant negative feedback eroded her self-confidence. In an effort to ingratiate herself to her mother-in-law, Ann wrote regularly to Elsie. The letter campaign seemed to have no effect. Billy was aware of his mother's disapproval toward his wife. Still when he found out that Ann was pregnant, he urged her to live with his parents in New York. He was being shipped out for duty and did not want Ann to be alone.

Ann had her son in 1944. Billy joined her at his parent's home a year later when he was discharged from the navy. His continual presence added to her insecurity. She was so eager to please that she hired a private tutor to coach her on the rituals of high society. She made countless trips to Paris to ensure she had the appropriate designer clothing for public appearances. Her purchases paid off when she was named to the best-dressed list. Yet, the announcement did little to bolster her confidence. While Billy had given Ann more expensive jewelry and over $500,000 in properties, he often treated her poorly or ignored her all together.

Ann was convinced that her husband was losing interest. Although they still slept together, their lovemaking usually took place after a fight.[39] Arguments were no longer confined to private quarters; they would scream at each other in public to the consternation of their friends. "In private the arguments crossed over into physical altercations with Ann fond of throwing ashtrays and Billy responding with a slap to the face," wrote Mark Gribben in his article "The Woodwards: Tragedy in High Society."[40] The stress took its toll on Ann. She began to drink heavily and take drugs.

Billy was now enjoying the life of a rich playboy. With access to his trust fund, he could emulate his father in doing whatever he wanted, when he wanted, including womanizing. Ann could live with dalliances. But Billy fell in love—with someone far superior socially to Ann. Billy's girlfriend was Princess Marina Torlonia. She outclassed Ann in every respect. Billy conducted his relationship with the princess discreetly for two years. By this time, he and Ann had a second son and their own mansion. Ann had taken it on herself to throw the best parties. Her guest list included the Duke and Duchess of Windsor, Ethel Merman, David Selznick, and other members of the glitterati. For some reason, Billy had invited his girlfriend to one of his wife's parties. Ann was livid. She created a public scene that embarrassed everyone present.

In 1948, Billy wanted to marry his girlfriend. He asked for a divorce. Ann was distraught with fear. She did not want to stop being Mrs. Billy Woodward. Begging him to change his mind, she screamed, "No please, no divorce . . . I'll never let you go."[41] Despite her protests, Billy was determined to have his freedom. He orchestrated an official separation. Unbeknownst to Ann, Billy also changed his will, so she would have less access to his money. Ann went off to Europe in an effort to pull herself together. Like many rejected women in need of a shot of self-confidence, she threw herself into an affair. Her partner was Prince Aly Kahn, an international playboy. Despite having a lover, Ann still wanted Billy. Billy may have decided it was better off financially to stay with his wife or may still have felt some love for her. He called off the divorce to Ann's relief.

Their relationship continued to drift along for the next half dozen years. They moved into an even larger mansion that Billy put in Ann's name. She spent her time and Billy's money redecorating it with priceless antiques. Intent on making it to the top of the social ladder, she attended charity balls and lavish parties. Her picture frequently appeared in the society pages. Always sensitive to the fact that she was older then Billy, Ann had cosmetic surgery. The couple continued to jet set around the world. They went shopping in Paris, sunbathing in the South of France, and tiger hunting in India. Both of them continued to have affairs. Ann had a relationship with a titled aristocrat from England.

His father's death in 1953 left Billy even richer. With nothing better to do, Billy became interested in the racing stables that were left to him. He soon got involved with the daily operations surrounding the champion thoroughbred Nashua that his father had purchased. Nashua continued to win races, and Billy was pictured in newspapers across the country. The horse eventually went on to earn over a million dollars in prize money. Ann wanted part of the attention, so she too made herself available for interviews. When Elsie saw the stories featuring Ann, she criticized her daughter-in-law for being a publicity hound. Periodically, Billy was proud of Ann's presence; from time to time, he was resentful that the spotlight was on her. It was possible that Ann's strategy was to cement her relationship with Billy in the public eye, so he would no longer think of divorcing her. With the intense media coverage of Nashua and the advent of television, their faces were now beamed into America's households throughout the country.

If this was Ann's strategy, it did not seem to be working. Billy had fallen in love again with a beautiful debutante. He told friends he was thinking of really divorcing his wife this time. Ann was a wreck over the turn of events. She increased the amount of drugs she was consuming. The two continued to have violent screaming matches followed by physical blows and rough sex.[42] Ann got drunk at parties, creating unpleasant incidents for everyone involved. Billy's friends whispered that Ann was mentally unstable. He did nothing to discourage the talk. In late October 1955, while on a business trip, Billy learned that Ann's father was still alive and working as a streetcar driver.[43] He cruelly taunted Ann over this fact. Ann may have been afraid that the lies she told about her background had finally caught up with her. Once again, Billy might threaten to end their marriage and legally cut her off. Discarded at 40, her life would be over as she knew it.

The couple continued their uneasy coexistence. Much of their time during this month was spent discussing the news of a prowler in the area. On October 28, 1955, the intruder had broken into the Woodward's garage. Ann was frightened and asked Billy to hire a guard. He ignored the suggestion, since they both had guns and knew how to use them. Two nights later, the couple attended a party in honor of the Duke and Duchess of Windsor. When the party ended, the Woodward's returned home and went to their separate bedrooms. Ann had her revolver loaded with shotgun pellets nearby. Around two in the morning, she woke up thinking she heard something. Ann picked up the gun in the dark, pointing it in the direction of the noise. Billy was standing in the hallway. On October 30, 1955, he was killed by a gunshot wound from his wife.

When the police arrived, she told the officers that she had shot her husband by accident, thinking he was the prowler. They scoured the area in search of the mysterious intruder. When more detectives showed up and the coroner arrived, Ann dissolved into hysterics. She was sedated, and then secluded. Although reports of the shooting reached the press, they were denied access to the site. Elsie did not learn about her son's death until later that morning. She always believed that Ann killed Billy on purpose; so did the Woodward family lawyer.[44]

News of Billy's death hit the papers immediately. Thanks to Nashua, he and Ann were well known to the public. *The New York Times* featured the case on the front page. Despite the fact that most coverage depicted the event as an accident, reporters were already discussing the possibility of murder and a cover-up. So was the Woodward's social set. Gossip spread that Ann had shot Billy deliberately. Cholly Knickerbocker, a prominent society columnist during the 1950s, made provocative comments on the nature of Ann and Billy's relationship. He noted that they had not been a happy couple. Unsolicited letters, presumably from friends, were sent to the police attesting to this fact. Whispers circulated that everyone knew Ann was a gold digger. As Billy's widow, people speculated that Ann had been hoping to inherit millions from the Woodward fortune. The press scrambled to dig up salacious stories about her past. Not surprisingly, Billy became canonized instantly. His funeral attracted thousands of curiosity seekers eager to glimpse members of New York's grandest social set. *Life* magazine commissioned an in-depth story, devoting 10 pages to the shooting. Despite all of the publicity, or probably because of it, both the public and press believed that the Woodward family protected Ann in order to avoid a scandal.

While Ann was spirited off to a hospital to recover from the stress and shock of the shooting, the police continued their investigation. Her story gained credibility with the arrest of Paul Wirths, a man suspected of being the mysterious prowler. Eventually, he admitted to being on the Woodward estate the night of the shooting. His statements appeared to clear Ann; however, some wondered if he was setup to be a scapegoat. When news of the confession became general knowledge, many people thought it was an example of the Woodward money being used to cook up an alibi for Ann. A rumor made the rounds that Elsie had spent hundreds of thousands of dollars to pay off the police to keep her daughter-in-law out of jail. Some wondered if Wirths was also paid off. Elsie had no love for Ann, but she did want to protect the family image. In the immediate aftermath of the event, she publically came to Ann's support and backed up the story of an accident. On November 25, 1955, less than a month after the shooting, a grand jury formally ruled that there was no evidence to suggest murder. Privately, Elsie was not convinced.[45]

Ann may have been exonerated, but her life and reputation never recovered. She learned about the 1948 changes to Billy's will, excluding her from most of his fortune. Her sons would eventually get the vast majority of it. Elsie made sure the boys were packed off to a Swiss boarding school to reduce the contact they had with their mother. Ann spent the rest of her years in a nomadic existence. She roamed dissolutely between Paris, London, Madrid, the Cote d'Azur, Italy, Switzerland, Morocco, Australia, and New York. She indulged herself with a series of boyfriends who became younger and younger. Although her vanity was at first satisfied by the attention, she later bitterly complained that the men only wanted her for the money they thought she had. Upon his release from prison, Paul Wirths tried to blackmail Ann. Former friends went out of their way to avoid her. Even though the two made a few public appearances together, Elsie spent the rest of her days telling people Ann was guilty.

Ann died a lonely embittered woman, committing suicide in 1975. But her death would do little to abate the public's fascination with the case. The well-known author Truman Capote was fixated on Ann's saga. His novel *Answered Prayers* featured a chapter on Ann, depicting her as a gold-digging social climber who killed her husband on purpose. The chapter was printed in *Esquire* magazine around the time of Ann's death and gained national attention. When it was published, Elsie commented, "Well that's that; she shot my son and Truman just murdered her, and so now I suppose we don't have to worry about that anymore."[46] A decade after Capote's book, Dominick Dunn wrote another quasi-fictional account, *The Two Mrs. Grenvilles,* which became a popular television miniseries. Dunn examined the case 20 years later in 2005 on his true-crime show, *Power, Privilege, and Justice.* To a whole new generation, in terms of popular culture, the former showgirl from Kansas City had officially joined the ranks of the rich and famous. Elsie would have been horrified; Ann may have smiled.

In 1955, the year Ann Woodward went on trial for killing her husband, it was hard enough to picture a woman with a heavy metal gun in her delicate hand, much less to envision her intentionally shooting two bullets into her husband's body—especially a high-society socialite like Ann Woodward. Most Americans had very specific ideas about what women would and would not do, what they were and were not capable of, and what roles did and did not hold promise for them. In the 1950s, acceptable roles for women were certainly more limited than they are now, and those limits made the options available all the more respectable, even if they didn't require the utmost integrity.

Although there were no websites in 1955 to offer step-by-step instructions to aspiring gold diggers, pop culture nonetheless made the lessons available to be learned, albeit with the suggestion that pursuing true love achieves better results than fortune hunting. One interesting example is the 1953 romantic comedy, *How to Marry a Millionaire,* which was adapted into a syndicated TV series later on that decade. The film starred Lauren Bacall as Schatzie, an enterprising graduate from the school of hard knocks; Marilyn Monroe as Pola, a pretty but self-conscious airhead; and Betty Grable as Loco, a naively effervescent dreamer.

Pola's refusal to wear glasses in the presence of prospective husbands demonstrates Gold Digger Rule #1—*Look your best*—while Loco's eagerness to accompany a horny businessman to the Elk's Lodge in order to meet eligible bachelors follows Rule #2—*Put yourself in places where there will be rich people.* Despite Schatzie's attraction to a sweet-talking guy named Tom, she instead pursues older widower J. D., whom she believes has a lot more money. Her unrelenting efforts to quell J. D.'s fears about their age difference finally earn her a marriage proposal, exhibiting Rules #3—*Come on strong*—and #4—*Get married.* But in the end, Schatzie's heart won't allow her to clinch the deal. At the last minute, she breaks it off with J. D. and marries Tom, whom she truly loves. But all ends well, since Tom, unbeknownst to Schatzie at the time, is actually a much wealthier man than J. D.

Another film of the same year, *Gentlemen Prefer Blondes*—best known for its signature song "Diamonds Are a Girl's Best Friend"—illustrates a more blatant sanctioning of women marrying for money. In one of the final scenes, Lorelei (played by Marilyn Monroe) makes a plea to her fiancé's father, who opposes her son marrying her. "I don't want to marry your son for his money," she says, "I want to marry him for *your* money." She argues that if he had a daughter, he would want the best for her, so it is only fair for her to want the same. Convinced after hearing this that Lorelei is neither stupid nor conceited, he gives the marriage his blessing.

Media images such as these serve to create some legitimacy for attractive, financially challenged women who marry wealthy men. But what about when these women kill the men they've married? Well, even in those instances, pop culture may play a helping role in their defense. Ann Woodward, for example, found an unlikely ally in her mother-in-law, Elsie Woodward, a prominent member of high society. Elsie's determination to preserve the family image was grounded in the belief that members of high society are held to a higher standard than common people—a message propounded by the cultural norms and purveyed by the media of the time. The covers of popular magazines like *Life, Look,* and *Time* often featured dignified photos of prominent upper-class figures, accompanied by idealized profiles inside.

Today our society retains its love/hate fascination with female fortune hunters. This is evidenced by the fact that "Diamonds Are a Girl's Best Friend" is still very much in the American psyche. In 2007, the American Film Institute listed the song as the twelfth most important movie song of all time.[47] Over the years, it has been reprised by such diverse artists as Eartha Kitt, Nicole Kidman, Emmylou Harris, and Beyonce Knowles. In her 2001 music video "Material Girl," Madonna conspicuously reenacts Monroe's performance in her appearance, set, costumes, and choreography. Clearly, we're still working this out.

Anna Nicole Smith—the voluptuous, platinum blonde, self-admitted Marilyn Monroe wannabe—was introduced to the public in *Playboy* magazine as 1993 Playmate of the Year. From there, she gained notoriety as a model, an actress, and the star of her own reality TV show. Born in a small, rural Texas town, Smith carved for herself a niche in contemporary American culture by outrageously personifying the "rags to riches" fantasy when she was just 26. Her marriage to 89-year-old business Tycoon J. Howard Marshall began a media spectacle that lasted for years. When Marshall died in 1995, barely a year after the marriage, Smith initiated a highly publicized court battle against Marshall's son, claiming half of her late husband's $1.6 billion estate. The court proceedings spanned over a decade and several federal and state jurisdictions. In 2000, Smith was awarded nearly half a billion dollars, only for the decision to be reversed the following year, leaving her nothing. On appeal, a federal ruling reinstated $88 million in 2002, a decision that was deemed unenforceable two years later. In 2006, the U.S. Supreme Court affirmed Smith's right to pursue her claim in federal court, but then made an opposite ruling in 2011. The lengthy series of back-and-forth arguments and verdicts illustrates the country's continued ambivalence about a woman's entitlement to the assets of a husband she may have married expressly for fortune.

This dual perspective is illustrated in fictional portrayals as well. Toni Childs, for example, is a central character in the popular, long-running TV sitcom *Girlfriends* (2000–2008). Toni is one of the four female 20-something comrades, seeking love and fortune in the fast-paced culture of Los Angeles. She is the one for whom money is the most important. A successful realtor and brokerage owner, Toni regards her own financial success as all the more reason for seeking a wealthy mate. As a child, she grew up poor, and as an adult, she makes regular deposits into her "never go back to Fresno" fund in order to ensure that she never has to repeat that experience. After several years of dating only those who fit her image of an ideal husband—usually tall, dark, and handsome professional athletes, entertainers, or business moguls—Toni meets Todd Garret, a short, white, Jewish plastic surgeon, who woos her and eventually proposes. Though Todd has great earning potential as a doctor, Toni discovers that he's also in considerable debt. In a move that seems out of character, she marries him anyway, choosing to follow her heart rather than be held back by her fears.

Toni's predicament is precisely the opposite of Schatzie's in *How to Marry a Millionaire*. Schatzie married a man she believed to be poor, only to discover that he was rich. Toni married a man she had originally thought was rich, even after she discovered that he was not. But the message is the same: Money may be important, but love is a better guiding principle when choosing a mate. Toni Childs is evidence that, despite the passage of more than half a century, we are still struggling with the role of money in partner relationships. As psychotherapist Olivia Mellan points out:

> For most people, money is never just money, a tool to accomplish some of life's goals. It is love, power, happiness, security, control, dependency, independence, freedom and more. Money is so loaded a symbol that to unload it . . . reaches deep into the human psyche. Usually, when the button of money is pressed, deeper issues emerge that have long been neglected.[48]

No wonder money has been and continues to be such a prevalent theme in stories about relationships. No wonder it is a commodity that some women kill for.

What can we conclude from the Woodward and Rutterschmidt/Golay stories? Woodward followed the four-step, tried-and-true gold-digger instructions to the letter, and she was exonerated. Being older and less desirable, Rutterschmidt and Golay were not in a position to exploit standard gold-digging technique, so they veered from the traditional path. They were convicted. Is the moral just to stick to proven, time-tested methods when kill-ing men for money? That it's best to leave gold-digging to the young and the beautiful? That it's prudent to keep murder within the sanctity of marriage? Perhaps. But it's really not as simple as that. In the decades following the Woodward case and leading up to the Rutterschmidt/Golay case, American society has, in fact, changed in a very significant way.

Americans are fascinated with high society—always have been and prob-ably always will be. In the 1950s, members of this elite group were still ideal-ized as pristine and honorable. When actress Grace Kelly married the Prince of Monaco in 1956, she became styled as *Her Serene Highness, the Princess of Monaco*, and redubbed "Princess Grace." The press called the event "The Wedding of the Century," and MGM took advantage of the widespread publicity by coordinating the release of Kelly's last film, *High Society*, with her exit from Hollywood into the majestic bliss of European royalty. During that same period, Jane Wyatt, the daughter of a prominent Wall Street investment banker and descendent of an "old wealth" East Coast family, began her act-ing career as an understudy in a Broadway play. Wyatt went on to win Emmy awards for her roles as the doting mom in the 1950s TV sitcom *Father Knows Best* and as Dr. Spock's mother, Amanda Grayson, on the sci-fi TV series *Star Trek*. But one role that she lost when she accepted the Broadway gig was that of real-life debutante. Her pursuit of an acting career resulted in her removal from the *New York Social Register* list. Such was the vigilance of effort at the time to protect the pure image of those privileged to be deemed "upper class."

Things are different now. Being an actress actually *helps* to elevate a wom-an's status. These days, class is more about money than heritage. And while wealth is still glamorized, the American public is now fed details of its down-side as well. Reality TV has exposed the ugliness that can often grow hand in hand with fortune. Yes, now we know that rich people are really no better than anyone else. Today, programs featuring the wealthy "elite" fill cable pro-gramming slots. On *The Real Housewives of Orange County*, an enormously popular reality TV show that has spawned no less than five copycat spin-offs, typical statements by the starring women show them to be petty, superficial, and self-aggrandizing: "I'm smart, I'm sexy and I'm confident. Of course people are going to talk about me" (Gretchen Rossi), "I want the power and the money, and I want the boat" (Vicki Gunvalson), "I'm not the new girl anymore, so watch out" (Tamra Vieth-Barney), and "Am I high mainte-nance? Of course I am. Look at me" (Alexis Bellino). Tabloid newspapers like *The National Enquirer* and celebrity gossip websites like *TMZ* offer nonstop coverage of rich, young female celebrities like Paris Hilton and Lindsay Lohan, in trouble with the law. With the advent of streaming video, we now know that there is no shortage of young women willing to post their com-plete, unedited daily activities on the Web for all over the world to ogle. And the exploitative video series *Girls Gone Wild* demonstrates in graphic detail how easy it is to get attention-starved females to do whatever it takes to get noticed.

All this attests to the fact that female brazenness—once considered crude—is now a routine, accepted part of American culture. While in 1955, it may have been hard for the public to imagine Ann Woodward's shooting of her husband to be brashly intentional, today it doesn't seem at all inconsistent with the images we have of pretty young women, whether they be part of high society or not. While at first, it may appear that the opposite verdicts in the Woodward and Rutterschmidt/Golay trials are due exclusively to the differing events and circumstances of the killings, one can't help but wonder to what extent those outcomes are also a product of media depictions that reflect, disseminate, and shape the values of changing times.

Women Who Kill Because They Are Crazy

The noted comedian and actor W. C. Fields wrote, "All women are crazy, it's only a matter of degree."[1] Although humorous, the quote sadly reflects the statistical fact that more women than men tend to suffer from various forms of mental illness.[2] Unfortunately, if the disorder becomes pathological, insanity can result. Aileen Wuornos and Andrea Yates were both labeled crazy. Their inability to handle life, cope with stress, and make appropriate choices led them to commit murder. Aileen, who took her hatred of men out on seven hapless victims, went raging to death row as a female serial killer. Andrea, who systematically drowned her five children in a bathtub, became a poster child for mental illness. Their tabloid cases raised the question: If you are mad, can you be bad? And if you are bad, can you be mad? It's a debate regarding the meaning of insanity that still goes on today.

AILEEN WUORNOS

Aileen Wuornos told police officers, "I'm a good person inside. . . . When I was a little girl I wanted to be a nun."[3] It's hard to reconcile this statement with the impression we have today of an angry psychotic who showed no remorse at her trial declaring, "I'm one who seriously hates human life and would kill again."[4] Somewhere along the way, the child who dreamed of being a nun grew up to lead a troubled life filled with promiscuity, drinking, drugs, violence, prostitution, and murder. While nothing can take away the horror of the senseless acts she committed, one wonders if the neglect and abuse so prominent in her early life had been mitigated, would she have turned out differently.

Aileen's story illustrates the sad reality of how a victim can turn into a predator. The psychopathic nature of her personality can be traced back to a traumatic upbringing filled with elements of "The Bad Seed." Born in 1956, Aileen was unaware that her birth mother was actually the woman she thought of as her older sister. Fourteen-year-old Diane Wuornos had eloped with local "bad boy" Leo Pittman. Predictably, the union was short-lived. Leo was often drunk, fooled around with other women, and thought nothing of beating up his wife. By the time she was 17, Diane was a divorced mother with two children, Keith a toddler and Aileen a baby. The situation proved so overwhelming that one day Diane just walked out effectively abandoning the children. Aileen grew up thinking until she was 11 that her grandparents, who had quietly adopted the siblings, were actually her parents. Although Diane came in and out of her daughter's life, Aileen never met her birth father. Leo Pittman graduated from being a small-town hood to becoming a pedophile. He was arrested and convicted for raping a child in 1962. Seven years later, he committed suicide while locked up in jail.

The depiction of the Wuornos household in Troy, Michigan, where Aileen grew up, is filled with contradictions. Some viewed it as just a typical large family governed by Lauri Wuornos, an authoritarian but loving man, and his wife Britta. Others heard rumors of Lauri's alcoholism, his cruelty toward his wife, and the bizarre punishments he would concoct to keep the kids in line. What is confirmed is that Aileen was often at odds with her father/grandfather. The two had a volatile relationship filled with constant screaming matches. Aileen would claim that Lauri physically and sexually abused her. While immediate family members denied her version of accounts, others thought it was very possible. The one person she had a good relationship was with her brother Keith. The siblings were emotionally close and seemed to exist at times in a private world.

Aileen was labeled a difficult child. Siblings and relatives depict her as a perpetually angry person with an explosive temper and destructive tendencies. She tried to commit suicide more than once. Branded early as a misfit, Aileen took to acting out on a regular basis. At different points in her life, she became a ward of the court, spending time in juvenile hall. She constantly ran away from home, smoked, took drugs, and drank. Her family knew she was not above stealing or causing fires. The most disturbing aspect of her wild ways was her overt sexual behavior. Her first encounter occurred at the age of 11. It didn't take long for her to hook up with many of the neighborhood boys. In *Lethal Intent,* author Sue Russell noted that Aileen had written to one of them, "For a pack of cigs I will suck and fuck."[5] By the time she was 12 years old, it was a well-known fact that Aileen regularly exchanged sexual favors for money. If the troubled girl hoped it would gain her acceptance, she was mistaken. Instead, her pubescent sexuality brought taunts and condemnation. Rumors in the neighborhood floated around that she was even sleeping with Keith, a charge she didn't deny.[6] Eventually, growing tired of local boys, Aileen became sexually active with an adult neighbor. Apparently, he had no reluctance getting involved with an underage teen.

Bored easily, she often skipped class—a move that resulted in low grades. Fellow students either called her cruel names or ostracized her completely. Privately she may have felt humiliated, but publically she covered it up by adopting a tough attitude. Aware of her undesirable activities and concerned over the teenager's hostile manner, school officials urged Aileen's family to get professional help. Russell's account presents an assessment report stating, "It is vital for this girl's welfare that she get counseling immediately."[7] The advice was ignored.

Shortly after this report, Aileen became pregnant. The 14-year-old with the tough persona was actually so terrified she kept it secret from her family for months. When her grandparents found out, they were livid. They quickly shipped her off to give the baby up for adoption. No one knew the paternity; it was doubtful she even did. It's very possible that she was raped, a refrain she later used repeatedly to justify her deadly actions. Aileen's grandmother died shortly after she returned home. In her own limited way, Britta had tried to reach out to Aileen, providing her with kindness while she was growing up. Britta was often the buffer between Lauri and Aileen. Now she was gone. The 15-year-old left home for good in 1971.

With no money, little education, and few skills, Aileen decided to support herself the one way she knew she could—by prostitution. Her life became a nomadic pattern fueled by a restless spirit. Days were filled with hitchhiking; nights were filled with biker bars and tricks. She was appealing enough to generate income beyond the cigarettes and chump change of her childhood, although her existence was still filled with financial uncertainty.

The 1990 movie *Pretty Woman* depicts the story of a hooker who meets up with a wealthy businessman. He showers her with material goods, makes her over, and ultimately rescues her from a life on the streets. It's a romantic fairy tale that seems to bear little resemblance to reality. Surprisingly enough, a version of this scenario actually took place for Aileen. Hoping to attract a paying customer, or at least get a ride to a more desirable location, Aileen stuck out her thumb along a Florida highway in 1976. Lewis Getz Fell noticed the attractive woman and picked her up. During the ride, Lewis told Aileen about his background. She quickly became alert when she realized she had hit pay dirt. Fell was a wealthy businessman from a blue-blood background in need of companionship. But not just companionship, at 69, he was looking to share his life with someone on a permanent basis. Aileen was smart enough to offer a sanitized version of her current circumstances. Whatever she told him, Fell saw Aileen as a damsel in distress. He was willing to be the knight who came to rescue her, in spite of or perhaps because of their 50-year age difference.

Aileen got married at 20 in March 1976. Certainly Fell's money was a huge factor in her decision. He was president of a yacht club and owned valuable real estate and shares of railroad stock. Perhaps, he also represented the father figure she never had. Uncharacteristically, Aileen may also have seen this as a chance for respectability and stability. Whatever Fell was expecting must have caught him up short when his bride revealed her true colors: violent temper tantrums, physical altercations, and volatile mood swings. The May–December marriage lasted only a few months. In the Wuornos and Berry-Dee account, "Her husband promptly filed for divorce after she beat him with his walking stick and pointed a meat skewer close to his throat."[8] Aileen later laughed at her ex-husband and characterized him as a cheap old goat.

While Aileen may not have been emotionally upset with the dissolution of her marriage, she was totally distraught with the death of her brother Keith from cancer in the summer of 1976. Keith had been the closest person to her, a confidant, and one true friend. He accepted her as she was, without making judgments. Although she had minimal contact throughout the years with other family members, she never developed any significant connections with them. They often felt bullied and terrorized, especially when she threatened to physically harm them. Russell's book indicates that following a visit, Aileen's birth mother Diane stated, "I could see the violence in her and she frightened me to death."[9]

The next 10 years indeed reflected the violence in Aileen. Unable to establish lasting relationships, uninterested in complying with societal norms related to civility, and unwilling to follow rules related to law and order, Aileen embarked on a life of crime. Her outlaw existence took her from the highways of Colorado to Florida. Fueled by drugs and alcohol, she did whatever she wanted, when she wanted. She was fined for assault and battery, arrested for passing forged checks, charged with auto theft, and arrested for grand larceny.[10] In 1982, she robbed a store at gunpoint, memorably wearing a bikini as she brandished a .22 caliber pistol. Treating the incident as a comedic crime caper, Aileen thought she would be given probation. Instead, she received a three-year sentence. With little to do behind bars, Aileen passed time by reading the bible. The good book's message didn't seem to have much impact on her attitude, since she was written up six times for bad behavior. Whether she was seeking redemption or just looking for a way to keep busy, this embracing of the scriptures would portend her quest for spirituality later in life as she faced the death penalty.

Most criminals don't serve their full sentence and Aileen was no exception. Her stay in jail lasted only 18 months. During the next three years, she engaged in small-time criminal activity, drifting from one unsatisfying relationship to another. There were two new aspects of her persona. The first was the adoption of the nickname Lee. Its clipped androgynous nature was more in line with the image she wanted to project than the feminine, more graceful name of Aileen. The second was her proclaimed interest in women. Although Aileen had steered clear of lesbian activity in prison and roundly condemned it, she now told people she was gay. In 1986, while hanging out in a Florida biker bar, Aileen met the person who became the love of her life.

Twenty-four-year-old Tyria Moore seemed the antithesis of Aileen. At 30, Aileen was a loner with few social skills, whereas Ty was fun loving and gregarious. Aileen had a criminal record; Ty was a regular churchgoer. Aileen's brittle, dour nature alienated most people; Ty had a wide circle of friends and was close to her family. Aileen had a dark hostile attitude, while Ty seemed to embrace the world in an easygoing manner. Perhaps, it was a case where opposite personalities attracted one other. The two became lovers that night.

Although Aileen had initially told her girlfriend she was a drug dealer, Ty soon learned that Aileen supported herself through prostitution. Ty was nonjudgmental about the source of money. If Aileen chose to use sex with men as a way to make a living, it was no reflection whatsoever on their relationship. After all, money was money. The two settled into their version of domesticity. Aside from her relationship with her brother Keith, Aileen had never felt closer to anyone, indicating "It was love beyond imaginable. Earthly words cannot describe how I felt about Tyria."[11] Showering Aileen with affection, quietly listening as she opened up to share her feelings, respecting her vulnerability, and being emotionally supportive, it's easy to imagine that Ty made Aileen feel good about herself. The two often referred to each other as "my wife."

A pattern emerged over the years. More often than not, Ty would have steady, although low, paying employment, going to work at a set schedule every day. Aileen would lounge around in bed, finally getting up in the afternoon. She would leave to do a few tricks by posing as a hitchhiker, and then offer sex in return for money, usually $30–$100 depending on the act. When she returned, Ty would have cleaned up the place and made dinner. The two of them would then party throughout the night, whether alone or at bar. Not surprisingly, Aileen's habits eventually rubbed off on Ty. Sensing that her lover was jealous over time spent with others, Ty began to distance herself from family and friends. Since Aileen wanted Ty to be around more often, she cut back on the hours she worked. Without any steady income between the two, they often got evicted. The peripatetic couple was forced to move from one low-level dive to the next, causing Ty to be more aimless and Aileen became more belligerent. By this time, Aileen's brushes with the law included an arrest for grand larceny and carrying a concealed weapon. On December 1, 1989, she set in motion a series of events that transcended her previous record and brought her universal notoriety.

Richard Mallory was a white, middle-aged, electronics repair business owner on his way to Daytona when he spotted Aileen hitching a ride along the I-4 Florida highway. He stopped the car to let her in. The two drank beer and smoked some pot. When Aileen eventually offered to give him a blow job for $30, Richard agreed.[12] What actually happened next and why it happened is unknown. According to Aileen's account, he tried to torture and rape her. She had no recourse but to pull out the gun she carried for safety, shooting him four times. After she watched him die, she took the keys to his Cadillac and drove off. Hikers found Richard's naked body 10 days later. The police carried out an investigation, but with so few clues, they chalked his death off as an isolated murder.

If Aileen was traumatized by the event, she did not show it to Ty later that day. Instead, she coolly told her about the killing, showing off the automobile she now had. Aileen dumped the contents of Mallory's car at a pawnshop, abandoning the vehicle after carefully wiping off all of her fingerprints. Thus, a deadly pattern began that lasted for nearly a year.

From December 1989 through November 1990, Aileen picked up seven white, middle-aged men while she was hitchhiking. She ended up shooting each of them multiple times, and then drove off with their possessions. The victims included Mallory, David Spears, Charles Carskaddon, Peter Siems, Troy Burress, Dick Humphreys, and Walter Gino Antonio.[13] One man was a business owner, one a construction worker, one a rodeo worker, two were former police officers, one a part-time missionary, and one a sausage salesman.[14] Some were loners with shady pasts, others respected family men.

While police may have initially looked at Mallory's death as an isolated incident, it didn't take long for them to suspect some connection when corpses of white, middle-aged men who had been shot and robbed started showing up along the highways of Florida. The similarities between the killings caused authorities to wonder if a serial killer was operating. While they first hypothesized a male perpetrator, a startling thought occurred to them— what if it was a female? Although females account for less than 10 percent of serial killers, it was certainly conceivable that these cases could be attributed to a woman.[15] Police theorized that a female could have been posing on the side of the road in need of help.[16] The thought of a female perpetrator was bolstered by the fact that witnesses had seen two women driving the car of one of the victims after his body had been found.

Following her modus operandi, Aileen had taken Peter Siems's car after his death. She and Ty were using the car one day when they had an accident in it. Aileen was adamant that they just leave the car where it was. Although bystanders came to help out, Aileen refused all assistance. When police eventually found the abandoned car, they discovered both women's prints. In due time, sketches of the women were released to the media naming them as suspects in a series of murder cases. Hundreds of leads came pouring in after the sketches appeared in national newspapers and on television. During the last months of 1990, Ty told Aileen that she wanted to break up and went home to visit her family.

Although Aileen had used an alias when hocking the items belonging to her first victim Richard Mallory, her inked fingerprint was on the pawn ticket. This fingerprint matched the one in Siems's car. After pulling up Aileen's criminal record, they concluded that she was the mastermind behind the murders, not Ty. On January 9, 1991, Aileen was arrested at the Last Resort, a biker bar she frequented. Not wanting to tip their hand, they told the 34-year-old woman that she was wanted for illegal possession of a firearm, taking her into custody.

Police approached Ty a day later. Although she acknowledged knowing about the Mallory murder, Ty steadfastly denied her involvement in this or any of the other deaths. Given her limited options, she agreed to cooperate with authorities. In a series of orchestrated phone calls, Ty told her former girlfriend that she was afraid that she would end up taking the rap for Aileen's actions. Aileen was aghast. Despite their break up, Ty had meant the world to her. In a letter to Ty just days before her arrest, Aileen had written, "You're my left and right arm, my breath, I'd die for you."[17] Now over the phone, she assured Ty, "Honey, I wouldn't put your life in jeopardy. . . . You've never done a thing wrong in your life when you were with me. . . . I'm not gonna let you get in trouble."[18] On January 16, 1991, Aileen confessed.

Her first comments exonerated Ty. Then in a three-hour session filled with incoherent ramblings, self-pity, declarations of love for her girlfriend, and anger toward her victims, Aileen admitted to six killings. Her constant refrain throughout the meeting centered on how she had been the one to suffer and how she had acted to save herself. Claiming to have sex with over 250,000 men without any incidence, her excuse was that these particular strangers were either going to hurt her, kill her, or rape her.[19] The police doubted the story, but let her talk. Once she started talking, she would not stop—even when her appointed attorney suggested she keep quiet. Aileen had center stage, and she was not going to give it up. She ended her confession by indicating that she wanted to make her life right with Jesus. No one present believed her.

The next day, Aileen was charged with Richard Mallory's murder. As news of the confession spread around the police station, officers involved in the investigation smelled money. It's likely they considered Aileen a certified psychopath whose statements and chilling crime spree would capture the public's attention. Although she was not the first-known female serial killer, a lesbian prostitute who condemned her victims gained instant notoriety overnight. Within 3 weeks of Aileen's arrest, some of the officers approached Ty about a $2.5 million movie deal they had been offered.[20] Aileen was unaware of the potential deal and Ty's possible involvement. She was aware though of her own instant celebrity. As she awaited trial, newspapers were writing headlines about her, tabloids were interviewing former acquaintances, and her picture was plastered across television sets. Coauthors Roslyn Muraskin and Shelly Feuer Domash noted in *Crime and the Media* that a great deal of coverage centered on the fact that "She was a prostitute and a lesbian, two aspects of her life that made her more deviant in society's eyes and clashed with the social constructed role that women should fill of puritanical heterosexual wife and/or mother."[21] According to *Dead Ends,* a book written by Michael Reynolds, "The tabloid TV shows were quickest to respond— 'A Current Affair,' 'Inside Edition,' 'Hard Copy,' and 'Geraldo' was tailor made for their spin . . . Highway Hooker, Lesbian Killer, and Damsel of Death."[22] When a movie producer contacted her directly, Aileen agreed to sell her life story. Upon learning that she could not participate in any deals allowing her to profit, Aileen complained bitterly since she had bragged of making $3 million from the project.[23]

A bizarre turn of events added to the media spectacle with the involvement of a born-again Christian by the name of Arlene Pralle. Arlene had a background polar opposite from Aileen's sordid past. Still, Pralle claimed that Jesus urged her to reach out to the woman in jail. The two became pen pals and then regular visitors. Pralle eventually conducted interviews in Aileen's name, acting as her main cheerleader. She eventually formally made Aileen her daughter through adoption. One can only conjecture as to why Aileen agreed to the arrangement. Maybe she liked the attention or felt that she was finally getting the mother she never had. It's also possible that she was looking for a replacement to fill the emotional void left by Ty. By this time, Aileen had not spoken to her former girlfriend since the days leading up to her arrest and felt completely abandoned. She had learned that Ty had been pursuing her own production deal, causing Aileen to denounce Ty for mercenary interests. The two never spoke again. When news of the adoption became public, one can assume that many saw it as a sick publicity stunt. Pralle's round of appearances on talk shows only added to the cynical frenzy.

As Aileen sat in jail, lawyers from both sides had tried to agree on a plea bargain. When it fell through, the case went forward in January 1992, one year after Aileen's arrest. Although the prosecution tried her only for Richard Mallory's murder, their strategy was to introduce evidence of the other killings as well. This was permissible in Florida under the William's Rule. From the law's perspective, it was easy to depict Aileen as an evil, cold-blooded killer with an established pattern of deliberately murdering her victims, and then robbing them. If convicted, she faced either life imprisonment or the electric chair.

The prosecution witness that most people were interested in hearing from was Ty. Once on the stand, Ty made it clear that while Aileen had told her about the murder right after it occurred, she did not disclose that Mallory had raped her. Aileen wept as she listened to her lover's statement most likely feeling that Ty had truly sold her out. Jurors also heard evidence provided by the prosecution team that linked Aileen to the deaths of David Spears who was shot six times, Charles Carskaddon who was shot nine times, Dick Humphreys who was shot seven times, Walter Gino Antonio who was shot four times, and Peter Siems whose body was never recovered.[24] The most riveting aspect of the prosecution was the introduction of Aileen's confession. Trimmed down from its three-hour length, jury members watched a chilling videotape of Aileen acknowledging that she had killed Mallory. In her account of events, she showed no remorse whatsoever for the deed.

Sentiment appeared to be stacked against Aileen when she actually took the stand. As the only witness for the defense, she had been determined to have her day in court. After discussing her troubled upbringing, she launched into her familiar version of events. She embellished the story with sordid and violent details of how Mallory had tied her to the steering wheel, forced her to have anal sex, attempted to torture her by throwing alcohol in her rectum, beat and choked her, and then threatened to kill her.[25] The jury did not buy it. In less than two hours, they came back with a guilty verdict. Consumed with anger, Aileen lashed out, "Sons of bitches! I was raped. I hope you get raped! Scumbags of America!"[26] During the penalty phase, she was sentenced to die.

Many expected Aileen to demand a trial for the other murder charges that were brought against her. Instead, in a surprise move, she chose to plead no contest, resulting in additional death sentences. There were a number of troubling issues surrounding her case that played out in the media. The first issue revolved around the movie deal involving the police officers. Their race to capitalize on her notoriety shortly after her arrest was irregular at best, unethical at worst. Aileen maintained that law enforcement was in a conspiracy against her. The second issue centered on Aileen's claim that Mallory was a sexual predator who caused her to kill him in self-defense. As it turned out, there may have been truth to Aileen's story. Nearly a year after the trial, the television show *Dateline* revealed that Mallory had served time for attempted rape and assault. Unfortunately for Aileen's case, the event had occurred 30 years before their encounter and the Florida court denied her appeal.

The most troubling aspect of Aileen's case centered on whether she was mentally competent enough to be executed. In appeal documents, it was noted that during the sentencing phase of her trial, three defense psychologists concluded that Aileen suffered from borderline personality disorder and brain damage.[27] When examining her troubled life, one can observe classic textbook signs of psychopathology including juvenile delinquency, poor behavior control, pathological lying, lack of remorse or guilt, manipulation, and the failure to accept responsibility for her actions.[28] Clearly, her horrific childhood led to some of these characteristics. The philosopher John Locke espoused the theory that it is our experience that forms our character. Humans enter the world in a blank state; whether they become saints or sinners depends on their environment. One has to wonder if her life would have been different if she had been in an early atmosphere that offered love and support. Who knows what it took to set off the coil of rage that resided within? Perhaps, it was the memory of all the men who had treated her badly from the father who abandoned her, the grandfather who abused her, the boys who taunted her during childhood, and the failed relationships with men. Certainly, Aileen had her supporters, ranging from her adoptive mother Arlene Pralle to anticapital punishment groups. Even the noted feminist writer Phyllis Chesler weighed in. Her article "A Woman's Right to Self Defense: The Case of Aileen Carol Wuornos" stated, "Everyone in Wuornos life . . . conspired through acts of commission, omission, indifference and negligence, to deprive Wuornos of the most minimal justice."[29]

Aileen remained in the spotlight while she sat on death row for 10 years. At first, she kept a high profile due to general media interest of her troubled life. Entertainment programming as well as hundreds of websites often depicted her as either a raging man-hating maniac or a feminist hero acting out of self-defense in the Thelma and Louise mold. A made-for-TV movie was rushed into production shortly after the trial. This was followed by television episodes of *American Justice,* Court TV, and *Biography.*[30] Both a play and opera presented a version of her life.

Perhaps the most compelling portrait of her life came from a series of documentaries in which she participated. Nick Broomfield released *Aileen Wuornos: The Selling of a Serial Killer* (1993), followed by *Aileen: Life and Death of a Serial Killer* (2003). Aileen takes center stage as she rails against everyone whom she feels exploited her. Particular bitterness was directed toward the attorney she said had coerced her into making the no-contest plea as well as her adoptive mother, denouncing both as publicity hounds (together they demanded a $25,000 interview fee, but settled for $10,000 from Broomfield). Her anger was also focused on the criminal justice system for handing out a death sentence, and then for keeping her alive. Broomfield's interviews depict a complex woman of shifting moods. She could be articulate and likable one minute, filled with hatred and contempt the next. Ever constant was her boastful nature coupled with thinly veiled rage. Playing directly to the camera, she admitted killing the men out of hatred, and then fell back on her old story of self-defense in the case of each death.

Aileen eventually petitioned the court to cancel all her appeals and asked for the right to die—a request ultimately granted. In an article entitled "New Documentary Deepens 'Monster' exploration," reporter Phil Villarreal wrote, "days before her death, Wuornos was nearly a basket case, claiming that her brain was being controlled by sound waves, that her food was poisoned, and that mirrors were really computers surveilling her."[31] At 44 years of age, on October 9, 2002, the convicted woman was executed by lethal injection.

Throughout her disturbing life, Aileen craved fame and fortune. Hoping to impress an acquaintance, she once stated, "I'm gonna do something no woman has ever done before and everybody will respect me."[32] Thanks to the "cult of Aileen Wuornos," she seems to have gotten her wish.

Crazy. It's one of those words with a wide range of connotations, many of them principally positive. In the 1950s, _crazy_ was slang for good, interesting, or cool. Shortly after that, the term became widely used as a descriptor for being in love, as in Willie Nelson's love song "Crazy," made popular by Patsy Cline in 1961, and "Crazy 'Bout You, Baby" by Tina Turner during that same period. This meaning has endured, showing up in songs like Madonna's "Crazy for You" (1985), Beyonce's "Crazy in Love" (2003), and the country album "Call Me Crazy" by Lee Ann Womack (2008). Similar musings can be found in songs like "Hopelessly Devoted to You" by Olivia Newton John (1978) and the classic 1960s ballad "Goin' Out of My Head Over You." In this context, women confess that they're crazy, but the underlying message is that what they are most committed to—what dictates all their actions—is the love they feel for a particular partner, one who may not love them back. _Crazy_ can also indicate being wild, imaginative, eccentric, fun, passionate, and outrageous, albeit harmless. This is what Steve Martin and Dan Aykroyd meant in their 1970s _Saturday Night Live_ skit when they referred to themselves as "two wild and crazy guys."

Moving down the connotative scale, we find _crazy_ as synonymous with demented—being completely unreasonable. In a similar vein, the word is also used to describe a person or an act that is seen as weird, foolish, unwise, or senseless. The phrase "crazy like a fox" is based on this meaning, but implies that a person has the _appearance_ of acting foolishly while actually being quite sly, cunning, and tactical. In the most negative sense of the word, _crazy_ means disturbed, unbalanced, threatening, even fanatical, insane, mad, and dangerous. For this type of crazy, there is no understanding, no benign amusement, no sympathy, and no compassion. Aileen Wuornos was considered to be _this_ type of crazy.

It is evident that Aileen Wuornos _was_ influenced by certain media images. In her last statement before her execution, she cites a popular Will Smith film, likening herself to a group of aliens who invade the earth: "I'll be back like _Independence Day_ with Jesus, June 6, like the movie, big mothership and all. . . . I'll be back."[33] As far as media influence on the general public in the Wuornos case, the most profound effects most likely came not from depictions of serial killers, but from those of mental illness.

In the 1982 film _Frances,_ in which Jessica Lange plays troubled, real-life actress Frances Farmer, the heroine is portrayed as a hard-headed rebel whose increasing dependence on alcohol leads her to a nervous breakdown. Although she is eventually institutionalized, she steadfastly refuses to believe she is mentally ill. "If a person is treated like a patient," she declares, "they are apt to act like one." The film questions the accuracy of dubbing a strong woman's antisocial behavior as "mental illness." *Crimes of Passion,* a film released two years later, tells the story of Joanna Crane, a prostitute with intimacy issues who turns tricks indiscriminately, regardless of their gender or sexual proclivity. One of her clients, a deranged "reverend" named Shayne, becomes increasingly obsessed with her. In one of the final scenes, Joanna's boyfriend arrives at her apartment to find her cowering in the closet. But when the real Joanna emerges, dressed as Shayne, the boyfriend discovers that the figure in the closet is actually Shayne, dressed as Joanna. Both characters, it turns out, are not only completely amoral, but are also mentally unhinged. Frances, Joanna, and Aileen are all points on a continuum of questionable mental stability. Our hearts go out to Frances because although she is defiant, she is not immoral. Johanna is less sympathetic because she has questionable sexual morals. Aileen, a "man-hating lesbian prostitute," generates zero sympathy.

In 1988, Stephen King's psychological horror novel *Misery* won the World Fantasy Award for Best Novel. The story features Annie Wilkes, a former nurse who finds writer Paul Sheldon injured in a car crash near her home. Proclaiming herself as his "number one fan," she takes him back to her house, where she can nurture him back to health. But Annie doesn't like the way Paul's latest manuscript reads. She becomes angered to the point of cutting off his foot with an axe, cauterizing it with a blowtorch, amputating his thumb, and gruesomely killing a state trooper who comes to investigate. It turns out that Annie is, in fact, a psychotic serial killer—not exactly a poster girl for the cause of mental illness. No attempt is made to investigate the cause of Annie's mental illness. Consequently, the characterization connects mental illness with violent amorality, rather than unfortunate but explicable misperceptions.

When killers are portrayed as mentally ill, the condition is often coupled with sexual promiscuity, gender confusion, or sexual orientation ambiguity. In the award-winning 1958 film *I Want to Live,* Susan Hayward plays real-life prostitute, drug addict, perjurer, and convicted murderer Barbara Graham, a nonmainstream character with few sympathetic or redeeming qualities. The following year came Robert Bloch's novel *Psycho,* in which mentally deranged Norman Bates commits murders, dressed as and believing himself to be his dead mother, reinforcing the notion that people with questionable gender identities may have a proclivity for murder. The book, subsequently adapted by Alfred Hitchcock into a classic horror movie, spawned other projects associating homicide with gender issues. In the 1980 film *Dressed to Kill,* psychiatrist Robert Elliott (played by Michael Caine) murders women, disguising himself as a woman. At the end of the film, a "real psychologist" explains that Elliott's transgender alter ego, Bobbi, killed because she became threatened when Elliott was attracted to women. In this case, a presumed authority on mental illness presents a logical argument for the association between homosexuality—represented by Bobbi—and violent rage resulting in murder. That same year came a screen adaptation of Gerald Walker's 1971 novel *Cruising,* in which a New York policeman, Steve Burns, goes undercover to try and track down who is responsible for a wave of brutal killings of gay men. After a suspect is arrested and the mystery is believed to be solved, the end suggests that the real killer was actually the police detective himself, confused about his own sexual identity. The coupling of homosexuality with murder again delivers an underlying message that alternative sexual preferences often go hand in hand with social deviance. Such images may easily have paved the way for the unquestioned vilification of Aileen Wuornos.

In each of these projects, the mentally ill character is not merely troubled. He or she is dishonest and evil, conspicuously lacking in moral fiber. The portrayals further attribute those negative qualities to those with alternative sexual or gender orientations. Rather than evoking sympathy and compassion, these characters are hard for "normal people" to relate to, allowing us to feel that they may be more deserving of punishment than of help. Those performances served to set the stage for the main act, the real-life trial of Aileen Wuornos.

There was no question that Wuornos had committed the murders; she even confessed. The judgment to be made by the jurors, and subsequently sanctioned by the public, was simply what constituted an appropriate penalty for her actions. That determination could only be made by evaluating the various traits that defined her character. Wuornos was unrepentant. Having a female lover defined her as gay, putting her on par with the promiscuous Joanna Crane, and the sexually confused Steve Burns. Like Barbara Graham, she was a prostitute, and in light of inconsistencies in her testimony, a perjurer. She was a predator, every bit as dangerous as Norman Bates, as malicious as Robert Elliott, as deadly as Annie Wilkes. The public was all too familiar with this type of killer. Wuornos deserved to die, and the fact that she accepted that sentence willingly confirmed its legitimacy. Now Aileen Wuornos is remembered as a deranged, psychopathic lesbian who showed no pity or remorse for her brutal crimes. She is thought of, at best, as sad and pathetic—at worst, as malevolent and evil. Her legacy in American culture is that of being one of the most well-known, genuine, bona fide "female serial killers."

ANDREA YATES

Andrea Yates had a secret—a dark secret that was terrifying. It's easy to imagine how the secret could leave her anxious at night and fill her with dread throughout the day. Satan talked to Andrea. According to Suzanne O'Malley's book *Are You There Alone,* Andrea felt she was possessed.[34] Satan talked to Andrea. He whispered that she was a bad mother, unfit to take care of her children. She deserved to be punished because of her evilness.

Andrea kept the secret quiet until she was locked up in jail, charged with the murder of her four sons and baby daughter. Before the killings, Andrea had been in and out of mental hospitals, tried to commit suicide multiple times, and was taking powerful drugs to help her control her anxiety.[35] Despite the ministrations of health-care professionals, no one recognized that Andrea suffered a severe form of postpartum psychosis. By the time she finally told people about the voices, it was too late. This Texas housewife became the center of a heartrending case, dividing public opinion and raising concerns over the failure of the American health-care system.

When Andrea Kennedy married Rusty Yates in 1993, she knew she wanted to have lots of children. After all, she had grown up in a large Catholic family, enjoying the camaraderie of her four siblings. Large families can have many benefits—you always have playmates, you are never alone, you learn to share, and there is always something going on in terms of daily activities. Because everyone often has to pull their own weight, a person from a large family is often self-reliant; Andrea was no exception. She was always considered the serious one. This may have come from her background as a competitive swimmer in high school, a pursuit that requires drive and focus. Houston, Texas, where Andrea grew up may have had lots of larger-than-life characters, but Andrea wasn't one of them. The pretty teenager observed things quietly, concentrating on doing whatever task was at hand. She wasn't the type to stand out in a crowd. Instead, she was viewed as a nice, responsible person, possessing a maturity that many individuals her age lacked. Hard work and intellectual ability led to high-school academic honors. Her goal was to earn a college degree in a field that would allow her to help people. After graduation, she became a nurse at a leading cancer treatment center. This occupation seemed like the perfect choice for a young woman with a calm, compassionate manner.

While not quite the girl next door, Andrea lived in the same apartment building as Rusty Yates, a NASA engineer. Both were the same age. When the two started dating, she made it clear early on in the relationship that she had traditional values. This included not drinking and no sex before marriage. Fortunately, Rusty accepted her moral conviction presumably because they shared a similar worldview.

Like Andrea, Rusty had also been a smart, high-school athlete motivated by discipline. The teen with a sense of purpose became even more serious after his father died. While going to college, Rusty became close to Michael Woroniecki, a travelling minister espousing a message of fire and brimstone. It's possible that the preacher became a father substitute although Rusty did not accept the minster's more extreme statements. Rusty arranged a meeting for Andrea to learn about the man who had been so important in his life.

It's easy to imagine how Andrea wanted her boyfriend's mentor to like her and willingly accepted Woroniecki's moralistic pronouncements. The young couple remained in touch with the preacher throughout the next decade, a decision that had disastrous results for Andrea.

Rusty and Andrea dated for a couple of years. The two often spent time engaged in prayer, presumably discussing how to live a good Christian life according to biblical precepts. Young love eventually overcame religious constraints when Rusty convinced Andrea to live with him in 1992. A year later, they were married. Given their desire to start a family as soon as possible, the Yates were most likely thrilled upon learning that Andrea was pregnant.[36] Their son Noah was born in 1994. The tradition of giving their children religious names became a common motif over the years. Andrea quit her job to be a stay-at-home mother. Shortly after Noah's birth, she later claimed that she had a disturbing vision of a knife appearing to be stabbing away at an unidentified person.[37] It is quite possible that Andrea thought the vision was an aberration brought on by normal sleep deprivation typically suffered by new mothers. Whatever triggered the image, she preferred to keep any fears to herself. Taking care of the baby kept her days and nights busy. She became even busier with the birth of her second son John in 1995, merely 10 months later.

Now she had two children in diapers. Most parental duties belonged to Andrea. Knowing her traditional views, one can assume that she willingly accepted the responsibilities. To make more hours in the day, she spent less time with friends, less time exercising, less time on activities for herself.[38] Her sense of self-sacrifice became even more apparent in 1996. She and Rusty decided to take advantage of a job opportunity in Florida for six months. Announcing that it would be fun to eschew traditional living accommodations during this period, Rusty proposed living in a 38-foot trailer. Andrea went along with the decision. Upon their return to Texas, they took up permanent residence in a bus formerly belonging to Rusty's spiritual mentor. Although customized for living quarters, the bus was quite removed from the Yates former 2,000-square-foot home. Still, Andrea appeared to take the move away from suburbia all in stride. Downsizing with fewer possessions reflected a more spiritual living experience that repudiated a consumer-driven existence. In a way, the Yates were part of the voluntary simplicity movement—a lifestyle trend originated in the 1980s that espoused scaling back on possessions, living with less, and being more frugal.

By 1998, at 35, Andrea had two more children, Paul and Luke. It appeared that she was delighted with her growing family. The busy mother planned birthday parties for the kids, encouraged them in imaginative activities, and spent hours playing with them. Andrea was never too tired to answer their questions or read them another bedtime story, even if she had told it dozens of times before. The endless laundry of diapers, socks, and dirty little boy

T-shirts didn't seem to bother her. She was always ready with a hug to comfort a crying child or kisses to let them know how much she loved them. In *Breaking Point,* author Suzy Spencer wrote that friends admired Andrea's parental abilities with one recalling, "She was the most devoted, dedicated mother I have ever seen. . . . She wasn't selfish at all."[39] However, one wonders if trying to be the perfect mother was taking a toll.

On June 17, 1999, it was quite clear that Andrea was not fine. She tried to kill herself by taking an overdose of 40 pills. Doctors treating her learned that she had been suffering from classic signs of depression that include problems sleeping and eating, lack of energy, loss of interest in daily activities, and feelings of hopelessness.[40] But Andrea was not willing to open up about the crushing despair causing these symptoms. Instead, almost apologetically, she minimized what happened, acting as if she had just overreacted to a bad day. Zoloft, an antidepressant drug, was prescribed, and she was discharged within a week. A week happened to be the maximum time the Yates health-care insurance would cover. Sadly, Andrea tried to slit her throat a mere three weeks after her first suicide attempt.

Not surprisingly, when Andrea returned home yet again, she had difficulty resuming her daily activities. She seemed detached from the new baby. The other children didn't seem to exist. Rusty noticed that she made little attempt to engage him in conversation. Possibly in an attempt to stop her inner anguish, Andrea had begun cutting herself. Not content with the pain inflicted on her arms and legs, she also scratched at her scalp until it was bleeding. When she wasn't just staring into space, Andrea seemed to be moving about as if in a fog. Unbeknownst to her husband, she stopped taking the antidepressants. Without the calming effects of the pills, it is quite likely that she felt waves of hopelessness. Worse yet, she started to hallucinate. Charles Montaldo wrote an article entitled "Profile of Andrea Yates," which noted that Andrea thought there were video cameras in the ceilings and characters on television talking to her.[41] Overcome with anxiety, she grabbed a knife and told Rusty she wanted to die. The next day, he took her to the hospital.

This time Andrea opened up to the doctors. She told them of being frightened by violent thoughts. O'Malley's account reported her telling a hospital psychologist, "I had a fear I would hurt somebody. . . . I thought it was better to end my own life and prevent it (from happening)."[42] It was apparent that Andrea was suffering from postpartum psychosis. Her medications were increased, and electroconvulsive therapy was suggested. Andrea adamantly said no to the shock treatment. She stayed in the hospital for nearly three weeks. Between the new medication, the increased psychiatric attention, and the respite from her daily responsibilities, it did seem that Andrea was improving.

Andrea's mother was well aware that her daughter's depression was not to be treated lightly. Although not openly discussed, three family members were also suffering from the disease.[43] She had been the one to find Andrea after the first suicide attempt. Learning that her daughter had recently tried to kill herself yet again must have caused her profound sorrow. Expressing concern over Andrea's fragile state of mind, she urged Rusty to buy a house; his wife could not be expected to continue living in a bus with four small children. Agreeing that a lifestyle change might be good for Andrea, he purchased a three-bedroom suburban home. Reflecting their emphasis on family, the Yates put up a plaque in their new home stating, "Blessed are the Children."

The move seemed to lift Andrea's spirits. She reached out to former friends. Taking advantage of a nearby pool, she began swimming laps again. Once too shy to approach other mothers, she now sought them out on park visits with her children. Attempting to hasten his wife's recovery, Rusty made an effort to be more supportive. Instead of parking himself in front of the television set, he rounded up the boys for a game of T-ball. On some evenings, he would lead the family in Bible study discussions. He designated "Mommy Night," so his wife could have time for herself. Wanting to provide an environment that affirmed traditional values, Andrea and Rusty decided to homeschool their children. Sitting at the kitchen table, she would spend hours developing curriculum focusing on religious or moral themes.

In time, Andrea felt well enough to talk about discontinuing her medication. She also talked about having another baby. Doctors had warned the couple against both of these ideas. Health-care professionals are keenly aware of dangers befalling patients who stop taking prescribed drugs out of a sense of false wellness. It is also well documented that women with postpartum depression in a previous pregnancy are 50 percent more likely to get it a second time.[44] Undeterred, the Yates ignored the advice. Andrea had a fifth child, Mary, in November 2000.

Caring for a new baby and balancing the demands of four other children would be difficult for any mother. Andrea faced these challenges as well as other mitigating factors. By March 2001, she had been off her medication for over a year and had stopped visiting her psychiatrist, becoming out of touch with medical professionals. Anxiety often prevented Andrea from sleeping. Adding to the strain was the death of her father after a seven-year bout of Alzheimer's disease. She had been his primary caretaker. It must have been agonizing watching him descend into his own twilight world in spite of the quality nursing care she provided. One can imagine her feeling frustrated and inadequate. There was another disturbing element that troubled her mind. Andrea believed that the devil was behind her earlier collapse. Hoping to overcome any satanic influence, she once again spent excessive time reading the Bible. She never shared her fears with her husband.

Andrea may have been uncommunicative, but Rusty was still astute enough to know his wife was in crisis. He took her to the hospital where she was admitted for a psychotic breakdown. O'Malley noted in her account that while Andrea was unresponsive most of the time, she did tell staff, "I am not a good mother."[45] Unfortunately, she was unwilling or unable to elaborate on why she felt this way. A great deal of the discussion from doctors regarding her treatment once again centered on which medications to prescribe. In the past, she had been on Effexor XR, Haldol, Cogentin, Wellbutrin, Zoloft, and Zyprexa; another antipsychotic drug, Risperdal, was added to the mix.[46] Knowing that Andrea had a habit of refusing her pills, the hospital staff constantly monitored her to ensure she was taking them. However, no one commented on the irony when she was also assigned to drug-addiction sessions.

Convinced that Andrea had been "stabilized," health-care professionals were ready to discharge her in 10 days. Her husband was uncertain. Spencer's account reports that at a group therapy session the night before her release, Rusty had noted to himself that, "Andrea is the sickest person in here."[47] By this time, Andrea had seen a great deal of doctors, nurses, psychiatrists, and social workers. While they all noted her bouts of severe depression and psychotic state, none of them ever raised concerns that Andrea could harm someone. Instead, their fear was that she would succumb to continued suicidal tendencies, causing them to release her on the condition that she would not try to harm or kill herself.[48]

Rusty had made arrangements for his mother Dora to come over in the mornings. It is likely that he felt Dora's presence might lessen Andrea's anxiety about taking care of the family. Her mother-in-law could help with the daily chores of cooking, cleaning, and keeping the children occupied. One day, Dora found Andrea filling a bathtub with water for no apparent reason. This odd fact, coupled with her recurring refusal to eat, sent Andrea back to the hospital. It was her fourth admittance within a two-year period. In less than 14 days, she was released with a supply of Haldol and antidepressants. One wonders how much effort doctors made in understanding Andrea's illness, especially after she was told a month later that she could discontinue the Haldol. Without the Haldol, Andrea spiraled into a dark morass of inner madness. Her madness proved to be fatal.

Andrea's tenuous grasp on reality disintegrated over the next month. She was now under the disturbing belief that Satan had been communicating directly to her that she was a bad mother who needed to be punished—not just bad, but wicked.[49] According to Andrea, the devil taunted her, claiming that her personal failings as a parent were corrupting Noah, John, Paul, Luke, and Mary. This faulty thinking led her to conclude that in order to be saved, the children would have to die.[50]

The morning of June 20, 2001, started out in a normal fashion. Andrea prepared breakfast as usual to avoid arousing any suspicion. Once Rusty left for work around 9, she knew there was only a short window of opportunity before her mother-in-law arrived at 10. Heading into the bathroom, Andrea claimed she remembered Satan's jeering vituperations. His sinister comments regarding the children most likely echoed in her mind while she filled the tub nearly to the top.

Each child was brought into the bathroom and submerged into the tub: three-year-old Paul, two-year-old Luke, five-year-old John, six-month-old Mary, and seven-year-old Noah. One by one, they were drowned. Andrea removed Paul, Luke, John, and Mary from their watery grave, depositing the corpses on a bed to be covered with a sheet; she left Noah in the tub.[51] She made calls to 911 and her husband telling them to come quickly because she had done something to the children.[52] Andrea neglected to mention she had drowned them in less than an hour.

When police arrived, the 36-year-old mother led them to a grizzly sight. Spencer's account in *Breaking Point* indicates they found "four dead babies, their garments drenched, their bodies warm, their eyes wide open."[53] An officer later testified that he saw white, frothy substance coming from three of the victims' noses and mouths, indicating their lungs had burst.[54] The entire scene, with its combination of horror and poignancy, left the police reeling in disbelief. Andrea herself seemed inured to the grim situation. She appeared lucid and coolly detached, while she answered questions. By the time Rusty arrived at the house nine minutes later, the police already had her confession. Andrea had not only admitted to the murders, but also revealed that she had been thinking of carrying out the deed for two years.

Reporters quickly descended on the area with notebooks in hand and cameras ready to roll. Local spectators milled around attempting to find out what happened. Whispers of multiple dead children were at odds with the tranquil suburban setting and the image residents had of Andrea as an unassuming, quiet woman. A makeshift memorial filled with stuffed animals, flowers, and candles quickly sprung up on the Yates lawn, an outpouring of love and grief for the young lives that had been brutally ended.

Locked up in custody on charges of capital murder, Andrea was placed on suicide watch. Her mental stability came into question almost immediately as her behavior dramatically deteriorated. The stoic demeanor she initially displayed at the scene of the crime was replaced by catatonic muteness or incoherent bizarre ramblings related to Satan, a prophecy, and the ability of George W. Bush to overthrow the devil for her. Andrea was convinced that the number 666 was on her head, a biblical allusion to evil signifying the mark of the beast. According to Revelations, those with that mark would be tormented forever, with no rest day or night. This certainly seemed to describe Andrea. During the ensuing weeks, she continued to tell prison officials that she was possessed. She also revealed for the first time the full extent of the voices she had been hearing as well as the hallucinations. Health-care professionals interacting with her saw firsthand her psychosis.

Although racked with grief by the death of his children, Rusty did not blame his spouse. He blamed her doctors for failing to rescue Andrea from the chaos of insanity her mind had succumbed to. The day after the murders, he held a press conference on his front lawn. A portrait was in his hands. The picture showed a beaming, attractive Andrea next to her husband. Their four young sons, dressed in their best clothes and each wearing a big smile, surrounded the couple. Rusty spoke of his wife as a remarkable woman whose struggles with depression he shared. The woman who had committed the murders was not the same woman he knew and loved. Filled with emotion, he vowed to stand by her, pledging his support.

Andrea would need it. Texas is considered a "hang me high" state, allowing the death penalty when multiple murders occur or when the murdered victim is under 10 years of age. Harris County, where the trial was held, was known as the death-penalty capital of the United States. Prosecuting attorneys decided to depict Andrea as the worst type of cold-blooded murderer who systematically chose the most heinous way to strike back at a nonsupportive husband. Tales of depression and delusions did not justify her actions. Many of the general public felt the same way, as sensational news coverage revealed heartrending details about the children's murders.

No sooner had Andrea been whisked to the police station following her arrest than widespread cries of revulsion spread throughout the country. Accusations of selfishness and lack of accountability were immediately leveled against her. She was roundly criticized for having five children in the first place. The general sentiment was that if Andrea felt so overwhelmed and so inadequate as a mother, she should have stopped popping out kids like a rabbit. When rumors were falsely spread that Andrea was pregnant again, airwaves resounded with further condemnation. How could a woman who so clearly was incapable of handling children continue to reproduce?

Dateline and *Today* quickly rushed into production television shows addressing Andrea's case as well as issues surrounding postpartum depression. Still, many viewers struggled to understand how Andrea could kill one child, let alone five in such a methodological brutal fashion. Brian Wise, the author of the article "The Case against Compassion: Andrea Yates," stated, "Unless she is forced into a tub of water and her lungs fill with water until she dies, Andrea cannot possibly suffer enough."[55] To others, she represented a fundamentalist nutcase to be derided for her subservient passivity and religious zealousness.

Although he appeared on *Good Morning America* as a grieving, supportive husband shortly after the murders, Rusty came into his own fair share of criticism. Did he purposely keep Andrea barefoot and pregnant for years, forcing her to live in a cramped bus, isolated emotionally from friends and family? If so, this conservative viewpoint would naturally rankle parts of the country both geographically and culturally removed from the Bible belt. Fingers were pointed at Rusty accusing him of being controlling at best, abusive at worst. Hostile comments suggested that he was also criminally responsible for the atrocity. Although the district attorney opened an investigation against Rusty, it never went anywhere.

Extensive magazine attention thrust the Yates into the spotlight. *Newsweek* issued a cover with the blaring headline, " 'I Killed My Children' What Made Andrea Yates Snap?"[56] *Oprah* magazine also featured an in-depth portrait of Andrea's struggles. These articles helped spark a public dialogue raising awareness over the prevalence and devastation of postpartum depression. Singer Marie Osmond, long known for her squeaky clean image as one of "America's sweethearts," came forward to share her own experience with the disorder and offer supportive words to Andrea. Rosie O'Donnell, a popular talk show host at the time, also discussed her bouts of depression, while expressing sympathy for Andrea.

Upon learning more of the facts, popular sentiments began to shift. A growing sector of the public had empathy for the woman now sitting behind bars. While they did not condone her actions, their hearts went out to someone who until that fateful day had been seen as an exemplary mother. Research indicates that up to 85 percent of women suffer from baby blues, while 7–13 percent suffer from postpartum depression.[57] Given this, it's not surprising that many women could relate to Andrea's sense of helplessness. They were more than willing to donate money to the Yates legal defense fund, which had been established after the airing of coverage provided by Katie Couric on the *Today Show*. Feminists attempted to put the case in the context of a larger picture, providing a rationale for Andrea's actions by asking what took her to this place. They were also quick to condemn a health-care system that utterly failed an individual who so clearly needed help. In a press release for NOW, the president of the organization announced, "We hope a broader discussion about the mental health issues involved may prevent a similar tragedy in the future, and may increase the help available to other families coping with such a crisis before it turns deadly."[58]

With over 1,100 articles published on the case just one month after Andrea had been arrested, it's not surprising media interest continued to build.[59] When the trial began in February 2002, reporters descended like locusts on the courthouse. By this time, two distinctive camps had emerged in both the legal and public debate. Was Andrea a sinner who deserved the death sentence or a sick woman deserving of compassion?

Andrea's lawyers, led by George Putnam, decided to pursue a strategy of not guilty due to mental insanity. In "The Insanity Defense," an article discussing the history of the landmark M'Naughton edict of 1843, Charles Montaldo reported that "a person was not legally insane unless he is 'incapable of appreciating his surroundings' because of a powerful mental delusion."[60] From their perspective, Andrea's documented case of psychosis prevented her from being held responsible for criminal conduct. During the nearly four weeks of the trial, both sides of attorneys focused on whether or not Andrea had planned the murders in advance and if she truly knew what she had done.

The most damning piece of evidence was Andrea's confession. The fact that she had instigated the phone call to the police, and then calmly explained what happened once officers arrived, painted a chilling picture of someone completely aware of her actions. Jurors heard Andrea tell investigators that she had been having thoughts of hurting her children for two years and that she wanted the criminal justice system to punish her.[61] The case against Andrea was also strengthened when a noted forensic psychiatrist for the prosecution testified. He speculated that she might have seen an episode on the popular television show *Law and Order,* which depicted a woman who had been set free after claiming insanity when she drowned her children in a bathtub.[62]

The defense centered on Andrea's mental illness and troubled state of mind. Psychiatric experts noted that she had been paranoid as well as delusional before the murders took place and after she was locked up. This seemed to indicate that she had not known her actions were wrong.[63] Her hallucinations, schizophrenia, and severe depression were brought up as mitigating factors.[64] This seemed to indicate that she had not known her actions were wrong on the day of the murders. After hearing both sides of the case, on March 16, 2002, the jury brought back a verdict of guilty. However, they chose not to impose the death penalty. This was due in part to learning that the testimony regarding the *Law and Order* episode was false—it never existed. Instead, Andrea was sentenced to life imprisonment and would be eligible for parole in 40 years.

While public reaction to the verdict continued to be polarized, Internet and television polls showed most people preferred to see Andrea behind bars rather than executed. Rusty vowed to remain a champion for his wife, indicating that he would still stand by her. Advocating that she be given treatment, he and Andrea's lawyers stated there would be an appeal. By the time Andrea's conviction had been overturned in 2005 and a new trial scheduled for 2006, three major changes had occurred affecting her life. The first was that Rusty had actually sought a divorce and remarried. The second was a broader understanding of postpartum depression. The well-known actress Brooke Shields wrote a searing account of her experience after the birth of her daughter that soared to the best-seller list. When the superstar Tom Cruise criticized Brooke on the *Today Show,* suggesting that she should have chosen exercise to control her illness, he was roundly condemned by millions of women and suffered a huge drop in popularity. The third change was a shift in legal perspectives. Several prominent cases, including some in Texas, occurred where women who had killed their children had been found not guilty by reason of insanity. Andrea and her attorneys were so hopeful justice would prevail that she turned down a plea bargain of 35 years. This time on July 26, 2006, she was found not guilty. But Andrea could not walk away free. At 42, she was committed to a state mental hospital until doctors felt she was recovered. No one could predict when that would be.

Andrea disappeared quietly to receive treatment. The topic of mental illness and postpartum depression received national attention again with the success of the wildly popular television series *Desperate Housewives.* It seemed that creator Mark Cherry conceived of the show after he and his mother watched Andrea's second trial. When he asked his mother if she could imagine a woman so desperate she would hurt her own children, she replied, "Yeah, I've been there."[65]

At first glance, one would think that Andrea Yates was a less sympathetic defendant than Aileen Wuornos. After all, Wuornos had no emotional connection to her victims—they were men she didn't even know, although she alleged they were trying to harm her. Yates's victims, on the other hand, posed no conceivable threat to her. She killed her own, defenseless children. Neither person was in her right mind when committing the acts. Yet, Yates's state of mind was ultimately deemed a reason to acquit her, while Wuornos was convicted and executed. What accounts for this improbable turn of events?

Andrea Yates was diagnosed with postpartum depression, a clinical state lasting up to several months that is thought to affect a considerable percentage of women after giving birth. It is generally attributed to hormonal imbalance, although hormone treatment has not been found to help those who suffer from the condition. When it comes to judging a mentally impaired person's culpability, one of the operative words in describing her mental status is "state." The temporary nature of the condition renders it different from psychological trauma that may affect a person for a lifetime. It's not difficult to conceive of a single drowning incident as a transitory chemical reaction, tied to the physiological event of recently giving birth—very different from thinking of early childhood abuse as an excusable cause of adult homicidal behavior, and definitely more consistent with the concept of "not guilty by reason of insanity."

Given this foundation for a defense, it becomes easier to associate Andrea Yates's "craziness" with the more positive connotations of the term. Here was a mother who believed she loved her children so much that she would do anything to spare them the wrath they would surely evoke from God if they continued along the path of sinful behavior. To some people, Andrea Yates was *hopelessly devoted* to her children to the point that she was *going out of her head* over them—just *crazy in love.* And these references from pop culture only hint at the types of messages that may have influenced the public's perceptions of Yates.

In the 1961 film *Through a Glass Darkly,* the central female character, Karin, is a disturbed and mentally imbalanced young woman. Her behavior shows her anguish to be part psychological and part spiritual, as evidenced in the scene where she hears voices coming from the wall behind peeling wallpaper. She perceives these sounds to be the voice of God. In an interview shown in her 2006 retrial, Andrea Yates describes a similar episode: "I thought I heard some voices come from the wall, . . . and I believe it was Satan calling me."[66] The spiritual context of the messages received by both Karen and Andrea make their torment more heartbreaking, thus increasing public sympathy to their plight.

In 1998, just a few years before Yates drowned her children, Toni Morrison's Pulitzer Prize–winning 1987 novel, *Beloved,* was released as a film. The book is about a black woman named Sethe who escapes with her children from the house where they had been held as slaves. The slaveholder finds Sethe at her mother-in-law's house and tries to reclaim her and the children. Believing her children doomed to return to slavery, Sethe grabs them, runs to the tool shed, and tries to kill them. She succeeds in killing her two-year-old daughter. "I was trying to put my babies where they would be safe," she explains. The parallels to Andrea Yates are striking. Through Sethe, audiences could see how a mother's genuine fear for her child's well-being could lead her to conclude that killing the child would be preferable to the fate of certain suffering. How an act of repugnance could be perceived as an act of mercy? This similarity—combined with the two characters' shared remorse for their actions—creates a connection between them that could steer the public toward compassion for Andrea Yates.

Yates has forthrightly admitted being influenced by the 1995 crime film *Seven,* where a serial killer chooses his victims and their manner of death in order to represent the seven deadly sins: gluttony, envy, lust, pride, sloth, greed, and wrath. That film, Yates said in a 2001 interview, was how she learned about the seven deadly sins. It apparently validated her belief that her children *had* to be killed, like the victims in the film, because they had sinned. If they were allowed to continue their sinful ways, their final punishment at the hands of God would only be worse. She describes how she rationalized her own behavior at the time by concluding, "I felt I had done all the other sins, and now this one would be the last one, the last one of the sins."[67]

Recent history of American pop culture is filled with mixed messages about mental illness. While real and fictional perpetrators of violent crimes are often shown to be tormented by internal demons, the disgust we feel for the harm they inflict on others tends to override whatever sympathy may be possible to have for them. Increasingly, though, mentally ill characters have been portrayed in a more humanistic way, in stories that even end on a hopeful note. An early initiator of this trend was Ken Kesey, in his 1962 novel, *One Flew over the Cuckoo's Nest.* Rather than exploit the strangeness of patients in a psychiatric hospital, Kesey focused on the horrors of institutionalization, detailing the severity and inappropriateness of their treatment. At the end of the story, we are happy to find that one patient escapes, even though he is a convicted murderer. The ending offers a single ray of sunshine amid an otherwise bleak existential landscape. In the book *Sybil,* published in 1973, Flora Rheta Schreiber documents the psychotherapeutic journey of Sybil Dorsett, who suffered from dissociative identity disorder. Readers follow Sybil's 16 personalities as they gradually become conscious of each other, ultimately resulting in her victorious emergence as a single, integrated individual.

The Academy Award–winning 1980 film drama *Ordinary People* tells the story of Conrad Jarrett (played by Timothy Hutton), who accompanied his older brother on a boating trip that resulted in the brother's fatal drowning. Blaming himself, Conrad attempts suicide and is subsequently admitted to a psychiatric care unit for four months. Though Conrad is the only one with a clinically authenticated condition, both his mother and father also show signs of scarring from their son's death. Surprisingly, it is not Conrad, but his *mother* who, in the end, is unable to cope with the tragedy. Conrad finally grows to a point where he is able to reach out to his mother, but she is so emotionally shut down that she rejects him. After her husband confronts her about her rigidity, she finds it unbearable to remain in the house with her surviving family, so she packs her bags and leaves. It turns out that Conrad—the one officially diagnosed with mental illness—shows the most promise of leading a healthy, normal life.

Later works continue the trend of more sympathetic and relatable mentally ill characters. The 1988 film *Committed* tells the story of a psychiatric nurse who applies to work at a recognized institution but finds herself instead imprisoned there as a patient. This juxtaposition of roles allows the audience to experience what it feels like to be labeled "crazy." There, but for the grace of God, go I. *Girl, Interrupted,* Susanna Kaysen's best-selling 1993 memoir, documents the experiences of a group of young women institutionalized for mental disorders. Kaysen's stay in the treatment facility teaches her that "sanity is a falsehood constructed to help the 'healthy' feel 'normal.'" Michael Cunningham's book *The Hours*—adapted from Virginia Woolf's highly acclaimed story *Mrs. Dalloway*—won the 1999 Pulitzer Prize for fiction. It focuses on a day in the life of three female characters (one of them is Woolf herself) in three different time periods, each struggling with psychological problems. Though Woolf's depression actually led her to suicide, the book's overarching message is that there is beauty and profundity in even the most mundane activities of a person's life.

The year 2002, when Aileen Wuornos was executed, was the same year that Andrea Yates was found guilty of murder and sentenced to life imprisonment. If, at that time, punishment was seen as the right and moral consequence for these women's crimes, how is it that, a mere four years later, Andrea Yates was declared "not guilty by reason insanity" and transferred to a hospital for rehabilitation?

Ironically, one event that may have had a profound impact on the public's judgments of mental illness was the making of a biographical film about the life and times of Aileen Wuornos. Released in 2003—one of the intervening years between Wuornos's conviction and Yates's acquittal on appeal—*Monster* starred Charlize Theron, whose realistic and empathetic characterization of the lead character was heralded in superlatives and earned her numerous awards including an Oscar. In an interview with entertainment blogger Emily Blunt, Theron had this to say regarding how she felt about playing a "victimized killer":

> There's a certain amount of propaganda we get fed by the media— [like] the sensationalizing of the "first time female serial killer." Especially with her, every shot you see is of her when she's looking a little [Charlize makes a "crazy" face]. That's the photo they ran on the 7 o'clock news. . . . I wouldn't have done the movie—[except] that in watching that greater truth of her story, you do get to a place of empathy.[68]

The Andrea Yates case sparked philosophical, political, and religious debates over the issue of treatment versus punishment for the mentally ill. The Wuornos case also ignited a firestorm of controversy, particularly regarding the legitimacy of capital punishment. Expert witnesses at both the Wuornos and Yates trials testified to the defendants' mental illnesses. And many believed that, in their minds, both women committed their crimes out of love: Yates to save her children from Satan, while Wuornos to bring money home to her partner. But only Yates was able to mount a successful defense. By 2006, the year of Andrea Yates's retrial, there were signs that Americans' beliefs about "normalcy" were beginning to change. But beyond that were differences in media coverage of the two women, showing Yates to be a much more sympathetic figure than Wuornos.

Andrea Yates was able to serve as a sort of poster girl for mental illness because, unlike Aileen Wuornos, she could be viewed—apart from her criminal act—as a respectable, nurturing, God-fearing wife and mother. In a 2001 interview with forensic psychologist Dr. Park Dietz, Yates explained that she killed her children because she loved them. She didn't want them tormented by Satan, like she was. "I didn't want them ruined, and I was afraid being around him [Satan], they would continue to go downhill. I thought I should save them before that happened. . . . If I kill them, they went up to heaven to be with God and be safe."[69]

Contrast this with detailed depictions of Wuornos's unabashed belligerence in newspaper articles and television news reports. Her bravado inspired contempt, rather than compassion, in those who heard or read about her case. It helped jurors conclude that execution was indeed an appropriate punishment.

The first thing Andrea Yates did after she drowned her children was to call the police. When they arrived, she immediately confessed to the murders, and during the trials, though she attempted to explain and even rationalize her actions, she never once made any attempt to deny responsibility or to blame others for what she had done. Aileen Wuornos, on the other hand, emphatically asserted that nothing was her fault. She talked endlessly about her troubled upbringing to anyone who would listen, and at her trial, she charged detectives, attorneys, book and movie agents, and even her partner, Tyria Moore, with corruption and complicity.

While Yates appeared self-reflective and contrite, Wuornos was shown as vindictive and malevolent, evidenced in videos of her leaving the courtroom, exploding with rage after her guilty verdict was announced. In the article "Aileen Wuornos: Killer Who Preyed on Truck Drivers," writer Marlee Macleod noted that Wuornos hissed to the Assistant State Attorney Ric Ridgeway, "I hope your wife and children get raped in the ass."[70] Then she turned to Judge Thomas Sawaya, making an obscene gesture and calling him a "motherfucker."[71]

Though few could follow Andrea Yates's bizarre logic that she killed her children for their own benefit, Yates's account of the factual events of the incident was void of exaggerated drama, showing that she was honestly willing to acknowledge exactly what had happened that morning. In contrast, Aileen Wuornos maintained throughout her trial that each one of her killings was done in self-defense, insisting that every one of her victims had assaulted, threatened, or raped her. This claim rang untrue.

In the end, Andrea Yates's attorneys were able to paint a picture of her as momentarily delusional, while Aileen Wuornos was characterized as being consistently evil and positively culpable. Wuornos was put in an entirely different category than Yates. That classification forever framed the way she was seen, both by the jury and by the public.

Portrayed as belligerent, vindictive, malevolent, dishonest, and perverted, Aileen Wuornos didn't have a chance of acquittal—by reason of insanity, self-defense, or any other circumstance. Faced with the evidence of a series of gruesome murders, we are hard-pressed to rationalize these crimes or to sympathize with their perpetrators. Doing so means searching deep into our souls and expanding our hearts and minds considerably. The truth is that we can only stretch our boundaries in small increments. What was shown to us of Andrea Yates's demeanor gave us something to work with. We saw too much of Aileen Wuornos's that was unacceptable. Having compassion for her required a giant leap out of our comfort zones. Not until after her death did we begin to see images that might evoke compassion. Had Wuornos's cards been played differently in the media, perhaps she too would ultimately have been judged differently.

Conclusion: Her Trait, Her Fate

The women profiled in this book are all products of American society. Like the rest of us, they were influenced by the media in its various forms, and in turn, each one's moment in the spotlight has had its own effect on popular culture. For better or for worse, the stories of these women—their backgrounds, their mindsets, their crimes, their court trials, their sentences, their legacies—have already become part of our history and are now affecting others, as the cycle of mutual influence continues. The type of effect a particular female killer has had on the culture depends on whether she's been viewed sympathetically. And that is determined by factors in three basic categories: *Traits of the defendants, cultural environment,* and *societal issues* ripe for clarification at the time.

In the cases we've examined, each killer exhibited an assortment of traits that could genuinely be ascribed to her. And each was also perceived by the public to personify certain traits. While there is some relation between genuine and perceived traits, the correlation is not always exact, especially when perceptions are filtered through media depictions. Yes, we get it: Aileen Wuornos is hostile. But could she have another side as well? And of course, we see that Andrea Yates is sullen and confused. But might a woman who was driven to drown her five children not also be holding just a hint of anger? If so, we never saw it in her trials. Truman Capote's writings about Ann Woodward virtually labeled her as a cold-blooded murderer, even though a jury had acquitted her in a court of law. Could Capote's damning account of Woodward possibly have been inspired by a quarrel in which she called him a "little faggot"? We sometimes forget—especially in the context of a written exposé or documentary film—that any attribution of personal traits is not only about the person being characterized but also the person constructing the image.

Motive is a key part of our judgment of an alleged killer's guilt or innocence, and some motives are inherently more sympathetic than others. Self-defense, for example, need only be reasonably substantiated to tip the scales in a defendant's favor. Greed for money, on the other hand, is a motive that must be staunchly defended against in order to gain an acquittal. Other motives are highly variable. Revenge, for instance, can be seen in a sympathetic light if a callous husband has repeatedly wronged a devoted wife and mother—like, say, Betty Broderick. But if a professional scientist such as Amy Bishop feels deeply indignant about what she perceives as an injustice, we fail to understand how that sentiment could justify an egregious act against her colleagues. How one person's motive is judged by others depends entirely on the context in which that motive is presented. And depending on that presentation, public judgments may come quickly, or they may take some time. We can all identify, to some extent, with every woman featured in this book. But at a certain point in each of their stories, we part ways with them. That departure could come as late as the final, critical turn when Francine Hughes sets the bed of her sleeping husband on fire or at the very beginning when we wonder what Olga Rutterschmidt and Helen Golay are up to, befriending homeless men. It's all about context.

Why do media depictions highlight certain traits of the characters they present and downplay others? The reason is simple: Consumers want to be furnished with a coherent and cohesive picture that contains at least the *suggestion* of a message to walk away with. Truly multidimensional characters pose a problem for us. They're confusing and confounding. Encountering them is unsatisfying, since they require us to think too hard in order to form an impression of them. So good journalists, authors, playwrights, bloggers, and songwriters know that they must provide a perspective from which we can view the characters in their stories and decode the traits those characters represent. This practice is not some sort of evil plot or sinister conspiracy. It is simply the way things are.

The second factor affecting how the public evaluates female killers is the cultural environment—emerging political and social movements, prevalent ideological beliefs, and the stream of technological advances characterizing that period. The times may be favorable or unfavorable to the circumstances of the woman in question. In 1976, when Francine Hughes went on trial for murdering her husband, the "vixen/victim" dichotomy was still a common framework for viewing women, even as domestic abuse was beginning to be acknowledged as a serious problem. Given the choice of vixen or victim, Hughes clearly represented the latter, allowing her case to serve as a strategic tool for advancing the cause of women's rights. By 2001, the year of Liysa Northon's trial, abundant, in-depth investigative crime reporting bombarded the television airwaves, making the public sophisticated enough about the dynamics of domestic violence to look with suspicion at Northon's claim that her abusive husband was a threat to her life. And women's groups now sought high-achieving role models to showcase. They were no longer looking for martyrs.

When Ann Woodward shot her husband in 1955, rigid boundaries confined the public's conception of what would be plausible for a woman to do, and social class typecasting advantaged the elite with opportunities to escape punishment. A half-century later, gender, social class, and even age stereotypes had become fuzzier. The idea of women—even elderly women like Olga Rutterschmidt and Helen Golay—committing cold-blooded acts of murder no longer seemed extraordinary. And with the ubiquitous streaming of news on the Internet and opportunists routinely selling their stories to tabloid journalists, today there would be a much harder time for a reputable matriarch like Elsie Woodward to make a secret "backroom deal" by simply paying off a witness. In the late 1970s, the public was told the Francine Hughes story in a one-way stream of news reports and magazine articles by professional journalists. A quarter-century later, Liysa Northon's story was constructed interactively—with the full participation of anyone with an opinion—through the vehicles of blogs, websites, and chat rooms on the Internet.

Betty Broderick and Amy Bishop both killed out of revenge, but the cultural environment affected their cases differently. By 1989, when Broderick took revenge against her ex-husband and his new wife, the public had become quite familiar with fiery marital conflicts. That was the year that the 1981 novel *War of the Roses* was made into a film. The story showed how tensions and misunderstandings between a wife and a husband could escalate into unforeseen and unimaginable proportions. While neither party got a particularly sympathetic depiction, one could see how each incident led to the next, spiraling into a venomous and ultimately fatal series of events. Parallels to Betty Broderick's situation may have helped the public acknowledge Dan Broderick's contribution to the tragic end of the story. Popular culture gave no such assistance to Amy Bishop. There were no best-selling books about disputes between academic colleagues, no blockbuster films showcasing the arbitrariness of tenure decisions, or no biographical profiles of university professors that served to humanize them in the eyes of the public. Why would anyone make the effort to try and understand the demented actions of a comfortable and privileged occupant of the "ivory tower"?

A third factor plays a role in shaping public discussion of women on trial for murder—the prominence of a particular moral issue in the collective consciousness of the time. As a society, we continually struggle to define who we are, and that definition comes from clarifying the essential meaning and boundaries of acceptable action regarding certain key concepts. The cases of Francine Hughes and Liysa Northon, each of whom claimed to have killed their husbands in self-defense, highlighted the concept of *bravery*. With no readily available resources and no historic precedent to follow, Hughes was considered to have embodied courage and bravery by finally standing up to her abusive husband. In contrast, we concluded that Northon's act of shooting her husband on a planned camping trip as he lay in a sleeping bag was not brave at all. In deeming her a coward, we drew a line in the sand, making the accepted standards for bravery a bit clearer and a little more stringent.

The cases of Betty Broderick and Amy Bishop focus our collective attention on the issue of *fairness*. As a society, one important question for us to answer has to do with what an agreement legitimately entitles the parties to expect: What actions are fair, just, and reasonable when a contract is breached? The verdict in Broderick's case elucidated that, while there may be a number of appropriate penalties for reneging on a promised obligation to your wife, getting shot to death is not one of them. Next for us to grapple with is the issue that the Amy Bishop case presents: What is fair retribution for those who may have undeservedly blocked the road to a colleague's career advancement?

Our standards regarding *personal integrity* are put into question when crimes are committed in the name of love. When Kristin Rossum was convicted for poisoning her husband to ready herself for a new lover, society made the statement that love's nobility as a behavioral motive does not extend to murder. Susan Smith—perhaps the most publicly denigrated of all—violated our sense of personal integrity in multiple ways, starting with adultery, progressing to infanticide, and ending with a bogus plea to the public to find an imaginary criminal she claimed was responsible for kidnapping her children. Smith did us a favor by making it easy, for once, to draw some clear boundaries in a moral landscape that can sometimes get pretty murky.

There's no question that American society values *materialism*. But how far does our culture go in sanctioning the pursuit of money? How does our collective desire for the better things in life affect our moral judgments? Does a person's net worth determine the extent to which we value his or her life? When Ann Woodward was acquitted of killing her husband, the Woodward family fortune certainly played a role in producing that outcome, whether it was in providing the resources to hire the best defense lawyers or in society's refusal at that time to see a high-society figure as a common murderer. The case of Olga Rutterschmidt and Helen Golay presented us with the same issue from a reverse perspective. We're all aware that violations against the homeless are routinely given less attention than other crimes. Convicting these women of murder gave society an opportunity to take a solid step in the direction of humaneness. The guilty verdict affirmed our higher-order belief that there is sanctity in every human life—even the lives of those with no possessions to their names.

The different personas of Aileen Wuornos and Andrea Yates were made apparent in the coverage of their trials, and those differences were not incidental to their sentences. Wuornos received the death penalty not only because her crimes were numerous and gruesome, but also because her behavior after her arrest was perceived to be completely irreverent toward society. Her belligerent denials of guilt and her penchant for placing blame on others demonstrated an utter lack of *self-responsibility*. Andrea Yates's contrite admission that she had willfully and premeditatedly drowned her children was held as an admirable gesture, setting the stage for her to be judged with a degree of compassion, despite the horrific and unforgivable acts she committed. Taking responsibility for one's own actions is an issue that has come to light more and more in recent years—one that has been steadily creeping into American culture and may yet prove to have a truly transformational effect on what we stand for as a society. We are starting to take ourselves to task for travesties like polluting the environment, spreading communicable diseases, and ignoring teenage bullying.

Like research projects for students, high-profile murder cases provide an opportunity for us, as a society, to direct focused attention on issues that we know, on some level, need to be reevaluated. As interactive technology grows, these cases increasingly allow for public discussion in which values can be examined, arguments weighed, and when necessary, new boundaries drawn. Female murder cases, in addition to serving this general purpose, can also be catalysts for reflecting on our evolving notions about the status of women in our society.

As women have come to see themselves differently over the years, media images have been modified and developed to reflect those changes. Prior to the women's movement, which began in earnest in the 1960s, certain activities and behaviors were generally reserved for men only. If a woman was encouraged to work at all, it was only in particular professions, such as nursing, teaching, or home economics. Other types of work were considered either inappropriate for females or too difficult or dangerous for them to perform. Given the common view that women were delicate, emotional, unassertive, and dependent, it made sense that they would not be envisioned as construction workers, scientists, salespeople, or entrepreneurs. We were comfortable seeing Ann Woodward at an elite social gathering with a fruity drink in her hand—not so much at a bloody murder scene, clutching a smoking .45-caliber handgun.

The goal of civil rights movements of the 1960s and 1970s was to "liberate" oppressed groups by systematically challenging stereotypes that promoted discrimination. Just as African Americans embraced the label "Black" in order to show genuine pride in even the starkest perception of their skin color, women aggressively pursued roles in which society was not accustomed to conceiving of them. The public would just have to get used to seeing gals who were strong, powerful, independent, angry, and even brazen. And the more extreme the image, the more effectively this purpose was served. Thus, the image of Francine Hughes setting her husband's bed on fire was one that fit right in with a growing social and political trend of the times.

The seeds of female assertiveness that were planted during that period have been nurtured, and time has allowed them to grow, thrive, and mature. Many things that were once off-bounds to women are now accepted and even celebrated. Hillary Clinton is the country's third female secretary of state. Oprah Winfrey enjoys the distinction of being one of the most influential people in the world. Christie Hefner has been running the venerable Playboy Enterprises, a quintessential domain of men, for over two decades. And for better or worse, female *brazenness* has also taken solid root in pop culture. In their popular video "Goodbye Earl," the Dixie Chicks rejoice in the murder of a friend's abusive husband. "We'll pack a lunch and stuff you in the trunk, Earl," they proclaim. In Lady Gaga's video "Telephone," the pop icon maintains her glamorous mystique through bouts of raucous prison fighting and the merciless commission of mass poisonings. Rap sensation Missy Elliott, announcing that her "money-maker" is open for business, sings "Ching-ching, gettin' paid over here," in her sensual and hypnotic video "Ching-a-Ling: Step Up 2 the Streets." In this cultural environment, it doesn't seem so outrageous for Andrea Yates not to be condemned for her own brand of brazenness.

Yes, times have changed. Women can certainly do things now that would never have been accepted before. One troubling question, though, begs to be asked: Just because a woman *can* act a certain way, does that necessarily mean that she *ought* to?

Since the turn of this century, the frontier of murders committed by women has continued to expand, with boundaries pushed ever outward to new territory and unprecedented situations. In 2000, 16-year-old gang members Hacia Saucida and Janeth Christina Olarte shot aspiring hoodlums Mechelle Torres and Robin Rainey during what was supposed to be a routine "beat in" gang initiation.[1] Torres died at the scene, but Rainey survived, only to be arrested herself six months later, charged with the shooting and killing of another teenage gang-banger. In 2002, Clara Harris, dubbed "the Mercedes killer," tracked her husband and his female receptionist to a motel room where she mowed him down with her luxury sedan, then backed up and drove over him again to make sure he was dead. In 2009, 300-pound Mia Landingham got into an altercation with her husband and sat on him, causing his death by asphyxiation. The following year, when 3-month-old Dylan Lee Edmondson wouldn't stop crying, his mother, 22-year-old Andrea Tobias, shook him to death, angered that he was distracting her from a video game she was trying to play.

With female killers now in the public consciousness more than ever before, the idea of a woman committing murder, in and of itself, is beginning to lose its shock value. Some might say that it's becoming commercial: just another product line. A website called *Shooting Divas* sells T-shirts for women and girls that read "I love guns" and "My mom is packing heat." Their line of female killer Halloween costumes is selling briskly.[2] YouTube currently boasts over 4,000 search results for "female killer" videos. And the antics of high-profile murderers such as Susan Smith have become fodder for comedians like Steve Harvey, who parodies Smith's claim that a black man carjacked her car and drove away with her two kids:

> There ain't a black man in this country who'd steal a car, realize there were two white kids in the back seat, and keep going. We already know we're gonna get life for stealing that car. Why sign up for the electric chair?[3]

Susan Smith may deserve to be ridiculed for trying to divert the blame for her crime, but at the same time, we must also acknowledge the inconsistency of pop culture in modeling responsibility for our own actions. Reality television abounds with mixed messages about assessing and assigning blame. *Big Brother* is a popular, long-running reality show about a group of contestants living in the same house whose every thought and action is glaringly caught on videotape by strategically placed TV cameras. The show pits the house members against one another by setting constant "challenges" for them and regularly requiring them to banish someone from the house and, consequently, from the show. The last housemate remaining wins a cache of money. Audiences delight in seeing emotional dramas unfold and watching as, one by one, the contestants turn on each other in an attempt to avoid being eliminated themselves. When something goes wrong, you'd better blame someone else, because if it looks like it's *your* fault, you're out.

The same message drives *The Apprentice,* a competition in which one shrewd and clever contestant wins the prize of running a multimillion-dollar Donald Trump company for a year. In this show, two teams of contestants tackle business challenges that Trump lays out for them. One might think that the team effort format would encourage bonding and mutual support among the participants, but the reality is that each week, someone will hear from Trump the dreaded words, "You're fired!" Like *Big Brother* housemates, *The Apprentice* teammates would be foolish to take the blame for any screw up or misdeed. Whether the prize is a large sum of cash for *Big Brother* housemates, a career-boosting business opportunity for *The Apprentice* hopefuls, public vindication and absolution for Betty Broderick, or a new boyfriend for Susan Smith, the cultural directive is the same: She who best dodges blame is the one who wins the game.

Not all reality shows, however, espouse such a cynical message. Some actually encourage and reward self-responsibility. The TV series *The Biggest Loser* has spawned an entire mini-culture of clubs, books, videos, websites, diets, exercise programs, and commercial products. The show features overweight contestants competing for a cash prize through activities designed to help them lose weight. In the process, they're able to earn for themselves rewards of even greater value than cash: They become fit and healthy. To get on the show, not only do you have to be willing to acknowledge that you have a weight problem, but you must also commit to a regimen of exercise and healthy eating in order to achieve your weight loss goal. *You* have created your problem. *You* take responsibility for doing what it takes to fix it.

In the same vein, parents whose children have somehow spiraled out of control seek help from child behavioral psychologist Jo Frost on the popular reality show *Supernanny*. Each week, Jo visits a home where the children present an obvious and immediate danger to the harmony of the household. They fight with each other. They talk back to their mommies and daddies. They refuse to obey the rules. They throw hissy fits. When parents call Supernanny for help, they have taken the first step toward healing—admitting that they have a problem. What they don't often realize, though, is that, invariably, the parents themselves are the main cause of the problem. After first observing the interactions of family members, Supernanny diagnoses what she sees as dysfunctional patterns—an absent father, a frustrated mother, or a couple that fails to provide structure for their kids or teach them that actions have consequences. Jo holds their feet to the fire, showing the parents videotapes of themselves that brutally expose the behaviors they must change. And change, they do. At the end of each episode, Supernanny rides away into the sunset, while the family, once headed for certain disaster, waves a cheerful good-bye, both parents and children now securely on the fast track to recovery. While Andrea Yates's story ends less happily for her children, the fact that she took responsibility for the tragic outcome gives us hope that she will recover as well. Amy Bishop would be wise to use the time during her current leave of absence from teaching to master this basic lesson in media psychology.

Some reality shows feature people lodged at various points along the self-responsibility scale and let the *viewer* interpret whether particular individuals' attitudes present them in a positive or negative light. *Wife Swap* offers couples a two-week opportunity to experience a different way of looking at the world by pairing households with virtually opposite lifestyles and having them exchange partners. For the first week, the guest partner must abide by all the rules of the host household. The second week, the guest gets to set the rules that the hosting family must then follow. Couples appear to have agreed to the exchange mostly with the idea that they have something to teach others who are less enlightened, but they wind up facing their own lessons to learn when the guest partner confronts them about *their* shortcomings. After the two-week exchange is completed and the original couples are reunited, all the cards are put on the table when the four participants sit down and discuss the experience. Not until then do we get a real sense of the exchange's true impact.

We find that for some, the event has resulted in an epiphany. A mother who has coddled her children excessively comes to understand that tough love, modeled by the guest mother, will serve her children better in the long run. A husband who has passively allowed his wife to set all the rules learns from his guest wife that marriage is more fulfilling as an equal partnership. These are examples of people who were open to a critical assessment of their own behavior and willing to endure the discomfort of examining it. But there are also those who are just glad when the whole thing is over so that they can return to life exactly as it was. They claim that the domestic intruder did nothing but upset the balance of their happy home. As viewers, we are left to decide: Are these characters heroes, choosing to affirm the conviction of their beliefs, preserve their dignity and retain their integrity? Or are they just egotistic fools, denying themselves and their families the opportunity to learn and grow?

The People's Court is a syndicated television program in which a bona fide judge makes binding arbitration decisions in real-life small claims cases. One of television's first true reality shows, it has enjoyed widespread popularity since 1981 and is still going strong today. At the heart of each case is the issue of self-responsibility, in one form or another. Is the seller of a defective sofa obligated to return a dissatisfied customer's money, or does the "as is" clause at the bottom of the receipt exempt him from any such ethical duty? Can a young man get out of repaying money loaned to him by his ex-girlfriend by claiming it was a gift from a smitten lover? Must a Pitbull owner pay the inflated vet bills that his neighbor claims resulted from a brief encounter between his dog and her Chihuahua? In these matters, it is the judge, of course, who makes the legal ruling. But as with *Wife Swap*, viewers are left to decide for themselves what role self-responsibility plays in the serving of *moral* justice for each litigant. Public value judgments like these—in both direct and mediated venues—are ongoing, serving the continuous function of reshaping our notions of acceptable behavior. In pop culture, images that absolve self-responsibility are just as easy to find as those that promote it. It all depends on what you're looking for.

It's up to each of us, as individuals, to pick and choose the events for which we deem ourselves responsible. But one act of self-responsibility that we should all be able to commit to is this: Being aware when we consume information. These days, we're barraged at every turn with media images, so it is more important than ever to take a step back and examine the underlying messages that they may represent. To take information at face value, as it is presented, is to relinquish control of how that information influences us. The media will continue to produce and disseminate what sells. We can't expect this to change. But we *can* make conscious choices about the kinds of images we allow to permeate our thoughts and the types of dialogue we engage in to try and put those messages in perspective. Female murder cases deserve our critical and thoughtful attention. They give us an opportunity to ascribe reasoned value judgments to particular sets of circumstances. By considering those decisions carefully and articulating them responsibly, we can each help, in our own small and personal ways, to shape popular culture. It's up to us to frame *the murder mystique* for future generations.

—Richard Pfefferman

Notes

INTRODUCTION

1. U.S. Department of Justice, http://www.ojp.gov/bjs/homicide/tables/osextab.htm.

CHAPTER 1

1. Ann Jones, *Women Who Kill* (New York: Holt, Rinehart Winston, 1980), 282.
2. "'Urgent Voice' Led to Ex-mate Killing," *Bridgeport Post,* November 2, 1977.
3. Ibid.
4. Faith McNulty, *The Burning Bed* (New York: Harcourt Brace Jovanovich, 1980), 64.
5. Ibid., 77.
6. Lenore Walker, "The Cycle Theory of Battering," *Transition House,* http://www.transitionhouse.ca/THEORY.html.
7. McNulty, *The Burning Bed,* 94.
8. Ibid., 106.
9. Ibid., 137.
10. Ibid., 176.
11. Ibid., 185–91.
12. Ibid., 192.
13. Jones, *Women Who Kill,* 281, 282.
14. Michael Hirsley, "Battered Ex-wife Becomes New Murder Trial Cause," *Chicago Tribune,* September 11, 1977.
15. Jones, *Women Who Kill,* 283.
16. Ola Barnett, Cindy Miller-Perrin, and Robin Perrin, *Family Violence across the Lifespan* (Thousand Oaks, CA: Sage Publication, 2004), 291.
17. McNulty, *The Burning Bed,* 220, 221.
18. Hirsley, "Battered Ex-wife."
19. Cynthia Kyle, "Curious Spectators Flock to Hughes Murder Trial," *The Herald Palladium,* October 31, 1977.

20. Michael Hirsley, "Wife Freed in Slaying of Abuser," *Chicago Tribune,* November 4, 1977.

21. Susan Jacoby, "Is Francine Hughes a Good Example for a Woman's Right to Self-Defense?," *Bennington Banner,* December 2, 1977.

22. Jones, *Women Who Kill,* 289.

23. Trisha Cofiell, "Anatomy of a Murder," *Delaware County Daily Times,* November 15, 1977.

24. "The Law: A Killing Excuse," *Time,* November 28, 1977, http://time.com/time/magazine/article/0,9171,919176,00.html.

25. Jerrold Footlick and Elaine Sciolino, "Wives Who Batter Back," *Newsweek,* January 30, 1978, 54.

26. Robert Greenwald, personal interview, June 10, 2009.

27. Charisse Van Horn, "Farrah Fawcett's 'The Burning Bed' Brought Domestic Violence to the Forefront," *Examiner.com,* http://www.examiner.com/crime-in-tampa-bay/farrah-fawcett-s-the-burning-bed-brought-domestic-violence-to-the-forefront.

28. Lyn Hardy and Donna Hebert, *The Ballad of Francine Hughes* (Swinging Door Music, 1986).

29. Gary Fletcher, "Murder on the Lostine," *The Observer,* October 16, 2003, http://www.lagrandeobserver.com/News/Local-News/MURDER-ON-THE-LOSTINE.

30. Ibid.

31. Ann Rule, *Heart Full of Lies* (New York: Pocket Books, 2004), 21.

32. Ibid., 31.

33. Ibid., 97.

34. Ibid.

35. Ibid., 82.

36. Ibid., 98.

37. Ibid., 125.

38. Ibid., 136.

39. Richard Cockle, "Eastern Oregon Killer Liysa Northon, Featured in Ann Rule Book, Eyes New Life after Her Release from Prison Next Year," *Oregonian,* November 5, 2011, http://www.oregonlive.com/pacific-northwest-news/index.ssf/2011/11/eastern_oregon_killer_liysa_no.html.

40. Caleb Hannan, "What Rick Swart Failed to Tell Us About This Week's Cover Story (UPDATE)," *Seattle Weekly,* July 28, 2011, http://blogs.seattleweekly.com/dailyweekly/2011/07/what_rick_swart_failed_to_tell.php?page=3.

41. Ibid.

42. Gary Fletcher, "Judge Rejects Murder Suspect's Release," *The Observer,* June 28, 2001, http://www.lagrandeobserver.com/News/Local-News/JUDGE-REJECTS-MURDER-SUSPECTS-RELEASE.

43. Rule, *Heart Full of Lies,* 151.

44. Cockle, "Eastern Oregon Killer Liysa Northon."

45. Rule, *Heart Full of Lies,* 156.

46. Ibid., 160, 161.

47. Gary Fletcher, "Judge Denies Bail for Northon," *The Bulletin,* June 29, 2001, http://bbstage.sx.atl.publicus.com/archive/2001/06/29/judge_denies_bail_for_northon.html.

48. Rick Swart, "Ann Rule's Sloppy Storytelling," *Seattle Weekly,* July 20, 2011, http://www.seattleweekly.com/content/printVersion/1384981/.

49. Rule, *Heart Full of Lies,* 163.

50. Ibid., 193.

51. Swart, "Ann Rule's Sloppy Storytelling."

52. Ibid.

53. Gary Fletcher, "Plea Bargain Brings Trial to End," *The Observer*, July 20, 2001, http://www.lagrandeobserver.com/News/Local-News/PLEA-BARGAIN-BRINGS-TRIAL-TO-END.

54. Rule, *Heart Full of Lies*, 177.

55. Fletcher, "Plea Bargain Brings Trial to End."

56. Rule, *Heart Full of Lies*, 194.

57. Gary Fletcher, "Defense, State Lay out Cases in Murder Trial," *The Observer*, July 17, 2001, http://www.lagrandeobserver.com/News/Local-News/DEFENSE-STATE-LAY-OUT-CASES-IN-MURDER-TRAIL.

58. Rule, *Heart Full of Lies*, 205.

59. Ibid., 223.

60. Fletcher, "Defense, State Lay out Cases in Murder Trial."

61. Gary Fletcher, "Murder Suspect Will Claim Self-Defense," *The Observer*, June 28, 2001, http://www.lagrandeobserver.com/News/Local-News/MURDER-SUSPECT-WILL-CLAIM-SELF-DEFENSE.

62. Gary Fletcher, "Murder Victim Heavily Sedated, Toxicologist Says," *The Observer*, July 19, 2001, http://www.lagrandeobserver.com/News/Local-News/MURDER-VICTIM-HEAVILY-SEDATED-TOXICOLOGIST-SAYS.

63. Fletcher, "Plea Bargain Brings Trial to End."

64. "Wife Pleads Guilty in Husband's Death," *Honolulu Star Bulletin*, July 25, 2001, http://archives.starbulletin.com/2001/07/25/news/story10.html.

65. Cockle, "Eastern Oregon Killer Liysa Northon."

66. Fletcher, "Plea Bargain Brings Trial to End."

67. Tor De Witt, personal communication, November 14, 2009.

68. Cockle, "Eastern Oregon Killer Liysa Northon."

69. *Husband Killer Says Crime Writer Libeled Her*, Feedback, www.courthouse news.com/blogarchive/northon.htm.

CHAPTER 2

1. Joy Ciarcia-Levy, "Revenge Is Sweet and It's Everywhere," *ABC News*, February 1, 2007, http://abcnews.go.com/2020/story?id=2831618&page=1#.T-t9kI7GMdI.

2. Bob Burns, "Nutty Professor's Heart of Stone," *Globe Magazine*, March 8, 2010, 20.

3. *True Crime Stories: Cases that Shocked America* (New York: People Books, 2005), 43.

4. Bryna Taubman, *Hell Hath No Fury* (New York: St. Martin's Press, 1992), 6.

5. Alan Abrahamson, "Betty Broderick Tells How Marriage Fell Apart," *Los Angeles Times*, October 31, 1990, http://articles.latimes.com/1990-10-31/news/mn-3140_1_betty-broderick.

6. Bella Stumbo, *Until the Twelfth of Never* (New York: Simon and Schuster, 1993), 67.

7. Richard Serrano and Amy Wallace, "San Diego Killings Make Bitter Divorce Final," *Los Angeles Times*, November 7, 1989, http://www.latimes.com/la-me-broderick7nov0789,0,997740.story.

8. Stumbo, *Until the Twelfth of Never*, 47.

9. Taubman, *Hell Hath No Fury*, 22.

10. Stumbo, *Until the Twelfth of Never*, 50.

11. Taubman, *Hell Hath No Fury*, 35.

12. Stumbo, *Until the Twelfth of Never*, 59.

13. Amy Wallace, "Till Murder Do Us Part," *Los Angeles Times*, June 3, 1990, http://www.latimes.com/news/local/la-me-broderick3jun0390,0,1443012.story.

14. Stumbo, *Until the Twelfth of Never*, 112–113.

15. Taubman, *Hell Hath No Fury*, 57.

16. Joseph Geringer, "Betty Broderick: Divorce . . . Desperation . . . Death," *Crime Library*, http://www.trutv.com/library/crime/notorious_murders/family/broderick/1.html.

17. Wallace, "Till Murder Do Us Part."

18. Stumbo, *Until the Twelfth of Never*, 163.

19. Wallace, "Till Murder Do Us Part."

20. Stumbo, *Until the Twelfth of Never*, 171, 172.

21. Linda Deutsch, "Socialite Betty Broderick Seeks Parole in Murders," *San Diego Union-Tribune*, January 21, 2010, http://www.signonsandiego.com/news/2010/jan/21/socialite-betty-broderick-seeks-parole-in-murders/.

22. Amy Wallace, "La Jolla Woman Confesses to Murders in Crime," *Los Angeles Times*, March 28, 1990, http://articles.latimes.com/1990-03-28/news/mn-232_1_betty-Broderick.

23. Anne Kingston, *The Meaning of Wife* (New York: Farrar, Straus and Giroux, 2004), 191.

24. Stumbo, *Until the Twelfth of Never*, 252–54.

25. *True Crime Stories*, 53.

26. Stumbo, *Until the Twelfth of Never*, 372.

27. Connie Cass, "Woman Guilty of Slaying Ex-Husband, New Wife," *Winchester Star*, December 11, 1991.

28. Jennifer Furio, *Letters from Prison* (New York: Algora Publishing, 2001), 154.

29. Taubman, *Hell Hath No Fury*, 149.

30. Ibid., 205.

31. Alan Carter, "Guilty! Guilty! Guilty!," *Entertainment Weekly*, October 30, 1992, http://www.ew.com/ew/article/0,312231,00.html.

32. Amy Wallace, "One Angry Betty," *Los Angeles Magazine*, November 1, 2009, http://www.lamag.com/article.aspx?id=20936&page=2.

33. "For Those Tempted, Beware a Woman Scorned," *Hua Hin Observer*, http://www.observergroup.net/ob133back/stories.htm.

34. Debra J. Saunders, "Read the Right Books and You Too, Can Murder," *The Salina Journal*, January 12, 1993.

35. Stumbo, *Until the Twelfth of Never*, 363.

36. Tony Perry, "Mayflower Madam Will Return for Lecture Despite Vice Squad," *Los Angeles Times*, November 13, 1991, http://articles.latimes.com/1991-11-13/local/me-1239_1_mayflower-madam-will.

37. *The Oprah Winfrey Show: The 20th Anniversary Collection* (DVD) (Hollywood, CA: Paramount Pictures, 2005).

38. *True Crime Stories*, 53.

39. Amy Wallace, "One Angry Betty."

40. Linda Deutsch, "Betty Broderick Hearing: Parole Board Revisits Daniel Broderick, Linda Kolkena Broderick Murders," *The Huffington Post*, January 21,

2010, http://www.huffingtonpost.com/2010/01/21/betty-broderick-hearing-p_n_
431611.html.

41. "Betty Broderick Blasts Justice System in Letter to 10 News," *10News.com,*
February 22, 2010, http://www.10news.com/news/22638888/detail.html.

42. Robert Fein, Bryan Vossekuil, William Pollack, Randy Borum, William
Modzeleski, and Marisa Reddy, *Threat Assessment in Schools: A Guide to Managing
Threatening Situations and to Creating Safe School Climates* (Washington, D.C.: U.S.
Department of Education and U.S. Secret Service, May 2002), www.secretservice.
gov/ntac/ssi_guide.pdf.

43. Fred Hanson, "Classmates Recall a Smart, Quiet Girl," *Patriot Ledger,* February 16, 2010, http://findarticles.com/p/news-articles/patriot-ledger-the-quincy-
mass/mi_8043/is_20100216/classmates-recall-smart-quiet-girl/ai_n50245980/.

44. "Sister Kills Teenager in Shotgun Accident at Home," *Patriot Ledger,* December 8, 1986, http://www.enterprisenews.com/archive/x228087669/From-the-
Archives-Sister-kills-teenager-in-shotgun-accident.

45. Stephen Smith, "Ambition Fueled Smoldering Rage," *Boston Globe,* February 21, 2010, http://www.boston.com/news/local/massachusetts/articles/2010/
02/21/ambition_fueled_a_smoldering_rage/.

46. Police Report, Braintree Police, March 30, 1987, http://www.boston.com/
news/local/massachusetts/articles/2010/02/13/Full1986Policereport/.

47. Patricia C. McCarter, "What Happened to Amy Bishop's Brother? Two Conflicting Stories Arise," *Huntsville Times,* February 14, 2010, http://blog.al.com/
breaking/2010/02/post_207.html.

48. Patricia C. McCarter, "Amy Bishop 'Consumed' with University Tenure but
Was Pursuing Plan B, Husband Says," *Huntsville Times,* February 18, 2010, http://
blog.al.com/breaking/2010/02/post_212.html.

49. Ashleigh Banfield, Suzan Clarke, and Angela Ellis, "Alleged University Shooter's
Husband Thought 'Somebody Had Gone Crazy at the School,'" *Good Morning America,* February 19, 2010, http://abcnews.go.com/GMA/amy-bishop-husband-alleged-
university-alabama-shooter-loving-mother-wife/story?id=9883895#.UBjK8I7GMWw.

50. Shelley Murphy, "Witness Reported Talk of Revenge in Bomb Case," *Boston Globe,* February 23, 2010, http://www.boston.com/news/local/massachusetts/
articles/2010/02/23/atf_files_show_talk_of_revenge_from_bishops_husband_
in_93_bomb_case/.

51. Shalia Dewan, Stephanie Saul, and Katie Zezima, "For Professor, Fury Just
beneath the Surface," *The New York Times,* February 20, 2010, http://www.nytimes.
com/2010/02/21/us/21bishop.html.

52. John Guilfoil, "Ipswitch Neighbors Recall Confrontations with Amy Bishop,"
Boston Globe, February 15, 2010, http://www.boston.com/news/local/breaking_
news/2010/02/ipswich_neighbo.html.

53. "Amy Bishop Charged with 2002 Assault at IHOP," *Huntsville Times,* February 16, 2010, http://blog.al.com/breaking/2010/02/amy_bishop_charged_with_
2002_a.html.

54. Steven Doyle, "Amy Bishop Claimed She Was Victim in 2002 IHOP Assault,"
Huntsville Times, February 18, 2010, http://blog.al.com/breaking/2010/02/amy_
bishop_cursed_punched_woma.html.

55. Ibid.

56. Dewan et al., "For Professor, Fury Just beneath the Surface."

57. Ibid.

58. Paul Basken and David Glenn, "Accused Alabama Shooter Was a Bright Scientist with Career Ups and Downs," *Chronicle of Higher Education,* February 15, 2010, http://chronicle.com/article/Accused-Alabama-Shooter-Was-a/64202/.

59. Challen Stephens, Patricia C. McCarter, and Steve Doyle, "Why Did Amy Bishop Snap? A Picture of a Driven Woman with a Troubled Past Emerges," *Huntsville Times,* February 22, 2010, http://blog.al.com/breaking/2010/02/why_did_amy_bishop_snap_a_pict.html.

60. Thomas Bartlett and Robin Wilson, "The Fatal Meeting: Death, Heroism, and a Campus Changed Forever," *Chronicle of Higher Education,* February 18, 2010, http://chronicle.com/article/The-Fatal-Meeting-Death-H/64295/.

61. "Alabama Students Complained of Professor Amy Bishop before Fatal Shooting Spree," *New York Daily News,* February 17, 2010, http://www.nydailynews.com/news/national/2010/02/17/2010-02-17_alabama_students_complained_of_amy_bishop_before_campus_shooting.html.

62. Smith, "Ambition Fueled Smoldering Rage."

63. Dewan et al., "For Professor, Fury Just beneath the Surface."

64. Katherine van Wormer, "Amy Bishop and the Trauma of Tenure Denial," *Psychology Today,* February 16, 2010, http://www.psychologytoday.com/blog/crimes-violence/201002/amy-bishop-and-the-trauma-tenure-denial.

65. Burns, "Nutty Professor's Heart of Stone."

66. "Amy Bishop Arrested: University of Alabama Huntsville Shooting Suspect Is Biology Professor, Harvard Trained," *The Huffington Post,* April 14, 2010, http://www.huffingtonpost.com/2010/02/12/university-of-alabama-sho_n_460868.html.

67. Thomas Bartlett and Robin Wilson, "Amy Bishop Is Indicted in 1986 Shooting Death of Her Brother," *Chronicle of Higher Education,* June 17, 2010, http://chronicle.com/article/Amy-Bishop-Is-Indicted-in-1986/65970/.

68. Braintree Police Department News Release, "Comments from Chief Paul Frazier Regarding Amy Bishop," February 13, 2010.

69. "More Weird Amy Bishop Behavior," *Boston Globe,* February 17, 2010, http://www.halfsigma.com/2010/02/more-weird-amy-bishop-behavior.html and "Tiger, Amy and Entitlement," *Class Bias in Higher Education,* February 20, 2010, http://classbias.blogspot.com/2010/02/tiger-amy-and-entitlement.html.

70. Maggie Koerth-Baker, "Women Scientists on the Debate over Women in Science," *Boing Boing,* June 11, 2010, http://boingboing.net/2010/06/11/women-scientists-on.html.

71. Ibid.

72. Ibid.

73. Alec M. Gallup and Frank Newport, *The Gallup Poll: Public Opinion 2007* (Lanham: Rowman & Littlefield, 2008).

74. Joshua Green, "The Front-Runner's Fall," *The Atlantic,* September 2008, http://www.theatlantic.com/magazine/archive/2008/09/the-front-runner-8217-s-fall/6944/2/.

75. "About Barbara," *Barbara Ehrenrich's Official Website,* http://www.barbaraehrenreich.com/barbara_ehrenreich.htm.

CHAPTER 3

1. Billy Wilder, *Double Indemnity* (Hollywood, CA: Paramount Pictures, 1944).

2. Jamie Reno, "A Toxic Turn of Events," *Newsweek,* July 1, 2001, http://www.newsweek.com/2001/07/02/a-toxic-turn-of-events.html.

3. Caitlin Rother, *Poisoned Love* (New York: Kensington Publishing Corp., 2005), 23.

4. Ibid, 59.

5. John Glatt, *Deadly American Beauty* (New York: St. Martin's Press, 2004), 41, 42.

6. Ibid, 42.

7. Rother, *Poisoned Love*, 55.

8. David Kohn, "American Beauty," *CBS News,* May 7, 2009, http://www.cbs news.com/2100-18559_162-505815.html.

9. "Forensic Pathology," *WordNet Search 3.0,* http://wordnetweb.princeton. edu/perl/webwn/webwn?s=forensic+pathology&h.

10. Rother, *Poisoned Love*, 83.

11. Ibid, 84.

12. Robert F. Howe, "Deadly Dose," *Reader's Digest* (April 2003), 117.

13. Rother, *Poisoned Love*, 89.

14. Glatt, *Deadly American Beauty*, 67.

15. Ibid, 71.

16. "Toxic Love Triangle," *ABC Radio National,* January 25, 2004, http:// www.abc.net.au/radionational/programs/backgroundbriefing/toxic-love-triangle/ 3458290.

17. Ibid.

18. Glatt, *Deadly American Beauty*, 81.

19. Rother, *Poisoned Love*, 112.

20. "Woman Denies Killing Husband," *Los Angeles Times,* November 2, 2002, http://articles.latimes.com/2002/nov/02/local/me-rossum2.

21. Howe, "Deadly Dose," 118.

22. Glatt, *Deadly American Beauty*, 112.

23. Kim Zetter, "The Husband, the Wife, and the Lover," *The Age,* November 16, 2002, http://www.theage.com.au/articles/2002/11/15/1037080914373.html.

24. Glatt, *Deadly American Beauty*, 132.

25. Ibid, 152.

26. Ibid.

27. Rother, *Poisoned Love*, 220.

28. Reno, "A Toxic Turn of Events."

29. Joanna Powell, "My Daughter Is Innocent," *Good Housekeeping,* March 2002, http://www.accessmylibrary.com/article-1G1-83077235/my-daughter-innocent-kristin.html.

30. Glatt, *Deadly American Beauty*, 212.

31. Alex Roth, "Paper's Sealed on Judges Orders in Toxicologist Case," *San Diego Union-Tribune,* April 17, 2002, http://legacy.signonsandiego.com/news/metro/ 20020417-9999_2m17rossum.html.

32. Caitlin Rother, "Ex Toxicologist Denies Role in Denies Role in Death/ Killing Suspect's Former Lover Back in Australia," *San Diego Union Tribune,* July 15, 2001.

33. Michelle Morgante, "Jury Finds Former Toxicologist Guilty," *The Berkeley Daily Planet,* November 13, 2002, http://www.berkeleydailyplanet.com/issue/ 2002-11-13/article/16073?headline=Jury-finds-former-toxicologist-guilty.

34. "Toxic Love Triangle," *ABC Radio National.*

35. "Web Poll," *Cosmopolitan,* May 1, 2002, http://www.highbeam.com/doc/ 1G!-85677149.html.

36. Rother, *Poisoned Love*, 317.

37. Associated Press, "California 'Son of Sam' Law Struck Down," *First Amendment,* February 2, 2002, http://www.freedomforum.org/templates/document. asp?documentID=15773.

38. North County Times News Service, "Millions of Dollars Awarded to Family of Man Killed by Toxicologist Wife," *North County Times,* March 21, 2006, http://www.nctimes.com/news/state-and-regional/article_4428aa6b-fbb0-55a2-9221-9592d31fe6e5.html.

39. *Kristin Rossum v. Deborah Patrick and Edmund G. Brown Jr.,* United States Court of Appeals for the Ninth Circuit, No. 09-055666, http://www.signonsandiego.com/news/2010/sep/23/kristin-rossums-appeal-her-murder-conviction-reviv/.

40. "Toxic Love Triangle," *ABC Radio National.*

41. Rother, *Poisoned Love*, 433.

42. Diane Warren and Ric Wade, "Love Can Move Mountains," *Celine Dion* (New York: Epic, 1992).

43. Gregory Kirschling, "Stephenie Meyer's 'Twilight' Zone," *Entertainment Weekly,* July 5, 2008, http://www.ew.com/ew/article/0,20049578,00.html.

44. Maurine Proctor, "Stephenie Meyer's Vampire Series Makes Readers' Blush," *Meridian Magazine,* April 27, 2009, http://www.meridianmagazine.com/books/article/1829?&ac=1.

45. Andrea Peyser, *Mother Love, Deadly Love* (New York: Harper Collins Publishers, 1995), 19.

46. Maria Eftimiades, *Sins of the Mother* (New York: St. Martin's Press, 1995), 37.

47. David Smith, *Beyond All Reason* (New York: Kensington Publishing Corp., 1995), 101.

48. Ibid, 103–5.

49. Peyser, *Mother Love, Deadly Love,* 36.

50. Eftimiades, *Sins of the Mother,* 45.

51. Smith, *Beyond All Reason,* 118.

52. Charles Montaldo, "Susan Smith—Profile of a Child Killer," *About.com,* http://crime.about.com/od/murder/a/susan_smith.htm.

53. Eftimiades, *Sins of the Mother,* 50.

54. Smith, *Beyond All Reason,* 169–170.

55. Montaldo, "Susan Smith—Profile of a Child Killer."

56. Ibid.

57. Gary Henderson, *Nine Days in Union* (Spartanburg, SC: Honoribus Press, 1995), 117.

58. Peyser, *Mother Love, Deadly Love,* 53.

59. Henderson, *Nine Days in Union,* 121.

60. Ibid, 38.

61. Eftimiades, *Sins of the Mother,* 126, 127.

62. Peyser, *Mother Love, Deadly Love,* 119.

63. "Analysis of Susan Smith Confession," *LSI Laboratory for Scientific Interrogation Inc.,* http://www.lsiscan.com/susan_smith_s_confession.htm.

64. Smith, *Beyond All Reason,* 202.

65. Henderson, *Nine Days in Union,* 67.

66. Eric Harrison, "Town Unleashes Rage over Murder of 2 Boys Crime," *Los Angeles Times,* November 5, 1994, http://articles.latimes.com/1994-11-05/news/mn-58757_1_susan-smith.

67. Peyser, *Mother Love, Deadly Love,* 148.

68. Roslyn Muraskin and Shelly Feuer Domash, *Crime and the Media* (Upper Saddle River, NJ: Pearson Prentice Hall, 2007), 124.

69. George Rekers, *Susan Smith Victim or Murderer* (Lakewood, CO: Glenbridge Publishing, Ltd., 1996), 123.

70. The Associated Press, "Jury Quickly Convicts Smith of Son's Murders," *Santa Fe New Mexican,* July 23, 1995.

71. Norman Solomon, "Ginrich and the Susan Smith Case," *AlterNet,* April 26, 2000, http://www.alternet.org/story/8695/.

72. "Murderous Mommy Seeks Pen Pals," *The Smoking Gun,* July 10, 2003, http://www.thesmokinggun.com/documents/crime/murderous-mommy-seeks-pen-pals.

73. Brian Wilson and Roger Christian, "Don't Worry Baby," *Shut Down Volume 2* (Scranton, PA: Capitol, 1964).

74. *The Oprah Show,* October 12, 2010.

75. "Phase One, Complete," *Two and a Half Men,* November 17, 2003, Season 1, Episode 9.

76. "I Do," *Party of Five,* Fox TV, November 27, 1996, Season 3, Episode 11.

Chapter 4

1. *Quotations Book,* http://quotationsbook.com/quote/26965/#axzz1BN57Lum5.

2. Sonya Geis, "Two Elderly Women Jailed in Deadly Insurance Scam," *The Washington Post,* May 23, 2006, http://www.washingtonpost.com/wp-dyn/content/article/2006/05/22/AR2006052201359.html.

3. Jeanne King, *Signed in Blood* (New York: St. Martin's Press, 2009), 32.

4. Ibid, 33.

5. Ibid, 24–26.

6. Paul Pringle and Hemmy So, "Portrait Emerges of a Baffling Pair," *Los Angeles Times,* May 31, 2006, http://articles.latimes.com/2006/may/31/local/me-olgahelen31.

7. Paul Pringle and Hemmy So, "An Unlikely Friendship that Finally Unraveled," *Los Angeles Times,* August 19, 2006, http://articles.latimes.com/2006/aug/19/local/me-olgahelen19.

8. Karl Vick, "In LA a Case Straight out of 'Arsenic and Old Lace,'" *The Washington Post,* March 18, 2008, http://www.washingtonpost.com/wp-dyn/content/article/2008/03/17/AR2008031702489.html.

9. King, *Signed in Blood,* 26.

10. Paul Pringle, "Age, Sex of Defendants May Affect Verdict," *Los Angeles Times,* April 14, 2008, http://articles.latimes.com/2008/apr/14/local/me-olgahelen14.

11. Pringle and So, "An Unlikely Friendship that Finally Unraveled."

12. Ibid.

13. Pringle and So, "Portrait Emerges of a Baffling Pair."

14. Pringle and So, "An Unlikely Friendship that Finally Unraveled."

15. Ibid.

16. King, *Signed in Blood,* 17.

17. "Homelessness in Los Angeles County," *Los Angeles Almanac,* http://www.laalmanac.com/social/so14.htm.

18. King, *Signed in Blood*, 45.

19. *People v. Olga Rutterschmidt*, 176 Cal. App. 4th 1047-Cal: Court of Appeals, 2nd Appellate Dist., 5th Div. 2009, No. B209568, August 18, 2009, http://www.google.com/search?client=safari&rls=en&q=people+v.+rutterschmidt&ie=UTF-8&oe=UTF-8.

20. Ibid.

21. King, *Signed in Blood*, 53.

22. Ibid, 56.

23. Ibid, 79.

24. Dana Goodyear, "Post Cards from Los Angeles, Verdict," *The New Yorker*, April 17, 2008, http://www.newyorker.com/online/blogs/danagoodyear/2008/04/verdict.html

25. Pringle, "Age, Sex of Defendants May Affect Verdict."

26. King, *Signed in Blood*, 157.

27. *People v. Olga Rutterschmidt*.

28. "The Black Widows," *American Greed*, Episode 26, http://www.cnbc.com/id/34876268/.

29. Michael Idato, "The Great Escape," *The Sydney Morning Herald*, September 19, 2005, http://www.smh.com.au/entertainment/tv-and-radio/clinging-to-the-remnants-of-youth-20120914-25vmk.html.

30. "Chelsea Handler Quotes," *Search Quotes*, http://www.searchquotes.com/quotation/I_think_we_can_all_agree_that_sleeping_around_is_a_great_way_to_meet_people./267660/.

31. Jim Yardley, "Heir to a Fortune, and to Tragedy; Suicide Ends the Life of a Wealthy, and Haunted, Man," *The New York Times*, May 8, 1999, http://www.nytimes.com/1999/05/08/nyregion/heir-fortune-tragedy-suicide-ends-life-wealthy-haunted-man.html?pagewanted=all&src=pm.

32. Susan Braudy, *This Crazy Thing Called Love* (New York: Alfred A. Knopf, 1992), 21.

33. Carter B. Horsley, "Pocketful of Yesterdays: It Was and Is 'Nevertheless' New York in the 1930's," *The City Review*, 1997, http://www.thecityreview.com/sfuller.htm.

34. Braudy, *This Crazy Thing Called Love*, 105.

35. Mark Gribben, "The Woodwards: Tragedy in High Society," *Crime Library*, http://www.trutv.com/library/crime/notorious_murders/celebrity/woodwards/2.html.

36. Yardley, "Heir to a Fortune, and to Tragedy."

37. Braudy, *This Crazy Thing Called Love*, 67.

38. Ibid, 125.

39. Ibid, 159.

40. Gribben, "The Woodwards: Tragedy in High Society."

41. Braudy, *This Crazy Thing Called Love*, 168.

42. Ibid, 252, 253.

43. Ibid, 260.

44. Ibid, 305, 306.

45. Ibid, 305.

46. Ibid, 414.

47. "AFI's 100 Years, 100 Songs," *American Film Institute*, http://web.archive.org/web/20071027165808/http://www.afi.com/tvevents/100years/songs.aspx.

48. Olivia Mellan and Karina Piskaldo, "Men, Women, and Money," *Psychology Today*, January 1, 1999, http://www.psychologytoday.com/articles/199901/men-women-and-money.

CHAPTER 5

1. "Crazy Quotes," *ThinkExist*, http://thinkexist.com/quotes/with/keyword/crazy/2.html.

2. Mikaela Conley, "1 in 5 Americans Suffers from Mental Illness," *ABC News*, January 19, 2012, http://abcnews.go.com/blogs/health/2012/01/19/1-in-5-americans-suffer-from-mental-illness/.

3. Aileen Wuornos and Christopher Berry-Dee, *Monster* (London: John Blake Publishing, Ltd, 2006), 2, 150.

4. "Female Serial Killer Has Been Executed," *ABC Good Morning America*, October 9, 2002, http://abcnews.go.com/GMA/story?id=124614&page=1#.T_ok_47GMdJ.

5. Sue Russell, *Lethal Intent* (New York: Kensington Publishing Corp., 2002), 23.

6. Wuornos and Berry-Dee, *Monster*, 7.

7. Russell, *Lethal Intent*, 53.

8. Wuornos and Berry-Dee, *Monster*, 19, 20.

9. Russell, *Lethal Intent*, 104.

10. Wuornos and Berry-Dee, *Monster*, 237.

11. Ibid, 29.

12. Ibid, 41, 46.

13. "The Case of Aileen Wuornos—The Facts," *Capital Punishment in Context*, http://www.capitalpunishmentincontext.org/cases/wuornos.

14. Ibid.

15. "Female Serial Killers," *Family of Men Support Society*, April 7, 2012, http://www.familyofmen.com/female-serial-killers/#more-516.

16. Michael Reynolds, *Dead Ends* (New York: St. Martin's Press, 1992), 100.

17. Ibid, 162.

18. Ibid, 174.

19. Wuornos and Berry-Dee, *Monster*, 161.

20. Ibid, 238.

21. Roslyn Muraskin and Shelly Feuer Domash, *Crime and the Media* (Upper Saddle River, NJ: Pearson Prentice Hall, 2007), 131.

22. Reynolds, *Dead Ends*, 233.

23. Ibid, 238.

24. "The Case of Aileen Wuornos—The Facts," *Capital Punishment in Context*.

25. Reynolds, *Dead Ends*, 274, 275.

26. Russell, *Lethal Intent*, 464.

27. *Aileen C. Wuornos v. State of Florida*, Case No. SC00-1199, http://www.floridasupremecourt.org/clerk/briefs/2000/1001-1200/00-1199_ans.pdf.

28. Judith Aquino, "20 Signs that You Are a Psychopath," *Business Insider*, July 29, 2011, http://www.businessinsider.com/signs-that-youre-a-psyopath-2011-8#cunningmanipulative-5.

29. Phyllis Chesler, "A Woman's Right to Self Defense: The Case of Aileen Carol Wuornos," *St. John's Law Review* 66, no. 4 (1993), Article 1, http://scholarship.law.stjohns.edu/lawreview/vol66/iss4/1/.

30. Henry Frederick, "The Cult of Aileen Wuornos," *Special Reports*, news-journalonline.com, June 11, 2000, http://www.news-journalonline.com/special/wuornos/061100film.htm.

31. Phil Villarreal, "New Documentary Deepens 'Monster' Exploration," *Arizona Daily Star*, March 12, 2004, http://www.highbeam.com/doc/1P2-26992450.html.

32. Russell, *Lethal Intent,* 144.

33. "Wuornos' Last Words: 'I'll Be Back,'" *CNN.com,* October 15, 2002, http://edition.cnn.com/2002/LAW/10/09/wuornos.execution/.

34. Suzanne O'Malley, *Are You There Alone?* (New York: Simon and Schuster, 2004), 43.

35. Ibid, xvii, xviii.

36. Anne Berryman, Greg Fulton, Deborah Fowler, and Hilary Hylton, "The Yates Odyssey," *Time,* July 26, 2006, http://www.time.com/time/magazine/article/0,9171,1001706-14,00.html.

37. Ibid.

38. Ibid.

39. Suzy Spencer, *Breaking Point* (New York: St. Martin's Press, 2002), 122.

40. "Understanding Depression," *Helpguide,* http://www.helpguide.org/mental/depression_signs_types_diagnosis_treatment.htm.

41. Charles Montaldo, "Profile of Andrea Yates," *About.com,* http://crime.about.com/od/current/p/andreayates.htm.

42. O'Malley, *Are You There Alone?,* 38.

43. Berryman et al., "The Yates Odyssey."

44. Madeline Vann, "Who's at Risk for Postpartum Depression?," *Everyday Health,* http://www.everydayhealth.com/depression/whos-at-risk-for-postpartum-depression.aspx.

45. Spencer, *Breaking Point,* 182.

46. O'Malley, *Are You There Alone?,* 35, 40 and Spencer, *Breaking Point,* 119.

47. Spencer, *Breaking Point,* 119.

48. O'Malley, *Are You There Alone?,* 51.

49. Deborah Denno, "Who Is Andrea Yates? A Short History of Insanity," *Duke Journal of Gender Law and Policy* 10 (Summer 2003), 87, http://papers.ssrn.com/sol3/papers.cfm?abstract_id=452040.

50. O'Malley, *Are You There Alone?,* 77.

51. Berryman et al., "The Yates Odyssey."

52. Dale Lezon and Peggy O'Hare, "Jurors Hear Yates' Chilling Call to 911," *Houston Chronicle,* June 26, 2006, http://www.chron.com/news/article/Jurors-hear-Yates-chilling-call-to-911-1866104.php.

53. Spencer, *Breaking Point,* 2.

54. Lezon and O'Hare, "Jurors Hear Yates' Chilling Call to 911."

55. Brian S. Wise, "The Case against Compassion: Andrea Yates," *Intellectual Conservative,* February 20, 2001, http://www.intellectualconservative.com/page1015.html.

56. "Newsweek Cover: 'I Killed My Children' What Made Andrea Yates Snap?," *PR Newswire,* June 24, 2001, http://www.prnewswire.com/news-releases/newsweek-cover-i-killed-my-children-what-made-andrea-yates-snap-72297767.html.

57. Vann, "Who's at Risk for Postpartum Depression."

58. Kim Gandy, "Tragedy Focuses Attention on Postpartum Psychosis," *National Organization for Women,* September 6, 2001, www.now.org/press/04-01/09-06.html.

59. Manuel Gamiz, "2 Tragic Cases Show Marked Contrasts," *Los Angeles Times,* April 15, 2002, http://articles.latimes.com/2002/apr/15/local/me-adair15.

60. Charles Montaldo, "The Insanity Defense," *About.com,* http://crime.about.com/od/issues/a/insanity.htm.

61. Denno, "Who Is Andrea Yates?," 87.

62. "Yates, Andrea Pia v. the State of Texas—Appeal from 230th District Court of Harris County," *Justica,* January 6, 2005, http://law.justia.com/cases/texas/first-court-of-appeals/2005/81309.html.

63. Denno, "Who Is Andrea Yates?," 48.

64. Ibid, 61.

65. "Marc Cherry—Child Killer Trial Inspired Desperate Housewives," *Contactmusic.com,* August 24, 2006, http://www.contactmusic.com/news/child-killer-trial-inspired-desperate-housewives_1006202.

66. Park Dietz, "Excerpts from Interview of Andrea Yates by Dr. Park Dietz," *World of PDF,* November 6–7, 2001, http://worldofpdf.com/INTERVIEW-OF-ANDREA-YATES-(AY).

67. Ibid.

68. "Charlize Theron: The Beast within the Beauty," *Blunt Review with Emily Blunt,* http://www.bluntreview.com/reviews/theron.html.

69. Dietz, "Excerpts from Interview of Andrea Yates by Dr. Park Dietz."

70. Marlee McCloud, "Aileen Wuornos: Killer Who Preyed on Truck Drivers," *Crime Library,* http://www.trutv.com/library/crime/notorious_murders/women/wuornos/1.html.

71. Ibid.

Conclusion

1. Kent Kimes, "Girls in the Gang." *Creative Loafing Atlanta,* http://clatl.com/atlanta/girls-in-the-gang/Content?oid=1227679.

2. "What's Your Shooting Diva Halloween Costume?," *Shooting Divas,* http://shootingdivas.com/whats-your-shooting-diva-halloween-costume#.

3. "Steve Harvey on Susan Smith," *YouTube,* http://www.youtube.com/watch?v=zVWpQpNpuG8.

Selected Bibliography

Abrahamson, Alan, "Betty Broderick Tells How Marriage Fell Apart," *Los Angeles Times,* October 31, 1990, http://articles.latimes.com/1990-10-31/news/mn-3140_1_betty-broderick.

Aileen C. Wuornos, Appellant, vs. 1199 State of Florida, Appellee. http://www.floridasupremecourt.org/clerk/briefs/2000/1001-1200/00-1199_ans.pdf.

"Amy Bishop Arrested: University of Alabama Huntsville Shooting Suspect is Biology Professor, Harvard Trained," *The Huffington Post,* April 14, 2010, http://www.huffingtonpost.com/2010/02/12/university-of-alabama-sho_n_460868.html.

"Analysis of Susan Smith Confession," LSI Laboratory for Scientific *Interrogation Inc.,* http://www.lsiscan.com/susan_smith_s_confession.htm.

Banfield, Ashleigh, Suzan Clarke, and Angela Ellis, "Alleged University Shooter's Husband Thought 'Somebody Had Gone Crazy at the School,'" *Good Morning America,* February 19, 2010, http://abcnews.go.com/GMA/amy-bishop-husband-alleged-university-alabama-shooter-loving-mother-wife/story?id=9883895#.UBjK8I7GMWw.

Bartlett, Thomas, and Robin Wilson, "The Fatal Meeting: Death, Heroism, and a Campus Changed Forever," *Chronicle of Higher Education,* February 18, 2010, http://chronicle.com/article/The-Fatal-Meeting-Death-H/64295/.

Bartlett, Thomas, and Robin Wilson, "Amy Bishop Is Indicted in 1986 Shooting Death of Her Brother," *Chronicle of Higher Education,* June 17, 2010, http://chronicle.com/article/Amy-Bishop-Is-Indicted-in-1986/65970/.

Basken, Paul, and David Glenn, "Accused Alabama Shooter Was a Bright Scientist with Career Ups and Downs," *Chronicle of Higher Education,* February 15, 2010, http://chronicle.com/article/Accused-Alabama-Shooter-Was-a/64202/.

Berryman, Anne, Greg Fulton, Deborah Fowler, and Hilary Hylton, "The Yates Odyssey," *Time,* July 26, 2006, http://www.time.com/time/magazine/article/0,9171,1001706-14,00.html.

Braintree Police Department News Release, "Comments from Chief Paul Frazier Regarding Amy Bishop," February 13, 2010.

Braudy, Susan, *This Crazy Thing Called Love* (New York: Alfred A. Knopf, 1992).

Cass, Connie, "Woman Guilty of Slaying Ex-Husband, New Wife," *Winchester Star,* December 11, 1991.

Chesler, Phyllis, "A Woman's Right to Self Defense: The Case of Aileen Carol Wuornos," *St. John's Law Review* 66, no. 4 (1993), Article 1, http://scholarship.law.stjohns.edu/lawreview/vol66/iss4/1/.

Cockle, Richard, "Eastern Oregon Killer Liysa Northon, Featured in Ann Rule Book, Eyes New Life after Her Release from Prison Next Year," *Oregonian*, November 5, 2011, http://www.oregonlive.com/pacific-northwest-news/index.ssf/2011/11/eastern_oregon_killer_liysa_no.html.

Denno, Deborah, "Who Is Andrea Yates? A Short History of Insanity," *Duke Journal of Gender Law and Policy* 10 (Summer 2003), http://papers.ssrn.com/sol3/papers.cfm?abstract_id=452040.

Deutsch, Linda, "Betty Broderick Hearing: Parole Board Revisits Daniel Broderick, Linda Kolkena Broderick Murders," *The Huffington Post*, January 21, 2010, http://www.huffingtonpost.com/2010/01/21/betty-broderick-hearing-p_n_431611.html.

Deutsch, Linda, "Socialite Betty Broderick Seeks Parole in Murders," *San Diego Union-Tribune*, January 21, 2010, http://www.signonsandiego.com/news/2010/jan/21/socialite-betty-broderick-seeks-parole-in-murders/.

Dewan, Shaila, Stephanie Saul, and Katie Zezima, "For Professor, Fury Just beneath the Surface," *The New York Times*, February 20, 2010, http://www.nytimes.com/2010/02/21/us/21bishop.html.

Dietz, Park, "Excerpts from Interview of Andrea Yates by Dr. Park Dietz," *World of PDF*, November 6–7, 2001, http://worldofpdf.com/INTERVIEW-OF-ANDREA-YATES-(AY).

Doyle, Steven, "Amy Bishop Claimed She Was Victim in 2002 IHOP Assault," *Huntsville Times*, February 18, 2010, http://blog.al.com/breaking/2010/02/amy_bishop_cursed_punched_woma.html.

Eftimiades, Maria, *Sins of the Mother* (New York: St. Martin's Press, 1995).

"Female Serial Killer Has Been Executed," *ABC Good Morning America*, October 9, 2002, http://abcnews.go.com/GMA/story?id=124614&page=1#.T_ok_47GMdJ.

Fletcher, Gary, "Judge Rejects Murder Suspect's Release," *The Observer*, June 28, 2001, http://www.lagrandeobserver.com/News/Local-News/JUDGE-REJECTS-MURDER-SUSPECTS-RELEASE.

Fletcher, Gary, "Judge Denies Bail for Northon," *The Bulletin*, June 29, 2001, http://bbstage.sx.atl.publicus.com/archive/2001/06/29/judge_denies_bail_for_northon.html.

Fletcher, Gary, "Defense, State Lay out Cases in Murder Trial," *The Observer*, July 17, 2001, http://www.lagrandeobserver.com/News/Local-News/DEFENSE-STATE-LAY-OUT-CASES-IN-MURDER-TRAIL.

Fletcher, Gary, "Murder Victim Heavily Sedated, Toxicologist Says," *The Observer*, July 19, 2001, http://www.lagrandeobserver.com/News/Local-News/MURDER-VICTIM-HEAVILY-SEDATED-TOXICOLOGIST-SAYS.

Fletcher, Gary, "Plea Bargain Brings Trial to End," *The Observer*, July 20, 2001, http://www.lagrandeobserver.com/News/Local-News/PLEA-BARGAIN-BRINGS-TRIAL-TO-END.

Fletcher, Gary, "Murder on the Lostine," *The Observer*, October 16, 2003, http://www.lagrandeobserver.com/News/Local-News/MURDER-ON-THE-LOSTINE.

Fletcher, Gary, "Murder Suspect Will Claim Self-Defense," *The Observer*, June 28, 2001, http://www.lagrandeobserver.com/News/Local-News/MURDER-SUSPECT-WILL-CLAIM-SELF-DEFENSE.

Footlick, Jerrold, and Elaine Sciolino, "Wives Who Batter Back," *Newsweek,* January 30, 1978.

Furio, Jennifer, *Letters from Prison* (New York: Algora Publishing, 2001).

Geringer, Joseph, "Betty Broderick: Divorce . . . Desperation . . . Death," *Crime Library,* http://www.trutv.com/library/crime/notorious_murders/family/broderick/1.html.

Glatt, John, *Deadly American Beauty* (New York: St. Martin's Press, 2004).

Gribben, Mark, "The Woodwards: Tragedy in High Society," *Crime Library,* http://www.trutv.com/library/crime/notorious_murders/celebrity/woodwards/2.html.

Guilfoil, John, "Ipswitch Neighbors Recall Confrontations with Amy Bishop," *Boston Globe,* February 15, 2010, http://www.boston.com/news/local/breaking_news/2010/02/ipswich_neighbo.html.

Hanson, Fred, "Classmates Recall a Smart, Quiet Girl," *Patriot Ledger,* February 16, 2010, http://findarticles.com/p/news-articles/patriot-ledger-the-quincy-mass/mi_8043/is_20100216/classmates-recall-smart-quiet-girl/ai_n50245980/.

Harrison, Eric, "Town Unleashes Rage over Murder of 2 Boys Crime," *Los Angeles Times,* November 5, 1994, http://articles.latimes.com/1994-11-05/news/mn-58757_1_susan-smith.

Henderson, Gary, *Nine Days in Union* (Spartanburg, SC: Honoribus Press, 1995).

Hirsley, Michael, "Battered Ex-wife Becomes New Murder Trial Cause," *Chicago Tribune,* September 11, 1977.

Hirsley, Michael, "Wife Freed in Slaying of Abuser," *Chicago Tribune,* November 4, 1977.

Howe, Robert F., "Deadly Dose," *Reader's Digest* (April 2003).

Jones, Ann, *Women Who Kill* (New York: Holt, Rinehart Winston, 1980).

King, Jeanne, *Signed in Blood* (New York: St. Martin's Press, 2009).

Kohn, David, "American Beauty," *CBS News,* May 7, 2009, http://www.cbsnews.com/2100-18559_162-505815.html.

Kyle, Cynthia, "Curious Spectators Flock to Hughes Murder Trial," *The Herald Palladium,* October 31, 1977.

Lezon, Dale, and Peggy O'Hare, "Jurors Hear Yates' Chilling Call to 911," *Houston Chronicle,* June 26, 2006, http://www.chron.com/news/article/Jurors-hear-Yates-chilling-call-to-911-1866104.php.

McCarter, Patricia C., "What Happened to Amy Bishop's Brother? Two Conflicting Stories Arise," *Huntsville Times,* February 14, 2010, http://blog.al.com/breaking/2010/02/post_207.html.

McCarter, Patricia C., "Amy Bishop 'Consumed' with University Tenure but Was Pursuing Plan B, Husband Says," *Huntsville Times,* February 18, 2010, http://blog.al.com/breaking/2010/02/post_212.html.

McCloud, Marlee, "Aileen Wuornos: Killer Who Preyed on Truck Drivers," *Crime Library,* http://www.trutv.com/library/crime/notorious_murders/women/wuornos/1.html.

McNulty, Faith, *The Burning Bed* (New York: Harcourt Brace Jovanovich, 1980).

Montaldo, Charles, "Susan Smith—Profile of a Child Killer," *About.com,* http://crime.about.com/od/murder/a/susan_smith.htm.

North County Times News Service, "Millions of Dollars Awarded to Family of Man Killed by Toxicologist Wife," *North County Times,* March 21, 2006, http://www.nctimes.com/news/state-and-regional/article_4428aa6b-fbb0-55a2-9221-9592d31fe6e5.html.

O'Malley, Suzanne, *Are You There Alone?* (New York: Simon and Schuster, 2004).

Peyser, Andrea, *Mother Love, Deadly Love* (New York: Harper Collins Publishers, 1995).

Police Report, Braintree Police, March 30, 1987, http://www.boston.com/news/local/massachusetts/articles/2010/02/13/Full1986Policereport/

Powell, Joanna, "My Daughter Is Innocent," *Good Housekeeping*, March 2002, http://www.accessmylibrary.com/article-1G1-83077235/my-daughter-innocent-kristin.html.

Pringle, Paul, "Age, Sex of Defendants May Affect Verdict," *Los Angeles Times*, April 14, 2008, http://articles.latimes.com/2008/apr/14/local/me-olga helen14.

Pringle, Paul, and Hemmy So, "Portrait Emerges of a Baffling Pair," *Los Angeles Times*, May 31, 2006, http://articles.latimes.com/2006/may/31/local/me-olgahelen31.

Pringle, Paul, and Hemmy So, "An Unlikely Friendship that Finally Unraveled," *Los Angeles Times*, August 19, 2006, http://articles.latimes.com/2006/aug/19/local/me-olgahelen19.

Rekers, George, *Susan Smith Victim or Murderer* (Lakewood, CO: Glenbridge Publishing, Ltd., 1996).

Reno, Jamie, "A Toxic Turn of Events," *Newsweek*, July 1, 2001, http://www.news week.com/2001/07/02/a-toxic-turn-of-events.html.

Reynolds, Michael, *Dead Ends* (New York: St. Martin's Press, 1992).

Rossum, Kristin v. Deborah Patrick and Edmund G. Brown Jr., United States Court of Appeals for the Ninth Circuit, No. 09-055666, http://www.signonsandiego.com/news/2010/sep/23/kristin-rossums-appeal-her-murder-conviction-reviv/.

Roth, Alex, "Paper's Sealed on Judges Orders in Toxicologist Case," *San Diego Union-Tribune*, April 17, 2002, http://legacy.signonsandiego.com/news/metro/200 20417-9999_2m17rossum.html.

Rother, Caitlin, *Poisoned Love* (New York, Kensington Publishing Corp., 2005).

Rule, Ann, *Heart Full of Lies* (New York: Pocket Books, 2004).

Russell, Sue, *Lethal Intent* (New York: Kensington Publishing Corp., 2002).

Serrano, Richard, and Amy Wallace, "San Diego Killings Make Bitter Divorce Final," *Los Angeles Times*, November 7, 1989, http://www.latimes.com/la-me-brod erick7nov0789,0,997740.story.

"Sister Kills Teenager in Shotgun Accident at Home," *Patriot Ledger*, December 8, 1986, http://www.enterprisenews.com/archive/x228087669/From-the-Archives-Sister-kills-teenager-in-shotgun-accident.

Smith, David, *Beyond All Reason* (New York: Kensington Publishing Corp., 1995).

Smith, Stephen, "Ambition Fueled Smoldering Rage," *Boston Globe*, February 21, 2010, http://www.boston.com/news/local/massachusetts/articles/2010/02/21/ambition_fueled_a_smoldering_rage/.

Spencer, Suzy, *Breaking Point* (New York: St. Martin's Press, 2002).

Stephens, Challen, Patricia C. McCarter, and Steve Doyle, "Why Did Amy Bishop Snap? A Picture of a Driven Woman with a Troubled Past Emerges," *Huntsville Times*, February 22, 2010, http://blog.al.com/breaking/2010/02/why_did_amy_bishop_snap_a_pict.html.

Stumbo, Bella, *Until the Twelfth of Never* (New York: Simon and Schuster, 1993).

Swart, Rick, "Ann Rule's Sloppy Storytelling," *Seattle Weekly*, July 20, 2011, http://www.seattleweekly.com/content/printVersion/1384981/.

Taubman, Bryna, *Hell Hath No Fury* (New York: St. Martin's Press, 1992).

"The Case of Aileen Wuornos—The Facts," *Capital Punishment in Context,* http://www.capitalpunishmentincontext.org/cases/wuornos.

"The Law: A Killing Excuse," *Time,* November 28, 1977, http://time.com/time/magazine/article/0,9171,919176,00.html.TRIAL-TO-END.

The Oprah Winfrey Show: The 20th Anniversary Collection (Hollywood, CA: Paramount Pictures, 2005).

"Toxic Love Triangle," *ABC Radio National,* January 25, 2004, http://www.abc.net.au/rn/talks/bbing/stories/s1010011.htm.

"'Urgent Voice' Led to Ex-mate Killing," *Bridgeport Post,* November 2, 1977.

Vick, Karl, "In LA a Case Straight out of 'Arsenic and Old Lace,'" *The Washington Post,* March 18, 2008, http://www.washingtonpost.com/wp-dyn/content/article/2008/03/17/AR2008031702489.html.

Villarreal, Phil, "New Documentary Deepens 'Monster' Exploration," *Arizona Daily Star,* March 12, 2004, http://www.highbeam.com/doc/1P2-26992450.html.

Walker, Lenore, "The Cycle Theory of Battering," *Transition House,* http://www.transitionhouse.ca/THEORY.html.

Wallace, Amy, "La Jolla Woman Confesses to Murders in Crime," *Los Angeles Times,* March 28, 1990, http://articles.latimes.com/1990-03-28/news/mn-232_1_betty-Broderick.

Wallace, Amy, "Till Murder Do Us Part," *Los Angeles Times,* June 3, 1990, http://www.latimes.com/news/local/la-me-broderick3jun0390,0,1443012.story.

Wallace, Amy, "One Angry Betty," *Los Angeles Magazine,* November 1, 2009, http://www.lamag.com/article.aspx?id=20936&page=2.

"Woman Denies Killing Husband," *Los Angeles Times,* November 2, 2002, http://articles.latimes.com/2002/nov/02/local/me-rossum2.

Wuornos, Aileen, and Christopher Berry-Dee, *Monster* (London: John Blake Publishing, Ltd., 2006).

"Wuornos' Last Words: 'I'll Be Back,'" *CNN.com,* October 15, 2002, http://edition.cnn.com/2002/LAW/10/09/wuornos.execution/.

Yardley, Jim, "Heir to a Fortune, and to Tragedy: Suicide Ends the Life of a Wealthy, and Haunted Man," *The New York Times,* May 8, 1999, http://www.nytimes.com/1999/05/08/nyregion/heir-fortune-tragedy-suicide-ends-life-wealthy-haunted-man.html?pagewanted=all&src=pm.

"Yates, Andrea Pia v. the State of Texas—Appeal from 230th District Court of Harris County," *Justica,* January 6, 2005, http://law.justia.com/cases/texas/first-court-of-appeals/2005/81309.html.

Zetter, Kim, "The Husband, the Wife, and the Lover," *The Age,* November 16, 2002, http://www.theage.com.au/articles/2002/11/15/1037080914373.html.

Index

About the Authors

LAURIE NALEPA, EdD, is a dean of Academic Affairs at Los Angeles Valley College. She has been an adjunct professor at Antioch University and National University, teaching a variety of courses in the context of popular culture. She has made numerous presentations relating to media culture and crime at the Hawaii International Conference on Arts and Humanities, the Film and History Conference, as well as the Popular Culture Conference. She loves to stay up in the wee hours of the morning watching reruns of *Power, Privilege and Justice, Body of Evidence,* and *City Confidential.* She mourns the loss of Court TV.

RICHARD PFEFFERMAN, PhD, is a retired dean of Academic Affairs at the Los Angeles Community College District. He received his doctorate in Communication from the University of Southern California, where his focus was on group and media communication in popular culture. He has been a frequent presenter at Speech Communication Association conferences analyzing messages of power, influence, and gender roles in television and film. Against his better judgment, he is mesmerized each year by *American Idol.*

For more information on *The Murder Mystique*, check out the website: rpfefferman.com/themurdermystique